By the same author

KILLING
FOR COMPANY

BRIAN MASTERS

arrow books

5 7 9 10 8 6

Arrow Books
20 Vauxhall Bridge Road
London SW1V 2SA

Arrow Books is part of the Penguin Random House group of companies whose
addresses can be found at global.penguinrandomhouse.com.

Penguin
Random House
UK

First published in the United Kingdom in 1985 by Jonathan Cape
First published in 1995 by Arrow Books
This edition published by Arrow Books in 2020

www.penguin.co.uk

A CIP catalogue record for this book is available from the British Library.

ISBN 9781787466258

Printed and bound in Great Britain by Clays Ltd, Elcograf S.p.A.

Penguin Random House is committed to a sustainable future
for our business, our readers and our planet. This book is made
from Forest Stewardship Council® certified paper.

*For Juan Melian
and Beryl Bainbridge
and also David Ralph Martin*

CONTENTS

I have now a guilt and punishment complex. I am convinced that I deserve everything that a court can throw at me.
                — *D.A. Nilsen, 13 April 1983*

FOREWORD TO THE 2017 EDITION

Well over thirty years have passed since the trial of Dennis Nilsen in Court One at the Old Bailey in 1983, and the publication of this book two years later. From the beginning he seemed to be a man of unfathomable depravity (I remember a woman in the front row of the jury staring at him in the dock with visible blunt incredulity, unable to attach the bureaucrat before her to the evidence she was hearing), accused on six counts of murder and two of attempted murder, with more charges that could not be brought because human remains had been reduced to ash mixed with earth, and would forever elude identification. On 4 November, the jury returned with majority verdicts of 10 to 2 on all counts of murder and one of attempted murder; their verdict on the remaining count was unanimous. Mr Justice Croom-Johnson sent Nilsen to prison for life, with a recommendation he serve no less than twenty-five years. A much later political decision by the Home Office determined that, in fact, he would never be released.

My own involvement with the case began almost immediately after Nilsen's arrest. Like everyone else I read about it in the morning papers, and especially of the bafflement of police officers whose task it was to question him. All their initial evidence was volunteered by him over several days of close enquiry. They did not have to elicit information through cunning. He would not stop talking. They elected to take the co-operative approach, supplying him with as many cigarettes as he could inhale, and listening to the relentless narrative of admission (not 'confession'). It was obvious that somebody would need to write an account of the crimes and trial, and I thought that perhaps I could attempt such an undertaking, since all the victims had been male, and it might require a homosexual sensitivity to unravel the sources of such derangement. I had no experience whatsoever, my previous books having been studies in French literature and an aristocratic history. But I wrote to Nilsen on remand in Brixton prison (not knowing one shouldn't, I was protected by my own naivety), saying that I would welcome the chance to analyse the case, but would not do so without his co-operation, which was quite true – a scissors-and-paste account would be quite worthless. My first letter from him began with a disconcerting sentence: 'Dear Mr Masters, I pass the burden of my life on to your shoulders'.

There followed eight months of contact before the trial. At least three times a week I would receive a closely-written letter on prison notepaper, demonstrating an eagerness not to waste any space, and it had presumably been passed by the censor. My replies were more leisurely and anodyne. In addition, I received from him a visiting order every few weeks, which permitted entry to the vast room where all prisoners gathered to receive friends and family for an hour. Nilsen and I sat opposite one another at a square wooden table, an ashtray between us. I noticed how other prisoners greeted him, without animosity or fear; he had helped them compose letters home. During the trial, I was taken to the cells underground at the end of each daily session. And finally, he filled more than fifty prison exercise books with reminiscence and reflection, not only on his crimes and how he had come to commit them, but on politics, literature, childhood, the army, and scorn for organised society. Knowing there would always be a danger that these might find their way outside, he planted one hideous story so preposterous that it was designed to appeal to editors of sordid newspapers. But it was not leaked.

All this exclusive access carried obvious responsibilities. The first was towards the truth which lay beyond judgement. Judge and jury would deal with the matter of guilt, whilst the writer must deal with matters of interpretation and accuracy. I started writing the book long before the trial, using material supplied by Nilsen as well as police archives, and very early on, I decided that my second responsibility would be to the readers. It was essential that I should eschew explosive adjectives ('repellent', 'disgusting', 'horrifying' and so on), because it was not my job to prod the reader into thinking in a certain way by using 'trigger' words. I had to say what happened, and the reader could supply his or her own adjectives to define it as he or she saw fit. I would be a recorder, not an assessor of moral worth or turpitude. Nilsen himself said, 'I am an ordinary man come to extraordinary conclusion'. The story would be told, and the reader would have to decide whether Nilsen was right or not. Even he himself claimed to be mystified at times. He told me that he was hoping I would be able to reveal to him why it all happened. Indeed, part of my responsibility would be to explain as best I could.

The simmering moral danger for me was that I might unwittingly become complicit, as many suggested was inevitable. I wasn't, of course, because I was aware of it, not blind, but I soon learnt to avoid using words that could easily be twisted against me. It was important that I did not 'understand' the murderer, which might sound sympathetic and is pregnant with peril, but that I should 'comprehend' what happened and why, which is safe and neutral. These are subtle, dodgy differences, but they are important if one needs to avoid being pelted with indignation, feigned or otherwise.

Another word I chose to smother was 'evil'. This is an occult word, meaning nothing precise or measurable, and is simply an excuse for not thinking. It signifies, in effect, 'I don't know', and therefore should not be part of a writer's vocabulary. I was shocked to hear the word used by the judge in his summing-up; that slip of judicial language deserved censure.

Nevertheless, some form of vocabulary had to be found to clarify the mystery of moral degradation. In one of our conversations, I told Nilsen that logic compelled me to allow that I might be capable of killing another person, though I hoped that such would never happen. After all, in battle it is almost a requirement, in anger, a constant risk. But I could never fathom how he could have afterwards dismembered the bodies, cut them into little bits and flushed them down the lavatory. His reaction was immediate and alarming. 'There is something wrong with your morals if you are more annoyed by what I did to a corpse,' he said. 'It was far worse for me to squeeze the life out of a living man; a corpse is a thing, and it cannot be hurt or suffer. Your moral compass is upside down.' That gave me pause for a while. It is, of course, the product of logical reasoning. But Nilsen could not see, or *feel*, that humans are much more than logic; they are creatures with imagination, which allows, nay *compels*, them to honour and respect that which had once been a life in full flow. Such a concept was totally foreign to him.

It was this same indifference to the emotional impact of his deeds, and of his words to me, that informed his remark one day, 'You know, you'd be surprised how heavy a human head is when you pick it up by the hair'. This was the man who had been capable of getting breakfast ready, buttering a slice of toast, then lowering the heat of a pot which had been simmering the head of his last victim during the night. He was still able, before taking the dog out for a walk, to eat his toast. The murders were consistent with this moral deadness; he knew very well that what he had done was wrong, but he did not know why it *mattered*, why people reacted so emotionally.

A lesser display of detachment was his failure to notice how much his mother would suffer when the full details of his crimes reached the newspapers. The weekend before the trial, I went up to Scotland to visit her, and prepare her for what was about to engulf her modest, terraced house within a day or two. It was a wretched experience, although she did her best to make it sunny by cooking me a splendid dinner and gossiping about Dennis' tender care for pet birds when he was a child. The distance between mother and son was astonishing.

The psychiatrists grappled with their conflicting definitions. Nilsen suffered from a 'personality disorder', some said, without offering an explanation of what might have caused the 'order' to be knocked askew in the first place. Had there been a priest in court, he would have said that he knew quite well what had done it, and they called him the Devil. That brings us right back to the occult, and the absence of explanation.

Nilsen told me he was surprised that people should be so fascinated by the macabre, and spend so much time talking about it even as they condemned it. I, too, was often accused of being 'fascinated', another word I reject. Fascination involves abnegation of thought, permitting unwanted impressions to be written on the memory. I have quite enough memories without adding to their weight. The police, unusually, showed me the file of photographs they had taken. There was a box containing, I guessed, over one hundred images, of graduating unpleasantness. I was told to say 'stop' when I had had enough. I looked at the first twelve, and could go no further. But they will never be wiped from my mind, and they may well come back to haunt me in senility.

Looking back now, it is the paradoxes that perturb. I am no longer prepared to accept Nilsen's disingenuous claim that he did not know what had caused him to be a killer. I now think he enjoyed it and the thrill it gave him. *Why* he should enjoy it is another matter. Moral vacuity is an insufficient answer. And yet, when I discovered the letter that had been written to the landlords complaining about blocked drains, I immediately recognised the distinctive handwriting. It was Nilsen's. The plumbers came, and found human remains. The murderer had engineered his own arrest.

For about ten years after his conviction, I visited him in prison about once every two months. I was chastised for this, too. My reason for so doing was simple: he had opened his memories and his character to me, giving me material with which to write this book. I could not then, in all conscience, say 'Thanks, but you are now by yourself'. The court had determined his fate; I could still be true to mine.

PREFACE

This has been in many ways a disturbing book to write, and some will no doubt find it an unpleasant one to read. Dennis Andrew Nilsen, having started life unremarkably enough in a fishing community in Scotland, at the age of thirty-seven admitted to the wilful murder of fifteen men over a period of four years, thus becoming the biggest multiple killer in British criminal history. This book attempts to show how such a calamity could occur.

The courts have already dealt with Nilsen by imprisoning him for life. In this there can be but scant comfort for the families of his victims, who must forever wonder why their sons were cut down before they had time to grapple with life's problems in their own way, in order to satisfy the obsessive needs of a stranger who has been adjudged sane. With this in mind, there can be no ambiguity about the moral response to his crimes.

By examining in detail Nilsen's life and attitudes, his emotions and reflexes, it might be possible to reach an understanding, albeit a scrappy one, of one dark and mysterious aspect of the human condition. That, at least, is my purpose. Any faulty interpretation of the facts is entirely my own responsibility.

I have used the biographical method to build a portrait of Nilsen before the crimes were committed, in the hope that one might discern clues in his life which point to the simmering of a latent conflict. As the biographer must select, I have given special weight to these 'clues', which were insignificant or unnoticed at the time but which assume gravity in retrospect. It is not until Chapters 6 and 7 that the murders themselves and the disposal of bodies are related. These are followed by a chapter on Nilsen's behaviour on remand in Brixton Prison, an account of his trial at the Old Bailey, and a final chapter on the various possible explanations for such gross distortion of conduct offered by psychiatric, philosophic and theological inquiry. My own amateur explanation is offered in conclusion.

I have tried throughout to be neither indignant nor exculpatory, but objective. I am aware that this aim is rendered difficult in two respects. Firstly, I grew to know Nilsen very well during the eight months preceding his trial, and this personal contact must necessarily have some hidden influence upon my own attitudes; I can only hope that, being aware of the danger, I have managed to avoid it. Secondly, my account of Nilsen's life is derived largely from his own words and reflections, written for me at great length in his prison cell. Wherever possible, I have corroborated his memory by researches in outside sources, and there are large sections (for example in Chapters 2 and 10) which owe nothing to Nilsen's own writing. Moreover, though he has given me full and extensive information, he has had no control over the text, and I have been free to discard or expand, to make my own assessments and draw my own conclusions.

Nilsen's co-operation has, I believe, been an advantage rather than a chain. It is extremely rare for a murderer to talk about himself as frankly and as extensively as Nilsen has done. In the nineteenth century Lacenaire revealed something of his motives in print. The Düsseldorf sadist, Peter Kürten, spoke openly to Dr Karl Berg in 1929 and their conversations appeared in a short book. Latterly, the American murderer Theodore Bundy has speculated about his crimes (while still maintaining his innocence) to two journalists. Most recently Flora Rheta Schreiber has examined in depth the case of Joseph Kallinger in her book *The Shoemaker*. But Nilsen is the first murderer to present an exhaustive archive measuring his own introspection. His prison journals are therefore a unique document in the history of criminal homicide, and afford us some opportunity to enter the mind of a murderer. He knows that some of his revelations are so candid as to be horrifying, but we must wonder whether, without them, we should ever be able to determine what forces operated to disfigure his emotional grasp of the world about him. And if we cannot so determine, then we are left with the miserable conclusion that a man becomes a murderer merely by chance.

A number of other people have helped me in the compilation of this narrative, and to them all I should like to express my gratitude. Dennis Nilsen's mother, Mrs Scott, has patiently shared her contemplation of a painful subject, and his step-father, Adam Scott, has been a source of strength to her and, by extension, to myself. Nilsen's two successive solicitors, Ronald Moss and Ralph Haeems, have been unfailingly courteous and helpful at times when they themselves were under strain. Detective Chief Superintendent Chambers and Detective Chief Inspector Jay have given me much co-operation and encouragement. Colin Wilson shared his allusive ideas on the subject of murder and directed me towards several useful books. The staff of the British Medical Association Library were constantly helpful. Juan Melian has listened to my reading the text for many hours and made helpful suggestions. My agent, Jacintha Alexander, has worked tirelessly to see the project through, and my editor, Tom Maschler, has curbed my excesses and consistently suggested improvements, some of which I accepted gratefully; if I did not accept more, that, I suspect, is my loss. Professor John Gunn and Dr Pamela Taylor were of particular assistance in pointing me towards some specialist journals, while Professor Robert Bluglass and Professor Keith Ward kindly responded to my request for advice. For sustaining encouragement, I must thank Michael Bloch, Selina

Hastings, Ian Romer, Stephen Tumim and Beryl Bainbridge.

I should like to express my gratitude to Messrs Chatto & Windus and to Miss Iris Murdoch for permitting me to quote one paragraph from *The Philosopher's Pupil*.

Others who have asked to remain anonymous include psychiatrists, social workers, and friends. My gratitude to them is not less for being addressed collectively.

Brian Masters
London, 1984

ARREST

The north London suburb of Muswell Hill is middle-class, residential, and almost intolerably placid. No events disturb its peaceful, thoughtless routine; there are no marches in the street, no pickets on the corner, rarely even the sound of a police and ambulance siren. The inhabitants of Muswell Hill get into their cars every morning, drive to work in central London, and drive back home at night. Their wives prepare dinner. They sometimes entertain. They enjoy a gin and tonic and pride themselves on knowing a little more about wine than the average supermarket shopper. And their weekends are spent gardening. Gardens are very important in Muswell Hill. As the name implies, it sits on relatively high ground overlooking the London basin and enjoys good, fresh air and full exposure to sun. Many of the roads slope, climb and undulate, making them unattractive to cyclists but enticing to the leisurely walker. More than one street is called 'gardens' rather than 'road'. One such, Cranley Gardens, has given its name to a kind of sub-district of Muswell Hill, marked on maps of London as a focal point. Cranley Gardens itself is long, fairly wide, bright and cheerful. You could quite easily imagine children disporting themselves with skipping ropes along the pavement, except that Muswell Hill

1

mothers do not approve of children playing in the street.

The houses of Cranley Gardens, built before the First World War, are semi-detached and stylish, with pointed roofs. Mostly painted white with beams and woodwork picked out in another colour, they are separated from the street by noticeably pretty front gardens, well tended and self-consciously aware of their charm. Gently they compete with each other. Except for one. The garden of Number 23 is woefully neglected, dank and brown without a splash of colour, overgrown and entangled by weeds. Even a daffodil would find it hard to thrust its way through to the sunlight. The house behind, too, is not in keeping with the rest of the street. White and pale blue, it looks rather scruffy, in need of a wash, lacking in the sparkle which emanates from neighbouring houses of the same shape and size. It looks haggard and forgotten.

While most of the houses in Cranley Gardens served their original purpose as family homes, Number 23 did not. At the beginning of 1983 it had for many years belonged to an Indian woman whose address was given as New Delhi and who may never have seen it since the day she bought it. The house was divided into six flats and bedsitting-rooms, and managed by Mr Roberts of Ellis & Co., an estate agent on Golders Green Road. Turnover of tenants was rapid and frequent, so that it was easy for the landlady and her agents to fall into the habit of neglect. No one was proud of the house, or gave it any attention. The stairs and hallways were unpainted and shabby, even unlit, for nobody took care to replace lightbulbs, and one had to use a torch in the winter months to find one's way upstairs.

In February 1983, there were five people living at 23 Cranley Gardens. Two rooms on the ground floor were occupied by Fiona Bridges, a barmaid at the Royal Oak pub in St James's Lane, Muswell Hill, and her boyfriend Jim Allcock, a builder. Miss Bridges had been there since the summer of 1982, and Mr Allcock had joined her some months later. Another bedsitting-room on the ground floor was shared by Vivienne McStay, a dental nurse from Wellington, New Zealand, and Monique Van-Rutte, a youth welfare worker from Holland. It was a room actually sandwiched between the two rooms let to Fiona Bridges, as she had taken over an extra room from a previous tenant who had moved out. Monique and Vivienne had moved in on 28 December 1982, and so had been tenants for only five weeks.

Nobody was living on the first floor, which had been vacant for some time, but right at the top of the house was an attic flat of two rooms, kitchen and bathroom, occupied by a civil servant and his dog. He had been in the house longer than the other tenants, over a year by now, but none of them knew him at all well, or had exchanged many words with him. Jim Allcock had lived downstairs for two months before he even saw him. Monique and Vivienne had been to his attic flat once for coffee and a chat, which was unusual, but no friendship had evolved from this. Judging by letters left in the hall on the ground floor for 'Des Nilsen' they had assumed his name was Desmond. But they had not asked. In fact his name was Dennis Andrew Nilsen, and he was an executive officer at the Jobcentre in Kentish Town, London. He simply preferred to be called 'Des'. The dog, a black and white mongrel bitch with a bad eye, was called 'Bleep'. The only time you could be sure to see Mr Nilsen was in the morning before he went to work at 8 a.m., or on his return at 5.30 p.m., when he would invariably put Bleep on the lead and take her for a long, healthy walk, after being left in the flat for hours. The mutual devotion of man and dog was obvious to behold, and not a little humbling. If one were tempted to feel sorry for this lonely, rather distant man, who appeared to have no friends, one remembered the dog and her loyalty. Yet there was always a lingering hint of despair about him.

Dennis Nilsen was tall and slim, slightly stooped, with shoulders that tended to jut forward, and thick brown hair. He habitually wore dark trousers and a pale grey tweed jacket, blue shirt, dark blue tie. Though clean and tidy, he was obviously not prone to sartorial vanity, for his wardrobe was severely limited. One rarely saw him wear anything new or different, except perhaps a scarf which might suddenly appear. He wore rimless spectacles and was clean-shaven.

Now thirty-seven years old, he was good-looking enough for one to judge he had been handsome when younger. A wide, generous mouth with a full bottom lip was spoilt only when he laughed, revealing uneven teeth, brown at the edges, which could do with some attention from a dentist. But that would be cosmetic, and vanity was not in Mr Nilsen's character. He struck one as sincere and straightforward, for there was nothing shifty in his eye. Unlike many people who avert their glance after a few seconds' concentration, Dennis Nilsen would look directly at you, and you would feel the penetration of his gaze. There would be little point in trying to dissemble. He had, too, a firm and honest handshake.

None of this was apparent, of course, to the other inhabitants of 23 Cranley Gardens, who had virtually no knowledge of the aloof tenant with the dog in the attic. But his colleagues at work were aware of his qualities. In his eight years as a civil servant he had interviewed hundreds of people looking for work, where his direct approach was a valuable asset. He was never known to shirk his duties, but would rather undertake a workload which would make less addicted colleagues tremble. Work did indeed appear to be an obsession with him, and some wondered whether his life might hide some crucial emptiness which work attempted to fill. In addition, he had until recently taken on the unpaid duties of branch officer for the civil service union (C.P.S.A.) and seemed to relish the responsibility. In any dispute with the management before an industrial tribunal he would always support the workers' cause with the passion of a born advocate. He quickly had gained the reputation of a 'trouble-maker' because his labours on behalf of the underdog would often make the dispute more acrimonious than it had been before. No one questioned his motives, only his manner. He was so articulate and fluent in debate that it was difficult ever to win a point against him. His intelligence and his powers of marshalling essential arguments were admired, as was his capacity for organisation. His sense of equilibrium was secretly deplored; there appeared to be no allowance made in his mind for the virtues of compromise. He was later to call himself a 'monochrome man', all black and white with no

4

gradations between extremes. Dennis Nilsen was also known at work for an anarchic, surprising, and often hilarious sense of humour.

None of Nilsen's colleagues visited the attic flat in Cranley Gardens which he shared with his dog. They were not invited, and they did not feel inclined to suggest dropping in. Des was amusing and bright, but not cosy; he was not the sort to attract a confidence. Besides, he tended to talk so much, about matters of political or union interest, that there would be little promise of an intimate chat. So he was left to go home alone, passing the strangers on the ground floor as he climbed three flights of stairs to his own front door. The scene beyond the door was frankly squalid. A tiny hall, immediately before you as you opened the door, served as a kitchen, with a gas stove on the left against the wall, and next to it a sink. The stove was thick with grease and fat left by a succession of previous tenants, which Nilsen had not bothered to clean. He never used the grimy oven, but confined his cooking to the rings on the top. Immediately opposite was the door to his bathroom, the bathtub on the right beneath a sloping ceiling in which was a large, square roof window, kept wide open. The two doors on the right of the hall/kitchen led to a front room and a bedroom at the back, both with sloping attic ceilings. Nilsen lived in the bedroom, which contained a double bed, a large television set, stereo equipment, some posters on the wall, pot plants, and a thick, tall candle with months of molten wax cascading down the sides. The room at the front had two plain wardrobes, a tea-chest in the corner, and two armchairs either side of the window. Little else. The carpets were not fitted, but lay squarely on the floor, dull, brown, patterned, not alluring. This room appeared never to be used, but was distinguished by one feature, clearly visible from the street and often commented upon; the front windows were always flung wide open. What you could not see from the street were the occasional joss-sticks in the room which struggled to disperse an indeterminate, unpleasant smell.

During the first week of February 1983, a problem arose at the house which was initially to affect all the tenants and eventually to have repercussions which would be felt far beyond the confines of Cranley Gardens. It was Jim Allcock who first noticed that the toilet, which he shared with Fiona and the two other girls on the ground floor, would not flush. This was on Thursday, 3 February. Twice he tried to clear the blockage, using an acid preparation which he bought from the ironmongers, but whatever was causing the obstruction resisted the acid poured down the lavatory pan and could not be made to budge by any amount of prodding with sticks. The water would rise in the pan but would not fall again. There was a danger of overflowing, a danger to health. Jim decided he would call Ellis & Co. the following day.

On Friday, 4 February, Fiona Bridges left a note in the lavatory to warn Vivienne and Monique not to use it in case there was a risk from the acid. She then tried to use another lavatory next to her usual one, and noticed that when this was flushed it made the water rise in the other one. It was especially inconvenient as her parents were coming to stay for the weekend (and Jim would have to move out). There seemed to be no lavatory in the house which was working properly. Jim called Ellis & Co., who gave him the number of a plumber, Mike Welch, who could see to the job quickly; he had been to the house before. At 4.15 p.m. Fiona called him and left a message with his wife. A couple of hours later, she bumped into Des Nilsen in the hall and asked him if he was having any trouble with his toilet, as hers was blocked. He said no, he had no trouble, and went upstairs to his flat. Mike Welch was home by 8.30 that evening, received the message about 23 Cranley Gardens, and determined to investigate the matter first thing on Saturday morning. Miss Bridges had been told not to expect him until then anyway. On Friday night they would just have to make do.

That same Friday night upstairs in the attic, Dennis Nilsen had other problems to cope with. In one of his wardrobes in the front room was the dead body of a young man he had met eight days before. Nilsen took a black plastic disposal bag, slit it up the side to make a sheet of it, and laid it on the floor of the front room, right in the middle. From the wardrobe he hauled the body and laid it face upwards on the

6

plastic sheet. He went to the kitchen and selected a long kitchen knife with a brown handle, which he sharpened briefly, then took it with him into the front room. Kneeling on the floor, he carefully cut off the young man's head. There was rather more blood than he anticipated, some of it flowing off the sheet on to the carpet, so he had to prepare another plastic sheet. From the bathroom he brought in a large cooking pot, placed the young man's head in it, filled it with water, and took it to the kitchen stove. He lit two burners so that the pot would boil more quickly, from the sides as well as from underneath. Back in the front room, he moved the headless body from one sheet on to the other, and took up the first. Some of the blood spilled off on to the white bathroom carpet as he was carrying it through. He tried to mop this up with paper towels, unsuccessfully, then covered the stain with a spare bit of brown carpet. By now he was getting fed up with his chore. He felt he needed a drink, and as he had the whole weekend in front of him to complete the job, why hurry? In the kitchen, the head was beginning to boil furiously, so he turned it down to simmer, called Bleep, and showed her the lead. She was naturally excited at the prospect of a walk. He did not pass any of the people downstairs on his way out.

Dennis Nilsen and his dog walked down to Muswell Hill Broadway and went to Shepherd's supermarket. While Bleep stayed tied up outside, Nilsen bought some cigarettes, a bottle of Bacardi rum and some Coca-Cola. They walked back to Cranley Gardens at a leisurely pace. They saw no one on the way upstairs, and the young man's head was still simmering gently. Nilsen listened to some music through his headphones (classical orchestral music had appeal at times like this, being soothing and peaceful; his favourite pop music, particularly Laurie Anderson's 'Oh Superman', was too suggestive of recent memories). He also watched some television, and managed to polish off three-quarters of his new bottle of rum. At the end of a long evening he switched the gas off under the simmering pot, and left the head there overnight. The rest of the body still lay in the front room. Dennis Nilsen went to bed, tired and slightly drunk.

7

He did not wake up until 11 a.m. the next morning, Saturday, 5 February, by which time the plumber Mike Welch was already investigating the blockage downstairs. He had arrived at 10.30 a.m. and having tried to clear the lavatory pan with his usual tools, which did not work, he went home to get a ladder so that he could have a look under the inspection cover on the wall outside where the pipes from all lavatories in the house converged. He cleared the junction of accumulated excrement and tried to reach down further into the vertical pipe but failed. At that point Mike Welch decided that this would have to be a job for specialists with sophisticated equipment; ordinary plumbers' tools were clearly unequal to the task. He told Miss Bridges and Mr Allcock that they should call Dyno-rod.

Jim Allcock called Dyno-rod at 12.40 p.m. on Saturday afternoon, while Fiona Bridges contacted Ellis & Co. Although Ellis & Co. agreed to pay the bill, they could not give authority for any work to be carried out until the following Monday. In view of the fact that they would all be stuck with a blocked drain for the rest of the weekend, Jim left a note on Des Nilsen's door asking him not to use his toilet lest it cause overflowing in the others. 'Plumber has been don't flush the loo,' it said. Later on Saturday Fiona saw Nilsen on his way out and explained the meaning of the note; she said she would let him know on Monday when it was all right to resume use of the toilet. Nilsen acknowledged and walked off, pensive. 'I began to realise that it could be something to do with my activities,' he later admitted.[1]

Those 'activities' had already caused Nilsen some embarrassment that afternoon. His doorbell had rung unexpectedly. He couldn't possibly let anyone in with a decapitated body on the floor. He turned the television down and held Bleep to keep her quiet. A little later there were knocks at his door. He waited until he heard footsteps down the stairs. 'I thought it could be someone I knew. It would have been silly of me to say "You can't come in," so I stayed quiet.'[2] The visitor was an old friend whom he had not seen in months, Martin Hunter-Craig. Hunter-Craig was one of the few people who had demonstrated to Nilsen that he enjoyed his company,

8

and he would normally have been a very welcome guest. He was passing through (he lived in Devon) and decided to surprise Des. According to his recollections, Des did answer the door without opening it. 'Don't come in, I'm tied up with someone here,' he said.[3]

Nilsen spent the entire evening on Saturday watching the television. On Sunday afternoon, 6 February, he braced himself to finish off the job of dismemberment. By this time he knew that on Monday some awkward questions might be asked. The least he could do was hide things away in the wardrobe. He took the knife again, sharpened it, and cut the body into four pieces: two sections of arm and shoulder, the rib cage, and the lower half of the torso up to the waist and including the legs. The first three sections he placed in plastic bags and put them in the cupboard. The legs were put in another bag and stuffed under an upturned drawer in the bathroom. He removed the partially boiled head from the pot, and put this into a plastic carrier bag and then into one of the black plastic bags which contained the other remains. On top of everything he placed a deodorant stick and locked both doors to the wardrobe. For the moment the problem was locked away and could be forgotten. But time was running out; Nilsen's mind would not be allowed to rest for many more hours. A few hours would make little difference to a mind which had been in sporadic and secret turmoil for over four years. The moment was approaching for taking stock and reaching decisions.

Monday, 7 February, did not bring the promised resolution of the drainage problem. Fiona Bridges called the agents again and was told the matter was in hand. Yet it was not until Tuesday afternoon at 4.15 p.m. that Ellis & Co. instructed Dyno-rod to conduct a thorough investigation of the premises. Meanwhile Nilsen went to work as usual at the Jobcentre in Kentish Town, where he was observed to dispatch his desk-load with his customary assiduity and energy. He was however a trifle short with colleagues, rather more impatient than usual. To one he apologised, remarking that he was under great pressure at the moment.

The Dyno-rod engineer eventually appeared at 23 Cranley

Gardens at 6.15 p.m. on Tuesday, 8 February. He was Michael Cattran, thirty years old and relatively new to the staff. After a cursory examination of the pipes he decided that the problem was most likely below ground level and would have to be properly investigated in daylight. It was already dark, but with the help of Jim Allcock, who held a torch, Cattran went to the side of the house, where there was a manhole cover, cracked across the top, leading directly down to the sewers. The drop inside was about twelve feet, and access was made possible by iron rungs in the wall of the manhole. Cattran went down the steps while Allcock held the torch. They both noticed a peculiarly revolting smell, which Cattran knew not to be the usual smell from excrement. To Allcock he said, 'I may not have been in the game for long, but I know that isn't shit.' In fact, he was convinced it was the smell of rotting flesh. There was a porridge on the floor of the sewer, eight inches thick, composed of about thirty or forty pieces of flesh, greyish-white in colour and of various sizes. As Cattran moved, more of the thick white substance fell out of the pipe leading from the house. He was deeply worried and knew straight away that he would have to report the matter to his superiors. Back in the house at 7 p.m. he telephoned his manager, Gary Wheeler, and told him his suspicions. By this time all the tenants were surrounding Michael Cattran and heard the conversation. Monique and Vivienne came out of their room, Des Nilsen came downstairs. Wheeler said they would have to take a closer look together in the morning, if the tenants did not mind waiting, but there was no need yet to call the police, in case they were making a fuss about nothing and the blockage could be satisfactorily explained. Cattran put down the telephone and said to Nilsen, 'You've got a dog, haven't you? Do you put dog meat down the toilet?' Nilsen replied that he did not, but the remark suggested to him a possible course of action.

Nilsen had already written and posted a letter to Mr Roberts of Ellis & Co., dated 8 February, asking that 'routine upkeep and maintenance' of the house be attended to in order to keep 'living standards at a tolerable level'. He specifically complained about lack of lighting in the common areas, and further, 'When I flush my toilet the lavatory pans in the lower flats overflow (since Friday 4 February). Obviously the drains are blocked and unpleasant odours permeate the building.'[4] Did he write this as a demonstration that he was as bewildered as everybody else in the house, to deflect the finger of suspicion? Or did he wish to bring matters to a speedy conclusion? His motives were undeniably mixed and confused. The desire to survive was almost irresistible, yet stronger still, perhaps, was the need to seek release from an intolerable nightmare. The struggle of opposing forces continued within him until about midnight, by which time he had made up his mind.

Before he left, Cattran took both Allcock and Nilsen to look once more at the blockage down the manhole, shining his torch and commenting that it looked like flesh. Nilsen went upstairs to his flat and pondered. At midnight he came down again, removed the manhole cover and climbed down to the debris, carrying a torch and carrier bag. 'I cleared the particles of white flesh and dumped them over the back garden hedge,' he later wrote.

> I had planned to go to the supermarket or Kentucky Fried Chicken and purchase a few pounds' weight of chicken pieces. These I would soak, cut up into similar chunks as that removed (being careful to leave easily identifiable wing-tips and drum-sticks). Any close examination in the morning would reveal in the open stretch of pipe an ordinary shattering of the imagination. The police and Dyno-rod would lose interest. The Dyno-rod man would not wish to appear foolish when the police were called again. I could see this plan easily succeeding. I could also see before me a situation where I could not guarantee that another death would not occur at some future time. I was sickened by the past, the present, and a doubtful future. I had found the whole mad burden of guilt intolerable.[5]

Nilsen drank lots of Bacardi that night. He thought of suicide, but rejected the idea because nobody would believe what he had to say in any note he might leave, so incredible would it seem, and besides he owed it to 'all the others' to let their fate be known; that fate would never be revealed if he were dead. 'Someone's got to know the truth about what happened to them,' he thought. He would also have had to kill Bleep, if he killed himself, and he knew he would never be able to do that. He could run away, disappear, but he could not escape from himself; he could not live with the notion that he was a coward, nor could he feel content that his deeds should forever remain undetected. A peculiar and paradoxical desire that he should not 'get away with it' compounded the torment of his mind as the hours dragged on. But at last he knew what he would do. He finished the rum, 'listened to some music and kept Bleep close to me (the last warm and lovely influence left in my life)'.[6] Finally, he slept.

Fiona Bridges and Jim Allcock were by now more than apprehensive; they were seriously alarmed. They had heard the footsteps on the stairs, the front door opening, the manhole being removed, more clanking and scraping, the sound of someone walking down the side of the house towards the garden. Fiona had said to Jim, 'There's somebody having a go at the manhole. I bet it's him upstairs.'[7] Jim took a pole and went to investigate, catching Nilsen as he came back in, his shirt sleeves rolled up above the elbow, a torch in his hand. 'Just went out to have a pee,' he said, but Jim had not believed him. Neither he nor Fiona slept well.

At 8.30 the next morning, 9 February, they heard Nilsen walk down the stairs. Jim looked out of the window and watched him disappear down the street. At 9.15 a.m. Michael Cattran arrived with his manager Gary Wheeler and went straight to the manhole. Cattran lifted the cover, shone his torch down, and to his utter consternation saw that the drain was clear. 'It's all gone,' he exclaimed. It didn't make sense; no amount of rainfall could have dislodged such a large amount, and he already knew the lavatories were not functioning well enough to have any effect. Cattran rang the front door bell; Jim Allcock had seen all the stuff last night, he could confirm it. In fact, Jim had gone to work, but he had seen all the confirmation he needed before he left. At the side of the house, he noticed that the crack in the manhole cover was now in a different position.

Cattran went down the manhole to have a closer look. He put his hand in one of the drains which led into the sewer and pulled out a piece of meat from the back of the interceptor. 'I've got something,' he said. Wheeler told him to bring it up. They put it on the ground and thought for a moment; it smelt like something from a slaughter-house, was greyish yellow, wrinkled, about six inches long, like a piece of chicken. There were also four pieces of bone which Cattran retrieved from the same source. Fiona Bridges came out and told the men about the noises she had heard coming from the manhole during the night. She admitted she was scared. At that point it was decided to call the police.

Dennis Nilsen turned in at the office as usual and tried to behave normally. But he knew he would never be back there. He tidied his desk and left a note in a plain brown envelope tucked at the back of the drawer, on which he wrote that should he be arrested, there would be no truth in any announcement saying that he committed suicide in his cell. This was all he left. He seemed cheerful enough, and was even wearing a blue and white football scarf, a quite uncharacteristic dazzle of colour. No one knew he possessed such a scarf. Later, he wrote about his thoughts on that day.

I was sure that I would probably be arrested when I came home or some time that evening. I was through running. I was totally resigned to this inevitability. I was worried about what was going to happen to Bleep. I was also worried about the shock my revelations would bring to the next of kin of those who had died. The night before I had thought of dumping the remains left in my flat but decided to leave everything exactly where it was. I even thought an arrest might not come until the next morning (10/2/83). By the time I arrived home on the evening of 9 February I was tired and prepared for what lay ahead. I thought that the police would either be outside waiting in a car, in another flat, or actually outside my flat.[8]

Detective Chief Inspector Peter Jay was waiting just inside

the front door. He had been to Cranley Gardens at 11 a.m. following the call from Fiona Bridges, had seen the flesh and bones hauled up from the drain, taken them in a plastic bag to Hornsey Mortuary, and finally taken them to Charing Cross Hospital where David Bowen, Professor of Forensic Medicine at the University of London and consultant pathologist, had examined them at 3.30 in the afternoon. Professor Bowen declared that the tissue was human, probably from the region of the neck, and the bones were from a man's hand. By 4.30 p.m. D.C.I. Jay was back at 23 Cranley Gardens, accompanied by Detective Inspector Stephen McCusker and Detective Constable Jeffrey Butler. They waited for Dennis Nilsen to appear. He arrived home at 5.40 p.m.

D.C.I. Jay introduced himself, saying that he had come about the drains. Nilsen expressed surprise that such a matter should be of concern to the police, and asked if the other two gentlemen were health inspectors. He was told they were police officers and given their names. All four men walked up to Nilsen's flat and entered the bedroom at the back. Mr Jay told Nilsen he was interested in the drains because they contained some remains which had been identified as human. Nilsen expressed surprise ('Good grief! How awful!'), but not for long. 'Don't mess about,' said Jay. 'Where's the rest of the body?' 'In two plastic bags in the wardrobe next door,' said Nilsen. 'I'll show you.' They went into the front room where Nilsen pointed out the wardrobe and offered his keys. Jay said he would not open the wardrobe for the moment, as the smell was confirmation enough. 'Is there anything else?' he asked. 'It's a long story,' said Nilsen. 'It goes back a long time. I'll tell you everything. I want to get it all off my chest, not here but at the police station.' D.C.I. Jay then cautioned him and arrested him on suspicion of murder. For Nilsen it was the end of a road fraught with bewilderment, anxiety, horror, and the keeping of a desperate solitary secret. For Inspector Jay it was the beginning of a case unlike any he had encountered in twenty-six years as a policeman. Indeed, it was to prove unlike any in the history of criminal investigation in Britain. He had a suspected murderer, and as yet had no idea who had been

14

murdered. The investigation would have to go backwards towards detection, rather than forwards towards arrest.

Butler was left at the flat, while Jay and McCusker took Dennis Nilsen by car to Hornsey Police Station. Sitting in the back of the car next to Nilsen, McCusker said, 'Are we talking about one body or two?' Nilson replied, 'Fifteen or sixteen, since 1978. I'll tell you everything. It's a relief to be able to get it all off my mind.' In the charge room at Hornsey Jay was still incredulous. 'Let's get this straight,' he said. 'Are you telling us that since 1978 you have killed sixteen people?' 'Yes,' replied Nilsen, 'three at Cranley Gardens and about thirteen at my previous address, 195 Melrose Avenue, Cricklewood.' 'That was the end of the beginning and the end of the killing,' wrote Nilsen later. 'The wheels of the law were beginning to spin and speed up down the long slope accelerating under the weight of their new unexpected load. It was all out.'9

The signs of shock sustained by experienced policemen who might have been impervious to such revelations was palpable. The causes were many. There was the apparent readiness of Dennis Nilsen to talk freely, openly, even volubly, about events which it was not to his advantage to reveal; his seeming emotional indifference; the fact that it was possible to kill undetected for four years in a London suburb. There would be later press allegations that the police had been offered clues over the past years which they had failed to recognise, clues often strewn by Nilsen himself.* But this is to anticipate. The implications of these thoughts revealed themselves gradually over the next few days. For the moment, on 9 February, shock derived from the grisly evidence found at 23 Cranley Gardens in the wardrobe.

That evening, while Nilsen remained in a cell at Hornsey Police Station, Professor Bowen accompanied the detectives Chambers and Jay to Nilsen's flat at 9 p.m. They removed from the wardrobe two plastic bags which they took to Hornsey Mortuary; Professor Bowen opened the bags and conducted the examination. In one bag he found four smaller bags,

* See Appendix.

three of them the kind of light shopping bag in everyday use and supplied by cashiers at supermarkets; one was a Sainsbury's bag. In the first shopping bag he found the left side of a man's chest, including the arm; in a second there was the right side of the chest, also with the arm attached; the third contained a headless, legless and armless torso, with no evidence of fractures or wounds but clear signs of skilful dissection. The Sainsbury's bag carried perhaps the most frightening load of all: a heart, two lungs, spleen, liver, gall bladder, kidneys and intestines, all mixed together in a disgusting, impersonal pottage. The stench, released from long-sealed bags, was overpowering.

Professor Bowen identified a knife wound in the heart, but drew no conclusions from it. When he read Bowen's statement weeks later, Nilsen reflected upon this himself, with unbelievable detachment: 'The stab wound to the heart was probably caused accidentally when I had my hands and knife inside the rib cage working blind and trying to cut it out [the heart].'[10]

In the second large bag, which also had many smaller ones within it, Professor Bowen discovered another torso, this time with the arms attached but the hands missing; a skull whose flesh had been boiled away, and a head which still retained much of the flesh and some hair at the back, though the hair from the top and front of the head had gone. It looked as if it had been subjected to 'moist heat', quite recently. This was the head that Nilsen had started to boil at the weekend, in a final rush to get rid of it.

At a quarter to eleven the next day, 11 February, the questioning of Dennis Nilsen began, in Mr Jay's first-floor office at Hornsey. It was to last over thirty hours, spread throughout the coming week, and was distinguished by a most unusual degree of full and thorough co-operation by Nilsen, who offered details, descriptions of technique, and aids towards identification calculated to help the police. Not only did he make no hindrance, but positively swamped the detectives with information faster than they could seek it. He barely required questioning; he spoke in an almost unbroken autobiographical monologue, as if to purge his conscience of a burden which he could no longer bear alone. Yet there were no irrelevant details, no digressions into personal life, no pleas for comfort or understanding. It turned out that one of Nilsen's previous jobs had been as a probationary police officer, which gave him some knowledge of how interviews of this nature should be conducted, and he had himself interviewed hundreds of people in the course of his work as a civil servant. Another striking aspect of this week was Nilsen's apparent lack of any hint of remorse; he admitted that he was astonished he had no tears for the people who had died at his hands. In the interviews he displayed no more emotion than the chair on which he was sitting. The police officers found this self-control chilling, but Nilsen would later reveal that he had to remain dispassionate in order for the evidence to be taken down in a proper manner, that his professional training enabled him to feign calmness and rationality while, privately, the rehearsal of his past actions disturbed a long-suppressed whirlpool of fear, pity and self-lacerating remorse within him. 'Nobody must see me weep for victims,' he wrote, 'that is our private grief.'[11] The question as to whether or not this 'grief' was genuine would prove crucial to an understanding of the man and to an assessment of the causes which diverted his personality down a path strewn with ghastly encounters. But for the moment, facts were all.

Within the first few minutes of the first interview, Nilsen had told the police that there were the remains of three different people at his flat, one whom he called John the Guardsman, one whose name he did not know, and the third, Stephen Sinclair, a young drug-addict and social outcast whom he had met on 26 January and killed that same evening. This meant that the police had a name and could, if they worked quickly on identification, keep Nilsen on one charge pending deeper investigation; otherwise they would have had to release him within forty-eight hours, and they knew enough already to view that prospect with alarm. He also told them, after they had challenged him with the contents of his wardrobe, examined the previous night, that they should look in the tea-chest in the corner of the front room, and under the drawer in the bathroom. Disconcertingly, he expressed relief that he had been caught. 'If I had been arrested at sixty-five years of age there might have been thousands of bodies behind me.'[12]

Accordingly, on 11 February Dr Bowen had the task of opening the tea-chest and a bag stuffed in the bathroom. The bag contained the lower half of Stephen Sinclair, from the waist down and including the legs. In the tea-chest, beneath a thick velvet curtain, sheets, and pages from the *Guardian*, there were several bags, including one from Woolworth. In these were found another torso, another skull, various bones, mothballs and air-fresheners.

It was now possible to assemble various pieces of Stephen Sinclair on the floor of the mortuary, a ghoulish reconstruction which caused D.C.I. Jay, for the first time in his professional life, to feel faint. D.C.S. Chambers, too, was affected as never before, although his years of experience outnumbered even Jay's. The remains were identified as belonging to Stephen Sinclair by fingerprints, which were on police files, Sinclair having been wanted for minor offences at the time of his death. Fingerprints from hands of dismembered arms matched.

On the same day, Nilsen went with the police to a house at 195 Melrose Avenue, Cricklewood, where he had lived from 1976 to 1981 and where, according to him, another twelve men had met their deaths. He pointed out an area of the garden where they might find some evidence of human remains. Furthermore, he told them that there were another seven people he had tried to kill and failed, some because he had stopped himself, others because they had escaped.

By the evening of 11 February, police evidence was sufficient for them to bring a charge against Dennis Nilsen, and he was advised that he should have a solicitor with him. (He had been offered this facility earlier, but had declined.) Accordingly, Ronald T. Moss of Moss, Beachley was approached and asked if he would represent Nilsen. Moss, an ebullient, cheerful man around forty years of age, had been involved in murder cases before, but never anything of this magnitude. Initially hesitant, fearful that the implications of the case might prove an unusually harsh emotional burden,

Moss needed only a few seconds' reflection before he accepted. 'I knew it was going to be the most worrying responsibility I would ever have,' he said, 'but it's my job.' As it turned out, his comparative youth and his straightforward approach, lacking any of the traditional deviousness one sometimes finds in lawyers, won Nilsen's confidence from the start, although the relationship was to collapse when the pressures of Nilsen's long remand began to tell. At 5.40 p.m. precisely, Nilsen was charged with the murder of Stephen Sinclair.

At 10 a.m. the next morning, Nilsen appeared at Highgate Magistrates' Court and was remanded in police custody for three days. Ronald Moss wanted to satisfy himself that Nilsen understood what was happening. Of this there could be little doubt. 'Defendant calm and rational,' he noted. Nilsen had been brought to the court at 8 a.m. in order to avoid the hordes of pressmen and photographers who were expected to gather. Gather they did, for the case, already reported in the newspapers as a result of police activity in Melrose Avenue, and also owing to the awkward coincidence that one of the witnesses who had just made a statement was related to a journalist, was arousing frantic interest. Some of the tabloid newspapers merrily referred to the 'House of Horrors' before there was any evidence that anything horrific had taken place within its walls. ('The only House of Horrors I know', wrote Nilsen in his cell, 'is Number 10 Downing Street.')[13] Within an hour of his having been charged, reporters had tracked down his mother in Aberdeenshire, a white-haired, attractive and extremely friendly woman, and invaded her house, demanding photographs. Bemused by such an overwhelming piece of news, she went upstairs to fetch what she could find, and had the precious snaps snatched out of her hand by people eager to get a 'scoop'. She insisted that she was only lending the pictures, not giving them away, but she later received word that some had been sold for large sums of money. (She herself would not accept a penny.) She later discovered that one man had a tape-recorder in his pocket which was switched on to capture her response at the moment she was told her son had been arrested for murder. When they dispersed, she was left trembling with shock. Other careful reporters, proud of themselves for having noticed that all the victims were said to have been men, hunted down people who had been at school with Dennis Nilsen twenty-five years earlier and asked if they had ever masturbated together. All this frenzied activity erupted long before the police had finished questioning their suspect, and on one occasion a Japanese crew was located in a house opposite the police station training highly sophisticated sound equipment on the walls and eavesdropping on Nilsen's amazing revelations.

Gradually, the newspapers ferreted out some basic clues to his past: he was homosexual, he came into contact with young men in the evenings, he was a radical left-wing trade unionist with a reputation for militant attitudes, and he appeared cold. Angry at the simplistic press attention he was receiving, Nilsen penned his own pastiche of a tabloid news report, a week after his arrest:

RED MONSTER LURES YOUNG MEN TO THEIR DEATHS IN HOMOSEXUAL HOUSE OF HORROR
Dennis Andrew Nilsen, 37, once believed to have close links with the Militant Tendency and the Socialist Workers Party (and personal supporter of Red Ken) appeared at the Old Bailey today to face 15 charges of murder and 9 charges of attempted murder.

Nilsen, who has been to East Berlin, sat in court in sombre suit and tie. He appeared unmoved and emotionless as the prosecution evidence was read out. It was revealed that Nilsen, a misfit and extremist trade union agitator, had butchered his helpless victims on his kitchen floor and burnt the pieces in front of neighbourhood children.

It is believed that during the Garners Steak House dispute he had 'bullied' staff at the Jobcentre into blacking of legal job vacancies. 'He always intimidated us,' said a spokesman for the staff at the Jobcentre. While maintaining a respectable front in the civil service he prowled the streets of London.[14]

The humour, which might appear misplaced, was to prove a welcome antidote to the catalogue of killing which Nilsen revealed in the course of that week. Policemen are as vulnerable as the rest of us to the shock of such a story, especially when delivered fluently, in a factual manner indifferent to its effect. Chambers, Jay and Nilsen all smoked ceaselessly throughout the interviews, leaving the non-smoker Ronald Moss to breathe his way through the fumes as best he could. Moss was perceptibly upset by what he heard. Nilsen told how he had cut up a body in the bath into small pieces of flesh, a few inches long, and flushed them down the toilet. When he asked what he should do with his cigarette butts in his cell, where there was no ashtray, and was advised by a junior constable to put them in the lavatory, he said that the last time he did that he was arrested. The police officers must be forgiven for bursting into relieved laughter. They needed it. They did not understand what manner of man they had before them and welcomed any respite, however short and however tasteless, from the labour of concentrating upon the dilemma with which they were faced. Who was he? How could he? What possible motive could there be? How was it possible that he escaped detection for so long? Why was he now telling them so much? Why did his long and vivid statement to the police make them feel sick, even physically ill at some points, and seem to leave him unmoved? Why, finally, in spite of his obvious self-confidence, the hint of arrogance, his unattractive stubbornness, did Messrs Chambers and Jay find that they did not dislike him, that they naturally fell into the habit of calling him 'Dés'?

There is no doubt that one of the reasons Nilsen co-operated so totally was that he felt at ease with Chambers and Jay. Before beginning the interviews, the two detectives discussed privately what sort of approach they should take with him. Should they be firm, authoritarian, heavy with him, or should they aim at a relaxed atmosphere? Mr Chambers instinctively felt that they would elicit more information from this man by the second approach, and Mr Jay confirmed that that was his impression too. They further recognised that his long experience in the army (see Chapter

21

4) would make him respect rank, but resist coercion. It was a professional decision born of long experience, and it paid off. Had they assumed a posture of attack, Nilsen would almost certainly have clammed up.

Still, the enigma deepened with each hour, the mysteries multiplied. Chambers and Jay tried to cling to the central threads of motive and manner, but could see no consistency. Superintendent Chambers, who asked all the questions throughout the week of interviews, at one point challenged Nilsen with the view that he was a cold, calculating killer: 'I think you went out looking for these people with the express intention of luring them back to your flat, plying them with drink and then killing them.' This, at least, would make sense, and would clearly establish, if true, that there was premeditation. Without hesitation, Nilsen replied:

> I can agree with a part of what you say. I do go out in search of company. When I voluntarily go out to drink I do not have the intention at that time to do these things. Things may happen afterwards drinkwise but they are not foreplanned. I'm certainly not consciously aware of what you are saying. I seek company first, and hope everything will be all right.[15]

Under further questioning, it emerged that there were far more people who had been to Nilsen's flat for a drink without any harm coming to them than there had been people who finished the evening dead. 'I've killed people, but I can't understand why those people. There's no common factor.' That was the problem, precisely: no consistency of purpose, no repetition, no easily recognisable pattern. Here was a man who had, by his own admission, performed monstrous acts, yet resented being called a 'monster' and was never treated as such by those who arrested him, a man whose company some had sought and paid a terrible price for, while others crossed his path unscathed many times, and yet others had been saved from death by him. Here was a man who until 1978 had been an estimable citizen and was still, in every other respect, a normal London resident going about his work. His activities had not terrorised the community; on the contrary, no one noticed the disappearance of most of his victims, a circumstance which astonished him as much as anyone; had it been otherwise, he would in all likelihood have been caught earlier, and would, again as far as one can make out, have welcomed arrest. (Superintendent Chambers was however convinced that he would never have walked into a police station and given himself up, which is also probably true.) Had they been privy to the poem which Nilsen wrote about his attitude towards the dismembered body of Stephen Sinclair on his last day before arrest, they would have been even more confused. The poem, entitled 'Sweet', indicates a softness and a gentleness which nobody who had come into contact with Nilsen in the past few days would have credited as being natural to him. It also shows a strange identity of murderer and victim forming an alliance against the authorities, and it undeniably shows a heart-stopping distortion of personality:

> Here in the hall of plenty there is nothing now.
> Just you
> Lying under my hands,
> With shadowy figures approaching
> With some formalities
> To take you into their 'system',
> And me.
> Think over
> The lonely life of you.
> It is tomorrow soon enough
> And they will meddle in our business.
> Privacy has no boundaries
> Which cannot be breached
> By the law's charges.

After this, wrote Nilsen,

> I dress and prepare for a final day of freedom. I take Bleep to the back garden. I replace the cracked manhole cover having refused to complete the cover-up. I knew the form

23

to follow that evening but would act as normally as I could. I put on his blue and white scarf, lit a Marlboro and stepped out into my last legend.[16]

Dennis Nilsen wrote more about his state of mind, as he understood it, after Sinclair had been killed, and this reflective confession will find its place later in this narrative.

He told the police everything they needed for a conviction, but no more; the rest, he felt, was still 'private' and not the business of the law to understand. Besides which, he was by no means sure that he was himself able to understand. 'I cannot unravel the complexities of this case.'[17]

When the interviews were completed and Ronald Moss had sat through days of graphic and awful description of death, pinching himself to regain the comfort of normal pain against a recital of Dostoievskian horror, he asked Nilsen one question: 'Why?' The reply was disarming. 'I am hoping you will tell me that,' he said.

The accused was removed to Brixton Prison on remand, whence he wrote an elegant letter of thanks to D.C.S. Chambers commending the Hornsey team on a professional job well done, producing yet another ripple of surprise from this enigmatic man. Attention from the press was now necessarily subdued, the case being *sub judice*. The newspapers could afford to keep silent for the next few months, having successfully implanted in the public mind an image of unmitigated depravity. In Brixton, Nilsen wrote:

> The train of words' digestion
> And answers from my head
> Cannot give the answer
> Or hope to raise the dead.
> Everyone wants labels
> Pinned neatly on my skin,
> A comfortable judgment
> Casting their stones at sin.
> Foaming Tory ladies,
> 'Rule Britannias' sung,
> 'Nilsen is a monster,

24

Should be bloody hung.'
Screaming mobs aplenty
Never knew Sinclair,
Wouldn't give him gutter-room,
Here or anywhere.[18]

To the present author he wrote, 'What can I ever say to turn
the unproductive past away? . . . my best moments of public
service may still lie ahead . . . I have judged myself more
harshly than any court ever could.'[19] Even before his arrest,
he had resigned himself to the humiliating realisation that his
many years of service, in the army, the police force, and the
Manpower Services Commission, would be judged much less
valuable than his necessary immolation as a result of his
crimes. At last the world was taking notice of him, listening to
every word, watching every move. The sad paradox of his
unremarkable life was to discover that he was, after all,
remarkable.

Nilsen warned me that I should find a full inquiry into his
life and deeds distressing; he admonished me with a quote
from *Georges Dandin* – 'Vous l'avez voulu, vous l'avez voulu.'
Certainly, there is always the possibility that if one seeks to
understand how such events as are related in this book
occurred, and even more if one seeks to feel from within the
motive forces of the man who caused them, one might oneself
become infected or contaminated by deeply-hidden streams
in the human psyche which are, in the normal course of
events, severely inhibited. Nilsen himself thought that public interest in his case (which genuinely took him aback) was
suspect:

I am always surprised and truly amazed that anyone can be
attracted by the macabre. The population at large is
neither 'ordinary' or 'normal'. They seem to be bound
together by a collective ignorance of themselves and what
they are. They have, every one of them, got their deep
dark thoughts with many a skeleton rattling in their secret
cupboards. Their fascination with 'types' (rare types) like
myself plagues them with the mystery of why and how a

25

living person can actually do things which may be only those dark images and acts secretly within them. I believe they can identify with these 'dark images and acts' and loathe anything which reminds them of this dark side of themselves. The usual reaction is a flood of popular self-righteous condemnation but a willingness to, with friends and acquaintances, talk over and over again the appropriate bits of the case.[20]

A just and subtle reflection, one might think, and not at all uncommon in people accused of vile murders who regard themselves as a cathartic release from the accumulated wickedness of mankind, and deeply resent the additional burden. Sympathy with murder is unthinkable. It is even safer not to understand.

And yet not to attempt an understanding is to abnegate a crucial responsibility. The murderer takes his place in the jumbled kaleidoscope of the human condition. So, too, does his audience. For them to enjoy the display of crime, detection, retribution, while refusing to be drawn into a steady contemplation of themselves as audience, and of the subterranean echoes which the case disturbs, would be fruitless and arid. To understand the steps which brought Dennis Nilsen and his victims to a lingering four-year catastrophe, one must go back to a fishing village on the coast of Aberdeenshire, Scotland, and beyond, and come forward to the war years in Fraserburgh, to school in Strichen, through bereavement, the sea, and on to a life of corrosive loneliness.

'No one wants to believe ever that I am just an ordinary man come to an extraordinary and overwhelming conclusion.'[21]

2

ORIGINS

Dennis Nilsen was born of a Scottish mother and Norwegian father in the town of Fraserburgh, on the north-easterly tip of Aberdeenshire, blown, buffeted, drenched and occasionally invaded by the fierce North Sea. His Norwegian inheritance is incidental, a postscript to a long legacy of Scottish ancestry which is fundamental to an assessment of his character. All the salient traits of his personality, including those which were apparent soon after his arrest, and many that lay hidden, are traceable to his strong Buchan roots. Sturdy independence, blunt honesty which despises compromise and forbids diplomacy, iconoclastic radicalism and contempt for privilege, garrulity, love of argument, distrust of the Church and faith in humanist logic, above all a deeply-ingrained and awesome respect for the irresistible forces of nature, especially the omnipotent and omnipresent sea, these are the characteristics of the rugged folk of the Buchan district from whom Dennis Nilsen sprang. A number of them, too, are readily prone to mental disorder of one kind or another, common enough in a community which has for centuries been turned in upon itself.

There is a clear difference between these Scots on the east coast and those on the west coast, a difference determined

27

ultimately by climate. The west coast, misty and gentle, produces mild, soft, trusting people; the east coast, with which we have to deal, is beset by constantly harsh and dangerous weather, which rears dogmatic character, unbudgeable opinions, and a fatalistic outlook on life. These are people who habitually keep their front doors closed, are suspicious of strangers, consider themselves outside the common run, and, in the fishing villages especially, are deeply and permanently aware of the dark side of their natures. Good and evil are realities for them, not thin religious concepts, and it is sometimes said, not fancifully, that the fisherfolk have markedly different personalities at night.

The district of Buchan, stretching southwards and westwards from Fraserburgh, is good farming land, crossed by stone walls and dotted with low stonebuilt farmhouses. The horizon is wide and low, and the trees have little chance to grow lush before they are punched by the wind and subdued. To the north and east there swells the sea, sometimes rising mountainously, always menacing and powerful. Yet it is the sea rather than the land which has historically given the Buchan people their livelihood, a fact which does not make it a friend, but rather a foe who has to be coaxed. Tamed it can never be, and to think of facing its mighty wrath and beating it would be absurdly presumptuous.

Fraserburgh, known throughout the area as 'The Broch', was built in 1592 on the site of a small village called Faithlie. It is the commercial and trading centre of the district, but it is a novice town compared to the string of fishing villages which stretch along the coasts west and south of it, and which have been inhabited, in one way or another, since the Ice Age. Names like Broadsea (or 'Bretsie'), St Combs, Cairnbulg, Inverallochy, have bred a people whose lineage ascends beyond time, and who have long since learnt that, when the men go to sea, they must not always be expected to come back. Thousands have not.

The boom in herring fishing, which reached its apogee in the nineteenth century, made the area prosperous, but the sea has always abounded in an endless variety of stock — cod, skate, turbot, mackerel, haddock, whiting, lobster and many more. The difficulty was not, for the most part, depletion of supply, but the constant risk involved in sailing, an exercise which has always been fraught with danger in these rough and unpredictable seas. To navigate a small boat by sextant and the stars required experience passed down through the genes, together with something more than courage. Every fishwife knew that half her family would be swallowed by the sea in time. There are cases on record which show a fishwife losing five of her menfolk, husband and sons, in five separate incidents spread over two years. The harshness of such a life does not breed optimism.

During the season, the fisherman's day would start at 3 a.m. and sometimes go on till midnight. The men were carried out to the boats on the backs of their wives to keep them dry, and a pretty sight it made, the women hoisting their colourful check skirts above the knee and wading out to sea. You could tell which village the fishwives came from by the distinctive colour of their skirt, or 'plaid'; it was a primitive kind of badge they wore. (Inverallochy's was red and black.) While the men were out tossing on the turbulent waves, the women would spend the day gutting and curing the fish, scores of them along the beach and over the rocks, covering every available inch with salt fish, and fighting off with stones the marauding seagulls who, screeching and swooping, could decimate a catch in minutes. On the roofs of the tiny cottages, hardly bigger than dolls' houses which one had to bend down to enter, the infants of the family would take a chair and cover all the tiles with gutted and split fish to dry in the sun. When the tiles showed moisture, it was time to turn the fish over. The colour, the noise, the smell, all combined to create a picturesque tableau which would entice any painter. What he would not see, or smell, or hear, was the utter exhaustion of the wife and her children at the end of the day, and their empty despair in the knowledge that, however many hours they worked, they would always be poor.

On certain days, the 'wifie' and her 'loons and quinies' (boys and girls) would travel to the 'near country' around Strichen, about seven miles inland, to exchange their fish for butter, eggs, cheese and milk from the farms. (The 'far country' was the Grampian mountains.) Also in Strichen and the Broch there were 'feeing markets', where the smaller children sometimes hired themselves out to a family which might need an extra pair of hands and be ready to pay for them. More often than not, however, the people of the village would organise themselves to maximum efficiency by adopting, for a few years, a neighbour's child if too many of their own had been lost and there was room in the bed.

The bed was a wooden box at one end of the cottage, or two wooden frames one on top of the other, into which everyone but the parents piled. At the other end was the open fireplace and the wooden table and benches for eating. All such cottages were known as 'butt and bens', and there are many of them surviving today; Dennis Nilsen's grandmother was born in one, and married from it twenty years later. Even the language spoken was unique to the Buchan people; it is not a dialect of the Scots tongue but a minority language known as 'Buchan Doric', completely incomprehensible to an Englishman, and only vaguely recognisable to a west coast Scot. This, too, helps to buttress the Buchan feeling of isolation, independence, and aloof superiority. They are not given to *politesse*, as they consider it a squandering of their precious energies to make time for the soft and the protected.

It is scarcely to be wondered, then, that the people of the Broch, of Broadsea, of Inverallochy, are distinguished by such sturdy pride in their race and their ancestry. They cannot bear to be patronised, and grow loudly indignant if anyone in authority should address them by surname only, which they consider profoundly insulting. ('In all my years as a public servant,' wrote Dennis Nilsen, 'I never regarded anyone, not even a road traffic victim, as only another face, name and number.')[1] Nor do they willingly grant obeisance to an aristocrat. Christian Watt, a fishwife from Broadsea whose papers were recently edited, wrote that her mother had told her never to depend on a living from landed proprietors, for it took away one's independence. It was preferable to be a poor fisher, she said, than a well-fed ladies' maid. 'Though a Lord or a servant, money will never make you if you are not right yourself.' Aristocrats who expected fishwives to bow to them were quickly disabused. 'Nowhere in north east Scotland have I seen this,' wrote Christian, referring back to the mid-nineteenth century, 'it is totally against the Buchan character to do such a thing. The Earl of Erroll tried to get folk at Cruden Bay to bow to him, he was feeble-minded. One wifie took his walking-stick and gave him a hiding.'[2]

There is in the fishing villages of Buchan a long tradition of radicalism brought down through the generations by verbal report and allied to an abiding sense of natural justice. Unlike radicalism of recent growth and political origins, theirs has its roots deep in Scottish history, in nationalist, Jacobite and anti-clerical bias. They were, for instance, angry at the famous Highland clearances, when the Duke of Sutherland's factor forcibly evicted hundreds of crofters to make way for a better use of the land. The clearances could be justified on economic grounds, but the fisherfolk (to whose villages some of the displaced and homeless crofters retreated) saw only greed and cruelty inflicted upon an ancient humble culture. Young Christian Watt with her acid tongue encountered Lord Macdonald (another intent on clearances) on the pier at Kyleakin on the west coast, and in front of an astonished audience shouted at him, 'You are lower than the outscourings of any pigsty, causing all that human suffering to innocent people.'[3] Had he lived on the east coast, she added, his castle would have been burnt to the ground.

Allied to this iconoclasm is a deep contempt for the divisions of class. It was widely thought that a public school education set the mind in treacle which only a hammering could break, and the strongest disapproval was reserved for those working people who crossed the threshold into a better world, then set up even higher barriers to keep their former fellows out.

Burnt castles were, and still are, a conspicuous feature around Fraserburgh. The castles of Inverallochy, Cairnbulg, Pitsligo, once solid defences against raiders from the sea, had been destroyed by government forces as punishment for Jacobite support in the Buchan district and left open to the sky, like ghastly skulls on the landscape. Children,

Dennis Nilsen included, have for generations played amongst the ruins of their people's past. They are never far from reminders of their history.

Radicalism has displayed itself also in a strong resistance to the established Church. The Presbyterian Church has never held the influence in the north-east of Scotland that it enjoys in the south and west. It has been estimated that four-fifths of the Buchan people were Episcopalian at heart, no doubt out of a desire, once more, to show their independence, the Episcopalian Church being allied to the Jacobite cause. Presbyterianism had eventually to be enforced, against much riotous rebellion (Presbyterian ministers were dragged from the pulpit), and those who clung to their chosen belief developed a nice sense of persecution which accorded well with their character. The Catholic religion held no attraction for them, and one would not expect it to. 'It struck me as a religion that may lend itself to a warm Mediterranean climate, where it began,' wrote Christian Watt, 'but not to cold northern climes. Cold and hunger sharpen one's desire for explanations.'4

On the other hand, there has always been a proliferation of minority sects to challenge the imposed orthodoxy, as if the need to resist must constantly find new outlets. 'The fisherfolk of the Buchan coast have been described as apt to embrace every new form of religion on offer.'5 'Born again' Christians and followers of the Faith Mission were by no means unusual from the nineteenth century onwards; one of Nilsen's distant relations on his grandmother's side, Jeanie Duthie, was well known and respected in Broadsea and the Broch for her good work on behalf of the Mission, and his mother belonged to the same sect for a time.

Perhaps this radicalism, demonstrable in so many ways, and curiously blended with congenital fatalism, accounted for the longevity of the Buchan race. There are many instances of fishwives living beyond their hundredth year, as blunt and argumentative as in their youth. You do not grow tired of living when you always have something to say. Their dry humour and loquacity rarely deserted them, and you could easily be detained for hours in conversation with a fishwife.

Almost the entire population of a fishing village was related through intermarriages stretching back centuries. In a very real sense, one might say that the village inhabitants were one large family of a few hundred individuals. A stroll through the well-kept and scrupulously clean cemeteries perched on high land overlooking the sea all the way down the coast reveals the same names over and over again — Stephens, Duthies, Whytes, Ritchies, Sims, Nobles, Watts, Buchans, often with the same Christian name recurring, to the extent that one can only distinguish one grave from the other by the dates.

Two consequences arose from this repetitive inbreeding. In the first place, there was the inevitable prevalence of both mental and medical disorders cropping up in the genes of one generation or the next. Some families had a history of dumbness, others of deafness, and some of insanity. Quite frequently, insanity would not be recognised as anything more than a quirk of character that relations merely became used to, or a tendency to depression which they tolerated, but five of Christian Watt's cousins were tainted with mental illness, and she herself spent the second half of her life in an asylum. She did not consider herself a lunatic, but wrote with plaintive intuition that the public should be educated to acknowledge that mental disorder was an illness. 'Probably the most tragic factor,' she said, 'is that the person can be as right as rain one day and tragically sick the next.'[6] It is a reflection worth bearing in mind when we turn to Inverallochy and the ancestry of Dennis Nilsen.

The second result of having so many families which bore the same name was that the name was finally hardly ever used. Nicknames, or what in Buchan are called 'tee-names', became the essential, the only mark of identity. If a street with ten houses harbours eight families called Duthie and, for example, half a dozen daughters called Elizabeth, the only way to distinguish them is to call them something else. Hence one might be called 'Jeanie's Betty' and another 'Kirsty's Leebie', while actually they were both christened 'Elizabeth Duthie'. Tee-names are sprinkled throughout the history of all these villages and endure almost to the present

33

day. It is only the generation born since the Second World War which has abandoned them.

Broadsea, to the west of Fraserburgh, has in the last thirty years been embraced and swallowed by the town, though it retains its distinctive Lilliputian character which astonishes the casual visitor who may wander off College Bounds, a main thoroughfare out of Fraserburgh, and find himself amongst houses scarcely higher than himself or in a square paved with sea-shells. Going out of The Broch to the south, however, after the broad, crescent-shaped beach of Fraserburgh Bay which offers four miles of pale yellow sand and long tides, the twin villages of Cairnbulg and Inverallochy remain unchanged and inviolate. Here the sand gives way to a rocky coast, and the houses huddle together in a haphazard way as if they had been thrown like dice and settled where they landed. In 1699 a list was drawn up of those men permitted to go to sea from Inverallochy as whyte fishers (i.e. not herring), and of these five were called Duthie, three were Stephens, and one bore the name of William Whyte. From all three families is Dennis Nilsen descended.

Willian Whyte (pronounced in Buchan Doric as 'Fyte') must be regarded as Nilsen's senior male ancestor on his mother's side. The Duthies and the Stephens come in by marriage, though how frequently before comparatively recent records it is impossible to tell (besides which, illegitimate births, mostly undocumented, were always a feature of village life). The Duthies were celebrated for their hard-working and ambitious character. Sir William Duthie of Inverallochy rose from a fishing butt and ben to become Member of Parliament for Banffshire, and Sir John Duthie of Cairnbulg was an eminent barrister who restored Cairnbulg Castle.

There were two Duthie sisters who bring us close to the present day and may be said to write the preface to Nilsen's story. Elizabeth was known as 'Wussell's Leebie', and Ann as 'Wussell's Anniekie'. Wussell's Anniekie married James Ritchie and gave birth to several sons, some of whom were unstable. Their tee-name was 'Pum'. William Pum tried to drown himself several times, while Jim Pum was a mental depressive all his life. Wussell's Leebie married James Duthie and had a son and two daughters. The son, Andrew Duthie, perished in the waves when his great-nephew, Dennis, was an adolescent; his body was washed ashore some time later, his small fishing-boat never recovered. Of Wussell's Leebie's daughters, one was called Christian Ann; she never married, but died in a mental hospital some fifteen years ago. The other daughter, Lily, known as Wussell's Leebie's Lily, is still alive (1984) and is the grandmother of Dennis Nilsen. Lily was born in Cedar Cottage, Main Street, Inverallochy, a house typical of the 'butt and ben' variety with its line stone protruding from the wall, on which was hung the basket of fishing-lines. Her mother, Wussell's Leebie, was one of the fishwives who carried fish into the 'near country' to sell and barter for farm produce. The house and its line stone can be seen today. Not far away, on the corner of Frederick Street, Inverallochy, is the house where Andrew Whyte and his three brothers lived. They had the tee-name 'Daw' (pronounced 'Dar'), so when Andrew Whyte married Lily Duthie, to the villagers it was Andrewkie Daw who wed Wussell's Leebie's Lily.

(Yet another strand in this complicated ancestry hauls in the most unexpected figure. Andrew Whyte's mother, known as 'Jeanie Mam', was a Stephen. She had a curious habit of staying indoors all winter and not appearing until the month of June, which led some villagers to call her 'the June rose'. Euphemistically, she was said to be a 'droll creature', but people knew well enough that the Stephen family had occasionally been prone to mental instability of one kind or another. At the same time, they were famous for intellectual brilliance. One branch of the Stephens had moved first to Ardendraught and then south to London, and produced at least one manic depressive, J.K. Stephen, who was eventually committed to hospital and never released. One account goes so far as to name him as the notorious Jack the Ripper. Another offspring was Sir Leslie Stephen, editor of the *Dictionary of National Biography* and father of Virginia Woolf. It is well known that Virginia Woolf suffered from depressive illnesses and committed suicide. Through his great-grandmother, then, Dennis Nilsen must be a very distant cousin of Virginia Woolf, in so far as the ancestry of both climbs back to a Stephen in Cairnbulg/Inverallochy.)

Andrew and Lily lived first at Inverallochy, then at Broadsea, and finally settled in a new house in Academy Road, on the very edge of Fraserburgh, backed by open fields. At the end of a grey granite terrace, the house was divided into two flats, one above the other, the Whytes occupying the top flat. In the meantime, they had had a son and two daughters, Lily and Betty; Lily would one day marry Robert Ritchie, and Betty would break ranks by marrying a Norwegian soldier called Olav Nilsen, but not before she had earned the reputation of being one of the most beautiful girls in The Broch.

The cycle of booms and recessions in the fishing industry had left some fishermen relatively prosperous by the middle of the twentieth century, others frankly poor. Andrew Whyte was one of the latter. A proud and honest man, much respected in the community, he attached overriding importance to the stern principles which had guided his life and left him incapable of compromise. He would not drink or go to the cinema, and habitually wore dark, sober clothes, with a fisherman's jersey and cap. As he was also tall and handsome, he cut a distinctive figure, and there were not many in The Broch who did not recognise the good-looking but sombre Andrewkie of Inverallochy. Unfortunately, his pride did him poor service, as it made him loath to take orders and reluctant to assume the subservient role necessary to hold down a job. A hard worker when respected, he would turn sullen if treated in what he thought was a cavalier manner. Consequently, he changed boats too frequently and found himself in time of poor harvest having to suffer the pain of seeking charity from the state. To many, signing on for unemployment benefit was a necessary nuisance, but to Andrew Whyte it was a humiliation. In times of hardship, his wife Lily would supplement the family income by cleaning other people's homes as a charlady.

It often happens that people who have no real achievement to boast of will boast of imaginary ones. Andrew Whyte was a man full of stories designed to impress. He had seen so much, he knew so much, he had so much to teach the young, or indeed anyone who would listen. He could claim kinship with people who were the subject of current interest lest he run the risk of being overshadowed, though the actual relationship might be distant. People were used to Andrew's 'blowing' and did not respect him the less, for he was a regular worshipper at church and brought up his daughters well in spite of a discouraging lack of funds. As he was so often away at sea, Lily spent more time with the children than he, but it was always his powerful influence that was felt in the house. He lit his pipe with a piece of paper, to save the matches. He was 'saving for a drifter' they said, to buy his own boat one day.

Their daughter Betty was a source of considerable pride and not a little anxiety. By the time she was twenty years old, she had grown into a young woman of beauty and natural elegance, the kind that men like to have as models or pin-ups on their walls. She enjoyed the attention which her prettiness provoked, and was not slow to feel the stirrings of rebellion against the excessively strict principles of her father which, were she to adhere to them fully, would keep her indoors most of the time. But he was away at sea, and her mother did not have the heart to prevent her going out to taste the frivolous pleasures of youth. Betty Whyte was one of the first to dare to go to cafés alone at a time when a young woman was expected to be escorted. She also had an absorbing passion for dancing, a passion that was unlikely to persuade her she could have a good time at home.

When the war came, it brought days of terror to Fraserburgh, an unaccustomed whirlpool of excitement, and a husband for Betty Whyte.

After the fall of France, Fraserburgh underwent a dramatic transformation, as thousands of soldiers and refugees swept in. As the nearest point across the North Sea from Nazi-occupied Norway, it was firmly expected that an invasion would be attempted on the Aberdeenshire coast, and an influx of Polish and Norwegian forces, together with Royal Scots, Argyll and Sutherland Highlanders, Lancashire Fusiliers, and a huge Pioneer Corps to serve them all, suddenly increased the population from 10,000 to about 40,000. The Fleet Air Arm and the Royal Air Force were nearby, and many radar stations were hastily assembled along the coast, as well as an Air Sea Rescue Unit at Fraserburgh Harbour. With Czech, Polish and Norwegian refugees to care for at the same time, the place was seething with strangers, creating a rare atmosphere of tense excitement and delight in the sudden change of pace. Every available inch of accommodation was taken for troops, many of whom were billeted in the wooden bothies of the fish-curing stations dotted along the coast from the harbour in both directions. Some schools were likewise commandeered, with the result that children were squeezed three or four to a bench in the remaining schools and were loud with enthusiasm when school was suspended for a day so that they might go down to the beach and help make sandbags. On such days the beach was black with people working, even making sandbags to protect the headstones at Inverallochy cemetery, and the new spirit of comradeship dislodged neighbourhood enmities which had endured for forty years.

The invasion never came, but the bombers did. In waves of fifty they flew over Fraserburgh so low one could see the pilots' faces, and more often than not Andrew Whyte would be in the street shaking his fist angrily at them. Of the many raids, certainly the fiercest took place on 5 November 1940, when it seemed as if the whole town would be flattened. The picture house, the Macaulay Institute, the Congregational Church, and hundreds of shops and houses were all on fire, sparks flying into the night air and flames pouring down chimneys into living-rooms. There were people streaming out of the town carrying blankets and suitcases when it looked as if the Germans would not pause till they had obliterated the town. In the morning, a heart-stirring reveille on bagpipes was heard in the chill November dawn, and the cemeteries were kept busy for three days.

Not surprisingly, when the fires had died down and periods of relative peace ensued, while the old folk gave thanks to God, the young were expressing their relief in other ways. All the cafés of Fraserburgh were packed nightly with soldiers and their girlfriends, bent upon enjoyment. There being a paucity of girls, a number of married women fell victim to the obvious temptation to flirt, and as in other towns during the war, illegitimate births increased measurably. One particular café called 'Hell's Kitchen' was the scene of excessive entertainment and frequent brawls, the novice whores of the town using it as their headquarters. (One of these women was notorious for taking mustard baths whenever she missed her period, an event which was never secret as the smell of mustard clung to her for days afterwards.)

Of the troops scattered in billets all over town, among the most popular were the Norwegians, for in spite of their apparent cold and aloof manner, they were observed to be very kind and helpful to the local population, particularly the elderly, and not commonly involved in fights. The Free Norwegian Forces, fighting against the occupation of their homeland by the German invader,* were housed in the Dunbar's Huts, the Highland Institute, Brucklay Castle, Fishfirs Mansion, St Peter's School, the Saultoun Hotel, Dalrymple Hall, and the Fraserburgh Academy Annexe. At this latter, the Academy Annexe, lived a Norwegian officer of striking good looks whose name was Olav Magnus Nilsen. Many of the Fraserburgh girls had noticed his brooding figure and heard romantic tales of his escape from the Nazis. A hint of cruelty about the eyes did nothing to diminish his attraction, and nobody was surprised when he eventually took up with Betty Whyte. The manner of their meeting was entirely accidental.

Betty Whyte had become something of a local celebrity. The Consolidated Pneumatic Tool Company of America had moved its entire operation and personnel from London to Cairness House, once the home of General Gordon, and was devoting considerable effort to devising recreation for the enlarged community. At a beauty contest they had organised, Betty Whyte had emerged the clear winner. She was a regular dancer at Broadsea Hall, packed so tightly every evening it was locally called 'The Battle of Britain'. One evening, as she

* The German invasion of Norway took place on 9 April 1940.

was coming out of a café in town, she was accosted by a soldier who suggested he would walk her home. She declined, but the soldier was persistent. A row developed on the street, the soldier gripped her by the arm, and Betty grew alarmed. At the moment she thought he was about to strike her, another man appeared from nowhere, pinned the soldier against the wall and made it clear he must leave the young lady alone. This was Olav Nilsen, and from that moment Betty fell in love with her rescuer. It was not long before there was talk of marriage; Andrew and Lily Whyte were not happy with the idea, but their daughter was a headstrong girl trapped by the compelling demands of emotion. She married Olav Nilsen on 2 May 1942.

From the first it was clear that Nilsen had but a scant idea of his responsibilities, and even that little could be suppressed beneath the immediate exigencies of his military duties. He always had a ready, and frequently genuine, excuse for his absence, with the result that he and Betty never formed a family unit and never made a home. There were three children — Olav, Dennis and Sylvia, conceived on brief visits — but Betty continued to live with her parents and sister, and the children therefore grew up in their grandparents' house. Betty afterwards said that she had rushed into marriage without thinking, that it was an unhappy episode which ought never to have happened and which spoilt her life. Her second son Dennis was later made painfully aware of the fortuitous nature of his birth, and listened to his mother's warnings on the sad tragedy of a failed marriage and ruined life. Olav Nilsen, he wrote, 'in the heat and uncertainty of war, married my mother primarily on lustful grounds and ignoring some irreconcilable cultural and personality differences which doomed the match to failure.'[7]

Betty and her three infant children shared one room at 47 Academy Road, a home within a home, and very tiny. In this room Dennis Nilsen was born, on 23 November 1945, and in this room, nearly seven years later, he would witness a sight which troubled him so deeply that he never recovered. Mother occupied one bed with Sylvia, while Olav Jnr and Dennis occupied the other. Dennis and his brother were never friendly, possibly because Olav had at least seen his father, which Dennis had not. He was closer to his sister Sylvia, but even that relationship had no profound source. In all essentials, Dennis gave the impression of a misfit, a child whose heart remained obstinately closed, whose secret imaginary life nobody could fathom. He was quiet, withdrawn, intensely private. 'As soon as I could toddle as a small child my mother was always in despair looking for me,' he has written, speaking of himself as 'a wanderer at odds with his fellows'.[8] Certainly he wandered. He made a habit of walking off without a word to anyone and disappearing, so often that his mother was forced to tie the garden gate with string to prevent his escape. Nor would this hold him in, for he soon devised a way of crawling under the gate and pattering uncertainly down the street. He was, by his own account, an 'unhappy, brooding child, secretive and stricken with inferiority'. Had a psychiatrist crossed his path, he might well have discerned the signs of a boy unsure of his identity.

Nevertheless, life at 47 Academy Road was apparently contented, and Dennis Nilsen retains vivid memories of his infancy there:

I remember the big china dog (a cocker spaniel) on the sideboard. Mother called it for some reason Tarzan. The wireless played 'Workers' Playtime', 'Have a Go', and 'Music While You Work', and while Mother went about her seemingly endless washing and housework she sang along with all the popular tunes. The open coal fire burned in the grate with a folding metal guard over it, with always something drying on it – towels or nappies, etc. It was a crowded but happy room.

Mum being on her own was a dab hand at interior decorating. She had become self-reliant in her daily struggles to make ends meet. There was always lots of washing hanging from the pulley-frame which hung from the ceiling. In the living-room there was a larger open grate with little compartments with doors at each side where 'kindling' was kept. There was no wireless in the living-room. Granny was ultra-religious and did not think

41

much of this invention. She always spoke out strongly against worldly things — cinema, drink, smoking, dances, modern music. [After church] we would return to Academy Road for Sunday dinner. Granny would prepare all the food the day before as she was loath to do anything on the 'Lord's Day'. I still have not known anyone to make a Scotch broth as good as Granny. I can still see her sitting in the living-room reading her *Christian Herald*. I never heard any of the adults swear or mention the word 'sex'. Babies just seemed to arrive late at night without any explanation.

In the summer, all the family, armed with picnic eats of sandwiches, biscuits, and bottles of lemonade, would descend upon Fraserburgh beach with buckets and spades. The 'Faith Mission' would set up their banner in the sand and preach their message to the assembled (mostly the kids). I would take a jam jar to the Kessock (a stream which flowed into the sea) and try to catch eels . . . on the hill above the waste ground off Dennyduff Road I would lie in the sun on a carpet of buttercups and daisies and look up to watch and listen to the shrill sweet larks rising. Or I would collect frog spawn and watch it slowly develop through the change via tadpole to small black perfectly-formed frogs. I would release them into the tall wet grasses near a pond or stream.

If there were any of life's luxuries to be scrounged then Gran was the bountiful source.

At Christmas, the children would write their notes to Santa Claus, set light to them, and watch them float up the chimney.

Although Betty Nilsen tried to be mother and father to her family, it was a task beyond her capacity, and not even practically sensible, as she was still young enough to enjoy a night out dancing. Inevitably, it was Lily and Andrew Whyte who became surrogate parents, and between Andrew and his grandson Dennis there grew a bond more precious to them both than any other relationship in the family. Dennis grew to resemble his grandfather (he still does) and to cherish the days when he was home from sea. Andrew Whyte became his only companion, the only person with whom he felt at ease and happy. He looked forward to his grandfather's coming home, and his going away again left a sense of deprivation which no solace could lift. He was proud to be in his grandfather's company, and proud of himself too, as it was always Dennis to whom the seafaring man came home. Dennis never asked after his own father, never showed any curiosity about him.

'I can remember nothing of my father but for a brown photograph of a man in army battledress standing with my mother, smiling, on her wedding day. She would try not to mention him.

'I remember being borne aloft on the tall strong shoulders of my great hero and protector, my grandfather.' Man and boy would go for very long walks down to the harbour, across the wide stretch of beach, up to the sand-dunes which rise thirty feet behind the beach, through the golf-course and on to Inverallochy. It was peaceful and exclusive, the two of them against the world, with only the elements to witness their affection. Eventually, Dennis would fall asleep and be carried home in his grandfather's arms.

Andrew would tell him stories of the sea and its dangers, of his own adventures, filling the boy's head with such tales as he would not divulge to anyone else for fear of contradiction or derision. Dennis, admiring and unquestioning, was his best audience. He went with him to the Fraserburgh dole office when times were bad and sensed his resentment, then with the proceeds was 'treated to a delicious ice-cream concoction at Joe's Café or taken to watch football at Belleslea Park or a local playing-fields'. One day a football missed the goal and hit Dennis, almost knocking him out, but Grandpa rescued him with 'a magic sponge. Taking a football full in the face is surprisingly painless.'

Olav and Sylvia tended to remain at home with their mother when grandfather and grandson went off for a walk to the golf-course above the dunes.

Grandad had an uncanny knack of finding lost golf-balls

on the course. He would take one apart and unwind the endless thread of sticky rubber and eventually come to the bag of liquid rubber at the centre. He had some friends whom he would meet out on these walks and he would walk and chat a lot to them. I was always exhausted on these long walks and he would have to carry me asleep on the last stretch home. He would also take me to Cairnbulg, Inverallochy and St Combs where we would meet various relatives whom I cannot now remember . . . I remember the smell of nets and fishing things . . . I went on the temperance marches between, I think, Inverallochy and St Combs accompanied by a flute band. Grandad sang in a male voice choir. He was a pillar of the religious establishment.

Andrew Whyte's stern morality fought hard against the new relaxed values of the post-war generation, and generally lost. 'It seemed that if you were not broody and miserable then you must be in sin.' Framed religious texts and pictures on the wall at 47 Academy Road recalled the older, harsher values.

My grandfather would make me a 'dragon' (he called it). It was a kite made from brown paper or newspaper and small, thin, supple branches tied or sewn with string. The balancing tail was made from an old, long thin piece of net. There were open fields beyond Dennyduff Road where we would test and fly the kite. Windy days were frequent up in Fraserburgh. Grandad would also take me around the harbour and on board the herring boats and to the repair slipway. I would see the herring-boats being built (entirely of wood) in the boat-building yards.[9]

People were only tangentially aware how deep ran the love of the small boy for his grandfather. For the most part it appeared a warm and cosy relationship for which one had to be grateful, as without it Dennis would have been completely withdrawn. But for Dennis it was the central core of his life, compared with which nothing else mattered. 'The work of a fisherman at sea was hard,' he writes, 'and the harshness of the wild elements tended to age a man long before his time. I would watch him, head down into the driving rain, go off to his boat. Life would be empty until he returned.'[10]

In 1951 Andrew Whyte seemed to be more tired than usual. He dropped out of the choir in which he had sung for years because he had not the strength to produce a note, and declared that he would never sing again. Even a little effort exhausted him. Still, there was a chance for work, and he could not afford to miss it, and besides no one had suggested he was ill. He said goodbye to the family, waved to Dennis and set sail. After he had put out the nets, he refused a cup of tea for the first time in his life, saying that he had a bad attack of indigestion. He went to his bunk and slept peacefully. When he failed to appear the next morning, his crew-mates went to rouse him and found him dead. They could scarcely believe it. The date was 31 October 1951, and Andrew Whyte was sixty-two years old. His grandson Dennis, waiting at home in Fraserburgh, was not yet six.

The body was brought ashore at Yarmouth, where there took place a quayside service and an inquest, always required when death occurs beyond the three-mile limit. Whyte was declared to have died of a heart attack. His body was then sent by train to Fraserburgh, and taken to lie in the house at 47 Academy Road. There was loud grief and tears in the house that day, but no explanations. Visitors came and went, Granny wept continuously, and nobody thought to tell the children what had happened. Dennis Nilsen never excised his vivid recollection of that day. 'I remember being in the large bed with my older brother and younger sister in the living-room, and my mother saying, "Do you want to see your Grandad?" ' They were then carried one by one into the small room where they had been born, lifted up in their pyjamas and held to peer into the open coffin set on trestles. 'Grandad was wearing glasses and expensive long johns. He was barefooted and needed a shave. He looked as if he was sleeping.'* Indeed, Mrs Nilsen said that he was just asleep.

---

* This picture owes much to Nilsen's imagination. Others present contend that Whyte was clean-shaven, in a shroud.

She was afraid to tell the truth lest it be too shocking for the children to contemplate. As it turned out, the shock of not knowing was far greater, for Dennis at least, and would provoke catastrophic consequences in years to come. 'I could feel my heart beating very fast as I was carried back into the living-room,' he recalls, yet he did not understand why he should feel such mysterious and fearful excitement. The next time he was carried back into the little room, on the morrow, his grandfather was gone. He was held by the window and watched a long procession of dark-suited men pass below. Someone told him to be a 'big man'. He did not weep.

For a long time afterwards, no one so much as mentioned Andrew Whyte's name. It was as if he had evaporated. The six-year-old boy was not told that he was dead, and was left to form his own impression, that Grandpa must be very ill for some reason which would eventually emerge. He would no doubt tell him himself when he came back. It was months before Dennis finally realised that this time there would be no home-coming, and his retrospective grief was so painful that he submerged it and refused to acknowledge its cause. Now, in the light of his arrest and conviction, he attributes the seed of his disordered personality to the numbing experience of that day. He can never forget the great mental shock of seeing his grandfather asleep for the last time, the light of his life taken from him.

My troubles started there. It blighted my personality permanently. I have spent all my emotional life searching for my grandfather and in my formative years no one was there to take his place.

It is the custom up there in Fraserburgh that when there is a death in a household they draw the blinds and curtains. When my grandfather died it seemed that these blinds had been drawn across my life . . . Relatives would pretend that he had gone to a 'better place'. 'Why', I thought, 'should he go to a better place and not take me with him?' 'So death was a nice thing,' I thought. 'Then why does it make me miserable?' Father and grandfather had walked out on me, probably to a better place, leaving me behind in this not so good place, alone . . . What storms of reasoning fury must have gone through my mind at that age. The blackness of women in mourning and their cries of triumph at the spiritual resurrection.[11]

The repercussions of this event may well be more complex and entangled than Nilsen himself can judge, and other interpretations must in time be weighed against his own recollection. But there can be no doubt that from that awesome day the boy retreated into an existence so fiercely private that no living person would ever be able to penetrate its secrets, and no dead one ever reveal them. Nor can it be questioned that his conception and understanding of death would henceforth remain equivocal, even bizarre: 'He took the real me with him under the ground and I now rest with him out there under the salt spray and the wind in Inverallochy Cemetery. Nature makes no provision for emotional death.'[12]

3

CHILDHOOD

From 1951 Dennis Nilsen became more moody than ever. His habit of wandering off alone grew compulsive, and when his mother remonstrated with him and attempted to keep him in, he responded defiantly that even horses were not tied up. He would go the short distance to Broadsea village, whose shore was built of forbidding, black igneous rocks constantly lashed by the waves. There was one deep mysterious fissure in the rocks, known as the Rumbling Goite (pronounced 'Gwite'), which the sea entered through a narrow channel then swirled, rising and falling, as the fissure broadened. It was said that the hole was bottomless (it certainly widens below the water-level) and that anyone who fell into it would never get out. The Rumbling Goite was a magnet for children who liked to challenge the unknown, and has been a grave for more than a few of the intrepid; Billy Skinner, a friend of Dennis's brother, fell in, bumped his head, and disappeared. Dennis would also go to Kinnaird Head, the promontory at the very tip of Fraserburgh, once the site of Fraserburgh Castle whose remaining tower had since been converted to a lighthouse. This, too, held a mystery, for everyone knew the legend of the laird's daughter who threw herself from a window to the

48

rocks below with the body of her forbidden lover in her arms.

But it was mostly to the rocks of Fraserburgh Harbour, and to the vast stretch of beach and sand-dunes to the south, that Dennis went on his solitary walks, a distance of some two miles from Academy Road. He spent a lot of time watching the herring boats sail past the pier or come into harbour, and stood on the pier as the fishermen walked past on their way home. Long after they had gone, he would remain there 'under the endless screams of the dog-fighting seagulls'. The cacophony of screeching gulls and the pervasive smell of fish still assault the senses today, and the wide expanse of sea has the power to humble.

> On the rocks I stood gazing at the all-powerful restless sea. I felt very akin to that great force, we reciprocated in a spiritual affinity of great love and great fear. I would stand for some time with a tear-filled face looking out there for Andrew Whyte to come and comfort me as he had always done.[1]

Dennis felt he could not show his grief at home, where the women (they were all women now — his grandmother, his mother, his aunt) were preoccupied with the re-organisation of their lives. His mother had to take on cleaning work to help make ends meet. So, 'I sought the silent lonely places where he had taken me, and prayed to my silent god on the horizon of the sea. It was a wonderful bitter pain.'[2]

At times, this respectful adoration was coloured by a more sinister current of will, a barely-understood wish to be embraced and cleansed by the sea in a consummation of freedom and sympathy:

> Many years ago I was a boy drowning in the sea. I am always drowning in the sea . . . down amongst the dead men, deep down. There is peace in the sea back down to our origins . . . when the last man has taken his last breath the sea will still be remaining. It washes everything clean. It holds within it forever the boy suspended in its body and the streaming hair and the open eyes.[3]

This probably refers to the occasion when he may have walked into the sea, aged about eight, and was apparently rescued by an older boy who was then aroused by his prostrate body:

On one of my treks along the beach to Inverallochy I was feeling pretty miserable. I stopped and took off my shoes and socks and waded up to my knees in the sounding sea. I was hypnotised by its power and enormity. I disregarded that my short trousers were getting wet, I moved steadily forward up to my waist. I could see a much older boy sitting further up the shore poking the sand with a stick. I must have stepped into a hollow because I suddenly disappeared under water. The retreat of the wave carried me out further. I panicked, and waving my arms and shouting I submerged. I could hear a loud buzzing in my head and I kept gasping for air which wasn't there. I thought that Grandad was bound to arrive and pull me out. I felt at ease, drugged and dreamlike under the silent green weight of water. I felt myself suspended in a void. I could hear a droning slowed-down voice in the distance (a mixture of every voice I had ever known, nothing recognisable). I felt a heavy weight upon me. I felt very cold at first, but this changed to a neutral feeling, then I could feel the warmth of the sun. I was vomiting and gasping. I became aware of blue and air and a breeze in a sandy hollow in the dunes. My clothes were spread out on the long sand grass and the sky was bright blue with wisps of white cloud. I felt a pressure on me and sank into a deep sleep. Later I could feel the dry sand's comforting support beneath me. I coughed a bit and felt my raw throat. I sat up and covered my nakedness with my hands noticing a white sticky mess on my stomach and thighs. I remember thinking that I had been fouled on by a seagull. I wiped it off with sand. I peered from behind the grass high on the dunes but there was no one about. My clothes were damp but not all that wet. It was quite hot so I put them on and wandered over the dunes and took the golf links road slowly home hoping that my things would soon dry out.[4]

He was scolded by his mother, constantly anxious about his disappearance, but he did not tell her what had happened. How could he? There was no one to blame but himself, and he was not even sure what he was to blame *for*. How to explain the irresistible compulsion to *join* the sea, to be part of it, to sink into the solace of its company? His mother would think him mad! A love for the sea has never ceased to feed his imagination in the years since he left Scotland. 'I am at one with visions of breaks in the dark wild sky,' he writes, 'with heavenly shafts of light searching the grumbling sea.' In prison he has found mental release by recalling these scenes of childhood and hearing again the voices of the gulls, 'the whole glorious sound liberated me from the irrelevant bounds of imprisonment. I stood on that imaginary crest with my arms raised to the sky and the tears of exhilaration of total natural unity.'[5] Nilsen now recognises that there is some fantasy, or retrospective editing, in his account of wandering into the sea. Some details are fashioned by imagination. But the basic event was real enough; so too is the strange imagination which has doctored it, probably adding the circumstance of the older boy. Both individuals, victim and rescuer, are self-images.* Oddly enough, Betty Nilsen used to have bad dreams that her son was drowning, and that there was no one to save him.

For Mrs Nilsen the struggle of bringing up three children without a father was at times brutal. She had long since allowed herself to be divorced by Olav Nilsen (in 1948), and was frankly glad to be rid of him. With Andrew Whyte also gone, she turned to the Church to offer penance for her ruined life and rediscovered the missionary zeal which she had inherited from her forebears. She became involved with the Faith Mission and took Dennis with her to faith meetings all over Aberdeenshire. 'I got quite used to falling asleep in

---

* See also the story in Chapter 10, p. 275. There was an actual case of a boy who drowned trapped beneath the pier at the harbour. When his body was recovered, the sea-crabs had eaten out his eyes. Dennis Nilsen had nightmares about this story afterwards, and the image of a boy in sea-water, whether himself or someone else, never left him.

buses,' is his comment on these days. He was disciplined to attend Sunday School and the Mid Street Congregationalist Church, which had its compensations when the Sunday School took a picnic to the lovely Philorth Woods for the day. He also enjoyed a small part in a Sunday School play. But Dennis had no need for anyone else's God.

On Saturdays he and his brother were given 7d each for the matinee at the Picture House, with an additional 2d for wine gums. (This is equivalent to nearly 4p in today's money, but it had much greater purchasing power.) There was no more pocket money for the week unless a visiting relation happened to drop an occasional coin. Still, the boys looked forward to this weekly treat as an escape from dull reality. Later, there was the television set at the Mission for Deep Sea Fishermen, which hypnotised the youngsters. They were dimly aware that their mother did everything she could to give them a decent life in the face of crippling adversity. It was a miracle she succeeded, thought Dennis.

After too many years of living with three children in one room, Betty Nilsen eventually persuaded the authorities to give her a flat of her own, and moved to 73 Mid Street, much closer to the centre of Fraserburgh. Part of a corner block of old tenement flats in a depressingly gloomy area, the flat did not lift anyone's spirits, but at least it was to give them an opportunity to live as a family unit for the first time. It was a pity that it was at the top of the block, and that there were steep stairs to climb. At the back there was a common area shared with other tenement blocks, containing old concrete air-raid shelters which served as a playground for the children. Dennis, however, rarely joined in; still melancholic, still drawn to the sea, he formed no close friendships with the children of his new neighbours.

Shortly afterwards, Betty Nilsen married again. Her new husband was Adam Scott, a quiet, solid and reliable man in the building trade, who gave her four more children in four years. The added burden of work was almost too much for her, and there were days when she cried with tiredness, probably too preoccupied to notice that the new disruptive element in the home pushed Dennis deeper into his sullen isolation. He was, in the local word, a 'skowkie' child, unsmiling and resentful of questioning by adults, to whom he gave a clear impression of distrust and reserve. His mother recalls that something prevented her from cuddling him. She wanted to, but he appeared to repel demonstrations of affection, so she kept her distance. She was an extremely good and caring mother, but, with Dennis at least, not tactile. He confirms that he felt cold towards the family.

On occasion I was a difficult child to manage. While at 73 Mid Street I had been brought to the attention of police in Fraserburgh. I once took a £1 note from my mother's purse and went to see the film *The Dam Busters*. I was taken from the cinema and got a good hiding from Adam Scott, my mother's new husband. Myself and a couple of schoolboy friends had been in the police station for breaking into an old iron steam drifter boat which was moored in Fraserburgh Harbour and used solely for 'barking' herring fishing nets . . . as kids we would stay out all day missing lunch and when we were hungry we would steal apples from gardens.[6]

Exasperated at her increasing inability to control him, Betty Scott once threatened her son that if he could not behave himself she would have to send him away to a 'home', to be taken into care.

In those days I could hate Adam Scott very easily. I was, I suppose, very jealous of him having a relationship with and the attention of my mother. I sometimes felt that we, the Nilsen kids, were an impediment to her fulfilment in her new life and family. I was a very lonely and turbulent child. I inhabited my own secret world full of ideal and imaginary friends. Nature had mismatched me from the flock.[7]

One activity he did share with two other boys — the rearing of pigeons. He, Farquhar Mackenzie and Malcolm Rennie would climb on to derelict buildings to find fledgelings to rear, then keep them in fish-boxes on the concrete air-raid shelters behind Mid Street. When they ran out of fish-boxes his mother had to find an old shoe box or two, but she would not let him bring them into the house. Two in particular he cherished — a black one he called Tufty, and another with white tips to his wings named Jockey. Every lunch and teatime he would visit them on top of the shelter. 'They would fly down from the roof when I called to them. My mother was always shooing them away when they landed on our kitchen window-ledge and tried to come in the open window (looking for food or me or both).'[8] One day he came in sobbing uncontrollably; another boy had killed the pigeons. There were no more birds after that, although years later, when he was in the army in the Shetlands, he would rescue young fledgeling gulls which had fallen from their high nests and rear them behind his living accommodation at base. He chewed unbreadcrumbed frozen fish fingers and stuffed the masticated mess down their throats until they were strong enough to be sent back into the wild.

It was unfortunate that the Scotts could not tolerate animals of any kind, for had Dennis been allowed to devote more attention to them he might have found some relief from the conviction that he was useless. Pity for the animal kingdom gradually supplanted his obsession with the sea, but it was not encouraged.

I felt close to the land and to all things animated upon it. I would be repelled by the shooting of crows and rabbits. A rabbit, to me, was one of the least offensive creatures which hopped about. I was horrified by the sight of rabbits infected by myxomatosis. I would kill them as they staggered blindly about with swollen eyes and dying of starvation. Adults told me that there were a lot of pests around that had to be destroyed. I was not allowed to have any pets, save once a white rabbit which I had to keep in a very small hutch with a wire window. It died in winter. I was accused by my parent and step-parent of starving it to death. This as a child hurt me deeply. My mother was very house-proud and I suppose she could not tolerate animal hairs around the house on the carpet. (I got the feeling sometimes that she didn't want me around on her carpet either.)[9]

The tension which this recollection suggests must not be laid entirely at Betty Scott's feet. She had, after all, other pressing concerns, not least among them the need to clothe and feed seven children, and now that Adam Scott was earning good money and she could at last start to build a decent home of which she need not be ashamed, it was natural that she should resist any plan to turn it into a zoo. To Dennis, in his own words 'a boy who could not hurt a worm or feel a tear',[10] such an attitude placed appearances above essentials, and he was entirely out of sympathy with it.

By the time the incident with the rabbit occurred the family was installed in a comfortable new council house at Strichen, seven miles inland from Fraserburgh in the 'near country'. They moved there in 1955 when Dennis was ten years old. Betty was relieved to think he would now be out of danger, far away from the treacherous rocks and the sea. Strichen is a small, grey, granite-built town with one main street, quite wide, half a dozen shops and one policeman. It stands on the River Ugie, surrounded by forest and farmland, and watched by the gentle slope of Mormond Hill, half a mile away. Strichen House, now derelict, was once the home of the Lords Lovat, a branch of the same Fraser family which had built Fraserburgh, and on the top of Mormond Hill are the ruins of Hunter's Lodge, which Lord Lovat used to take for shooting parties. An earlier member of the Fraser clan had entertained Dr Johnson and Boswell at Strichen House on their famous Scottish journey, but now it was no more than a haunt for youngsters. Dennis Nilsen was enrolled at Strichen School, and spent the next five years of his life growing into adolescence in a fairly normal way, making no special mark and causing no profound disturbance. He was, however, slowly maturing the reflections which would confirm his self-vision as an outcast and a radical.

I began life with an instinct and training for Christian

virtue. I believed in the justice of the establishment and in (what I thought to be) the reality of democracy. I felt that the injustice I encountered could only be some terrible mistake to be righted when the causes were exposed. Coupled with injustices which happened to me I felt that somehow it was my fault for being poor and shabby . . . I felt that poverty was a reflection of character imposed upon me through natural justice while those 'good' families were 'good' because of their background and deserving of rewards and advancement . . . I felt I should be grateful for the crumbs from the masters' table.

The most telling influence upon his growing social awareness was Robert Ritchie, who had married his Aunt Lily. A design engineer at the Consolidated Pneumatic Tool Company, Ritchie had made his own way through evening classes but had remained an idealistic socialist, despising privilege and power. Dennis would sit with him in front of the fire and listen entranced to his angry flow of information. It was his first education in social issues, and it formed an embryo of cynicism which would fester in the years to come and be distorted by lack of recognition. Ritchie also introduced the boy to the beauties of music on his Leak Hi-Fi system (in those days the most expensive system and most beloved of connoisseurs). Samuel Barber's 'Adagio for Strings' was the first recording to stir within Dennis Nilsen a primitive response to the stimulus of music which would one day bring cruel consequences upon those with him. Moreover, it was Ritchie who introduced his nephew to the delights of film-making, a hobby which in adulthood he would develop to the point where it became the refuge of his subconscious. Other important influences were the history lessons of Mr Shanks, and the huge local knowledge of the librarian Bob Bandeen.

Getting up early in the morning in a cold room to deliver papers and milk with inadequate breakfast weakened me. (I was always a skinny child.) I would feel tired at school and unable to concentrate. I was belted for this slackness. When I was about eleven or twelve I collapsed ill. I was rushed to Aberdeen City Hospital where I stayed for a time suffering from pneumonia and pleurisy. I bitterly resented my stepfather at first but later learned to like him . . . He was a good provider . . . an honest uncomplicated labourer with the Aberdeen County Council. I always felt ashamed when I was asked 'What does your old man do?' He liked fishing a lot and was a rustic lone fisherman in the rivers around Strichen. My mother was lucky to be his wife as he was kind and not a womaniser or drunk.[11]

In spite of his having school-mates — Bruce Rankin, Peter MacDonald, Hugh Harkness, Jimmy Gibb, and Plucky Simpson (crippled by polio), among them — Dennis would more often than not wander the fields and woods alone.

I would throw down my satchel after school and be out and about until late, often missing my tea (bread and syrup and a cup of tea) . . . I had the whole wild countryside as a huge magic garden. I loved the wildness of the land and the great ruins of Strichen House . . . the noise of the house at 16 Baird Road kept me away.[12]

His favourite spot was Waughton Hill (a local name for the nether slopes of Mormond Hill) and the high, empty ruin of Hunter's Lodge. There he could tame his growing wrath against what he saw as the materialistic standards of his mother, her façade of polish and sparkle to impress the neighbours and divert attention from the shoddiness of the children's clothes. 'I always felt they [Betty and Adam] were largely the willing architects of their own poverty chains. They were docile to authority and touched the forelock at the appointed moment.' This is unfair. When the schoolmistress Miss Lee led a school outing to Belmont Camp in Perthshire, Betty paid for Dennis to join. She could afford only ten shillings, which Miss Lee happily accepted.

At fourteen he joined the Army Cadet Force and frankly revelled in the equality which uniform provided. He also had his first beer and passed out. 'I felt proud and useful in my battle-dress.' On the football field he did less well; in fact he played so badly he was made goalkeeper and proceeded to let in six goals. He was not invited to play again. In school his best subject was art, even contriving to earn higher marks than Bruce Rankin, who subsequently became an art teacher. He also did well at English literature, but failed miserably in mathematics. 'I would go to pieces during those mental arithmetic sessions. I was too flustered and terrified to concentrate. I thought that coming from a poor family I must have been born dim, slow-witted, and unintelligent.' When the 'tattie' season came, Dennis would spend weekends picking potatoes, to be rewarded with a marvellous farmhouse lunch afterwards, better than anything he had eaten except at Christmas. Still, it was back-breaking work, yanking the potatoes from resistant, clammy earth, and he soon had to acknowledge that farm work would not suit him, given his congenitally weak spine and round shoulders.

Once a year came the excitement of 'bringing home the peats'. Between the villages of Strichen and New Pitsligo lay areas of peat where families could rent a small plot and dig from it as much as they wanted. Dennis and the other children would help pack the dried blocks of peat into jute sacks ready for delivery to 16 Baird Road, giving enough domestic fuel for the entire winter. It was Adam who did most of the work, and Dennis's admiration for him deepened and matured. It was tinged also with some mute envy; Dennis would have liked to emulate Adam, but did not feel he belonged to him.

There was no cinema in Strichen, but once in a while a travelling projectionist would set up a screen in the Town Hall and offer a rare show. Also, when Dennis was about fourteen, two evangelistic young ladies from the Faith Mission, Miss Wilkie and Miss Stafford, arrived in Strichen with their caravan and their squeeze-box music and anchored themselves there for a while. Dennis, his sister Sylvia, Hugh Harkness and James Gibb were immediate converts, singing their bright jolly hymns and enjoying their 'born again' sermons. It was not difficult for them to 'renounce' the cinema, so the four children converted a shed at the back of Hugh Harkness's house and had their own faith meetings there by candlelight. Dennis says he felt emotionally warm and good at these meetings, but they did not survive the departure of Miss Wilkie and Miss Stafford by more than two weeks.

There was one particular schoolday incident which caused Dennis to ruminate. An old man from Strichen, Mr Ironside, went missing. The village turned out in force to look for him. Dennis and another boy, Gordon Barry, searched the banks of the River Ugie behind the school and found his corpse. His sanity had cracked, and he had wandered out of his house in the middle of the night in his pyjamas, fallen into the river and drowned. Other children gathered round as his body was hauled from the river and carried up the hill to a Land-Rover. The boy Nilsen was more perturbed than most by the sight. 'He reminded me of my grandfather, and the images were fixed firmly in my mind . . . I could never comprehend the reality of death.'[13]

Images of death, and images of love. They were yet a long way apart, but they had begun to form themselves in the subconscious and to make the slow journey towards convergence and calamity. In all his years at school, Dennis Nilsen had no sexual encounter, not even of a minimal kind; this in itself is unusual enough in a pubescent boy to warrant notice. However, there was an emotional experience which burned deeply, never to be released or confessed. In his sister Sylvia's class at school there was one boy whom Dennis adored from afar. Of the entire school, no other person held this power to make him feel nervous. He was, to Dennis, beautiful, enigmatic, different. Being the son of a local minister, he spoke with a different accent from the other boys, and had about him an air of aloof confidence. Dennis felt inferior and ashamed; he did not dare to approach him, but merely hovered in the playground watching him and trying to get near him, his legs quivering like jelly. He never once spoke to the boy (whose name was Adrian), but did once manage to engage his mother in conversation, even going into her (his) house. Whenever he thought of this boy, guilt invaded him, a vague uneasy guilt without a reason.

His next attachment was even less open to declaration. It

was for a boy called Pierre Duval, an illustration in the book used for French lessons. Dennis found that his response to this illustration simmered with the same intensity as his earlier response to Adrian. The fact that it was inanimate did not remove its appeal; on the contrary, it enhanced it.

Throughout his early adolescence, Dennis shared a bed with his brother Olav, two years older. There came a night when his sexual imagination could no longer be restrained, and waiting until he thought his brother was safely asleep, he undid his pyjama cord and began to explore. The body beside him did not move, but remained still, lifeless. Olav must have woken, for when Dennis realised his brother's sex was aroused, he stopped. Neither of them ever referred to the incident.

As he lay awake at night, he would sometimes hear the springs creaking in his parents' room. He felt outrage and repulsion when this happened, and it would take some time for this extreme reaction to fade.

When Dennis Nilsen left school at the age of fifteen, he was sexually innocent, emotionally untried. He had had no 'best friend', no exciting discoveries with other boys, no desire to unravel the mysteries of girls. But his emotions had been aroused three times, in three ways where safety from rejection was ensured; with a distant idol, with an inanimate drawing, and with a sleeping body.

Nilsen's scholastic record was decent but not glorious. He had excelled in art and seemed destined for some kind of artistic future if only he could rid himself of a morose lethargy born of an indistinct but persistent belief that he needed above all to escape from the narrowness of Strichen and the complacency of his parents' unglamorous life. He knew only that he was in some way 'different'. The family urged him to join the Consolidated Pneumatic Tool Company and work his way up the ladder, as his uncle Robert Ritchie had done, through evening classes. That held little attraction if it meant spending the rest of his life in Aberdeenshire. To fill in for the time being he worked a few weeks at Maconochie's Fish Cannery in Fraserburgh, where his job was to take tins of herring in tomato sauce from a conveyor belt and stack them in metal drums. All the time he was thinking how best he could lift the restrictions and tedium of existence, as well as banish the shame which he still felt clung to him. The answer came one evening at home.

Dennis told his mother that he had decided to enlist in the army. It offered new opportunities, travel, a complete break with the past, and the occasion to train for a trade. He would be a chef. His mother said she thought he had wanted to do something artistic, to which he replied that cooking was as artistic as anything else. At the Army Recruiting Office in Market Street, Aberdeen, he passed the entrance tests and was given a date to start in September 1961, having signed on for a period of nine years. He was perky with optimism. Adam went to see him off.

I remember standing on the platform on the hill at Strichen Railway Station. I had a shabby suitcase and raincoat. I was fifteen years old. It was raining. The great steam train arrived and took me puffing slowly off to the start of a new life. I never looked back, and the old images and the mists lifted as the bright blue sky appeared ahead of me. I left Aberdeen on the 'Aberdonian' overnight express for King's Cross. I was impressed crossing the Tay Bridge with the tragic stumps of the fallen old bridge still there . . .

The next morning we arrived in London. I took a confusing route on the tube to reach Waterloo Station. There I took the train to Aldershot and took a taxi up to St Omer Barrack (Apprentice Chefs Wing), Army Catering Corps, 'A' Company Junior Leaders' Regiment.[14]

4

ARMY

For the next three years, from 1961 to 1964, Dennis Nilsen
was a boy soldier at Aldershot, in company with about twenty
other adolescent recruits all eager for adventure. By his own
account, he was 'a frail and skinny boy, very self-conscious,
introverted, and shy'.[1] There was scarcely a moment, as is
the way with army life, for introspection. The boys were
immediately issued with a mountain of kit, staggered over to
the 'spider' complex, and divided into V and W squads,
Nilsen being assigned to V squad. From the very first day
they were initiated into the iron discipline of army routine,
under a strict and smart instructor. The day started early,
stripping beds in the barracks and making a neatly-folded
'bed pack'. Then the scrubbing jobs, washing the floors,
corridors, lavatories until the linoleum shone like a mirror.
With not a second to spare, they toiled the rest of the day in
military, educational, and technical trade training, with kit
inspections likely to be called at a moment's notice. The boys
quickly grew accustomed to working as a team, the better for
each individual, and were transformed in a matter of days
from a disparate group of confused, undisciplined children
into an array of smart, alert, responsible young men. Dennis
Nilsen's confidence blossomed under the strain, and he, like

everyone else, did not object to speeding about all day. He regularly collapsed into bed and slept at once. To feel 'like everyone else' was both novel and exhilarating for him. 'On a final account, and in total, these days as a boy soldier were the happiest of my life.'[2]

His colleagues at Aldershot — Brian Wells, Eric Talbot, Chris Innerd, Dave Norris — accepted him at face value, and one in particular, Brian Brasher, became a confidant until, crushed by the harsh routine, he bought himself out. Nilsen managed drill and training well enough, but his one difficulty was with physical exercise. When the regiment put forward a team for the Ten Tors marches, sixty miles' tracking over hills in Dartmoor in thirty-six hours, he worked hard to train for the event, but felt he let the side down when he collapsed in the heather and failed to finish the course. Thereafter, he threw himself into cross-country running, determined that such a failure should never happen again, and made himself abundantly fit. This was the first occasion when both the strength of his will and his terror of failure manifested themselves as central aspects of his character.

The Ten Tors march took place during the hot summer months when the entire Junior Tradesman Regiment moved to camp at Fort Tregantle in Cornwall. 'It was a boy's dream of high adventure, rock climbing, and general excitement. I loved that part of the country, the cliffs and the sea.'[3] The warm air breezed in stark contrast to the cold bitterness of Aberdeenshire winds; it was another world entirely.

On other occasions at Aldershot, he took part in ceremonial parades. One such, held in celebration of the centenary of the Garrison Church, was attended by the Queen, whom Dennis was proud to see in close proximity (and amazed at her small stature), and before whom he marched past afterwards. Another celebrity who inspected him on parade was Field-Marshal Lord Montgomery; instead of staring straight ahead at attention, Dennis Nilsen looked his lordship in the eye, and was surprised not to be admonished.

On weekend leaves, the boys had seventy-two hours passes, and most would go home. Those who lived too far away to make a journey worthwhile, Nilsen included, would go camping, to Marlow on the Thames, to the New Forest, or to Stonehenge. On one occasion they found themselves in the grounds of Broadlands, Lord Mountbatten's home.

The most important man at Aldershot was the regimental sergeant-major who, whether he liked it or not, met the needs for paternalistic authority felt in varying degrees by all the boys. Dennis Nilsen was no exception. He warmed to the 'father-figure' appeal of R.S.M. 'Paddy' Dowd, a man whom he knew intuitively he could trust:

> I never met any R.S.M. in the army whom I didn't (although sometimes secretly) admire and respect . . . An R.S.M. is top man in any regiment, and they all have a hard abrasive vocal edge, with scrupulously fair-minded 'soft centres'. You know exactly how you stand with them — there are no uncertainties. They can be relied upon 100 per cent. I never knew an R.S.M. who didn't have a warm sense of humour and quick (sometimes acid) wit . . . in times of real personal problems the 'soft centre' always came to the fore and mountains could be moved to ease the pressure.[4]

After three years, Nilsen passed his senior education test (equivalent to 'O' Level) in five subjects — maths, English, catering science, map-reading and current affairs, passing in addition the important B II catering exam which confirmed the direction of his career. He completed full training on foot, arms and weapons drill, and took his passing out parade in the summer of 1964. At the age of eighteen, Nilsen was a young man with a career, a future, security. There was little that need trouble him. Even his pervasive sense of isolation had to a large extent been dissipated by the comradeship of army life. He could mix much more easily, and he had begun to find his tongue.

After Aldershot, Nilsen went home to Strichen for a brief period of leave. Anxious to see his grandmother, he hired a scooter and drove to Fraserburgh, then on south to Aberdeen. It was raining and the road was slippery. Dennis skidded, crashed into a lorry, and was taken to the infirmary where he was X-rayed and discharged. Apart from bruises, there appeared to be no serious damage, and if the heavy knock he sustained to the head caused an injury with hidden and delayed effects, certainly no one diagnosed anything of the sort at the time.

Nilsen's first posting as a private was to the 1st Battalion the Royal Fusiliers (City of London Regiment) at Osnabruck in Germany, whose commanding officer was Lt.-Col. Taylor. He took up his job on the team of SQMS 'Badger' Maitland, a likeable and easy-going fellow with a serious drink problem. The cook sergeant was Tommy Ibrahim, and Nilsen's contemporaries and friends at this time were Ginger Watson, Micky Duke, Bob Pears, Dumbo Howitt and Paddy Aherne. The company commander was Major Dennis. It was, again, a happy time, an extension and continuation of the domestic camaraderie begun at Aldershot, occasionally interrupted by military field exercises. Osnabruck also marks Dennis Nilsen's introduction to drink. 'We were a hard-working boozy lot who did not appear to miss one night's drinking in the two years I was there.'5 Some of his fellows noticed he was more frequently intoxicated than the rest of them. He returned to Aldershot briefly to pass the B I catering exam, and served with the brigade in Norway.

The happiness of these years was compromised by one increasingly serious preoccupation. While still at Aldershot he had been aware of being attracted to various other boys, and of the obvious need to repress these sexual longings. The repression carried with it a concomitant feeling of guilt, for if his desires needed to be hidden then there must be something wrong with them. He thought of himself as bisexual rather than homosexual, and as he was not in any way effeminate it was relatively easy for him to dissemble. He was careful never to let slip any indication of his sexuality, still less to declare himself, but was tormented by the awkward suspicion that his 'abnormality' must somehow be transparent. 'I never took a shower, always a bath. I was always afraid that I must somehow look different and that my innermost thoughts would be exposed with my nakedness.' Sleeping in barracks

with twenty other boys, he could only find relief in masturbation when alone in the bathroom.

As a young man in Osnabruck, the temptations were
greater, and had therefore to be the more severely contained.
Coming home drunk in the evening, he might frequently
have to be undressed and dumped into bed by one of the
other soldiers, or perform the same service for one of them.
No sexual encounter ever took place. If ever 'queers' were
discussed, it was invariably with derision and scorn, in which
Dennis Nilsen joined as heartily as the next man. All the time
he knew that he was deceiving his friends, and that his real
emotional identity was being smothered by pretence. The
strain of maintaining the deception was gradually depositing
a silt of unacknowledged pressure.

In 1967, aged twenty-one, Nilsen was posted to Aden,
attached to the Military Provost Staff Corps in charge of
terrorist detainees at the Al Mansoura Prison. The British
had on their hands a desperate defensive war against Arab
terrorists fired by hatred and oblivious to personal safety.
The prison, a walled fort with heavy gates and machine-gun
watch-towers, was under frequent attack from rioters, and
the sight of dead bodies littering the countryside was commonplace. Some soldiers, ambushed on their way back to
their barracks, lost their lives and were horribly mutilated;
others unwise enough' to be entertained by a local whore
might have their throats cut on the job. It was altogether a
searing experience in an atmosphere torrid with heat and
danger. Dennis Nilsen appears to have taken more than a few
risks, hitch-hiking back to Al Mansoura through terrorist-
infested terrain (and probably unmolested because the Arabs
thought he must be a decoy), and arriving at the prison on the
back of an Arab vegetable lorry. There was one incident
which ought to have proved fatal, when he had been drinking
in the Oasis Bar.

I was really drunk at the time. I hailed a black and yellow
cab and instructed the driver to go forth. I remember
passing Check Point Bravo and waving the taxi on. I must
have dozed off in the back of the cab. I felt a sharp pain on

the back of my head (on reflection I guessed that the driver had hit me with a cosh or something — to this day I cannot understand why he didn't cut my throat — maybe he was proud of his taxi and didn't want to make a mess of the back seat with my blood). I woke up naked in what I took to be the boot of the car. I was still a bit dazed. I felt around and my clothes were in the boot as well (or someone's clothes). The engine started (I couldn't open the boot). After what seemed like a short drive the vehicle stopped. In a flash I decided to 'play dead' as being the best way to sum up the situation and make a break for it. The boot opened slowly and through a squinted eye I saw a well-built Arab. He had a cosh or something in his hand. He stretched his arm cautiously towards me muttering something in Arabic. He touched my ankle and moved his hand up to my knee still muttering. He grasped my leg under the knee, raised it and let it flop limply back in place (I tried to be as limp as possible) . . . he stroked his hand across my buttocks . . . It was when he was manhandling me out of the boot that I felt the coldness of metal. I grabbed the jack-handle and sitting up hit him a hard blow full on the head. He dropped like a felled ox. I hit him two equally hard blows on the head. There was a lot of blood. He never made a sound. I was in a cluster of old buildings. I quickly put on my clothes (I couldn't find my underpants). My money was still in my jeans . . . I wiped the jack-handle with an oil cloth, put it in and closed the boot. There was no one else around, very quiet. A dog barked some way off. It was quite light under the strong moonlight. I stood thinking for a moment and decided that he would be less conspicuous actually in the boot himself.[6]

Nilsen managed to drag the Arab into the boot, scuffed the sand to disperse traces of blood, and started walking. He was not far from a main road, and soon recognised it as the road which would eventually lead to the prison. It was two in the morning when he arrived at the gates, was picked out by searchlights and brought in by foot patrol. He was reprimanded but never talked about the incident.

The next morning I was full of the horror of what had almost happened to me. I felt like the luckiest man in Aden. I had nightmares afterwards of being tortured, raped, murdered and mutilated, or other combinations towards the same end.[7]

The incident gains interest in the light of what we now know. Both a psychiatrist and the present author challenged Nilsen with the possibility that it might be a fantasy. He readily acknowledges that he is prone to embellish memories with imagined details (as indeed we all do to some extent), and is no longer certain which of his recollections are fantasy and which are fact. (Similarly, his portrayal of himself as a scruffy little boy in Aberdeenshire with romantic longings for the land owes something to the *post facto* shaping of a novelist or stage director — a fusion of Nilsen the boy and Nilsen the creature of his own imagination.) The psychiatrist said frankly that he thought the Aden incident was 'most unlikely' to be true. I believe it is based on an actual event and has been enhanced by subconscious editing (the nakedness and unconsciousness probably being the work of the subconscious). There may not even have been a death, but only the threat of one. The degree of factual truth is almost beside the point. What is significant is that he mentioned it to no one. His capacity to thrust the memory into a private compartment of his mind and proceed, outwardly unaffected, along the normal course of his life, was remarkable when set beside the ordinary compulsion that many would feel to confide such an unnerving experience. And if it is an imagined adventure, it is still remarkable that his fancies could thrive secretly, without interference from the side of him engaged in mundane reality.

Pending British withdrawal from Aden, in the summer of 1967 Nilsen was posted in charge of catering to the Trucial Oman Scouts Mess at Sharjah in the Persian Gulf. Despite some harrowing events (a pilot who crashed was brought back to his mess in pieces), this was a relatively more relaxing time with boozy evenings at the R.A.F. Flying Kunjah Club, jovial companionship and lewd songs, even cocktail parties on the roof. One of the drinking companions, known as 'Smithy', fell off a Land-Rover and broke his neck. He was buried in a simple desert grave. Dennis lamented his loss as they all did, but he nursed a secret fascination with the idea that to die young was in an important way enviable, that to be saved the vicissitudes of an uncertain future was perhaps more a cause for celebration than regret. Looking back, he reflected on 'the sand storm blowing over the disappearing grave of young "Smithy", terminated at the end of a happy day with his mates, instantly. There "Smithy" is forever as he was, ageless, while the rest of us totter on round our little circles of personal decay.'[8] Death is here conceived, not as an end, but as an endless pause in time.

At Sharjah, Dennis Nilsen was an N.C.O. with the crucial advantage of a private room. This was to have a lasting influence upon the development of his sexual nature. It was not particularly important that there was an Arab boy willing to go to bed with him, as he was with most of the officers, although this must have been the first time that Dennis had achieved tactile sexual contact with another person. The boy declared undying affection, pleaded to be taken back to England, and offered his services more frequently than they could reasonably be required. Dennis was not moved in any way. He felt rather ashamed of having sex with the boy, who was not even sure of his own age, but his thoughts did not dwell upon it or deepen into guilt. Far more important was his discovery of the mirror.

When I had the privacy of my own room as an N.C.O. sexual expression became more complex. The novelty of one's own body soon wore off and I needed something positive to relate to. My imagination hit on the idea of using a mirror. By placing a large, long mirror on its side strategically beside the bed, I would view my own reclining reflection. At first always careful not to show my head, because the situation needed that I believe it was someone else. I would give the reflection some animation, but that play could not be drawn out long enough. The fantasy could dwell much longer on a mirror image which was asleep.[9]

Thus began a distorted narcissism in which the desired object was, to all outward appearances, dead.

Years of concealment and guilt were now harvesting their crop of deep psychological damage, or at least beginning to. 'If the guilty feel like criminals, then I have been *all* my life a criminal.'[10] Nilsen was ashamed of his emotions and dared not declare them. As far as he knew, he was destined never to enjoy the warmth of a normal human relationship, for a variety of reasons which he only half admitted to himself. He would not marry, because he was stained with the genetic shortcomings of his unstable father, which made him peculiar even before birth. He felt no great stirrings of emotion or lust towards women, and those he felt towards men had necessarily to be hidden. He was an expert at concealment; nobody knew him, and his reputation as a 'loner' was gaining wide credence, in spite of his being chummy and loquacious with the crowd. As far as he was concerned, his very nature was marked with a scar of abnormality which he could do nothing about. Like a club foot, it would be with him forever, but at least it was not so visible. If he would have to continue suppressing his own nature, then he must indulge his private emotions in secret, where the imagination rules, not reality. 'The image in the mirror becomes your only friend and true lover.' He would not allow any emotional experience in reality, but would take more and more frequent refuge in fantasy. 'It starts in narcissism and ends in confusion.'[11]

Thousands of young men have had to cope with the same problems and have emerged triumphant from the struggle. Thousands more create a fantasy which often involves the use of mirrors, either for self-admiration or for the masturbatory appeal of an imaginary onlooker. What made Nilsen's fantasy unusual was the requirement that the body in the mirror be still, that the head not be visible. Dennis Nilsen was aroused by the image of himself, but of himself only as a dead man. Love and death were becoming dangerously mingled in his mind as the remembered image of his adored grandfather surged forward. Quietly in his quarters with his mirror, Dennis was dead, too.

In January 1968, Nilsen returned to England to be posted with the 1st Battalion, Argyll and Sutherland Highlanders, at Seaton Barracks, Plymouth, under the command of Lt.-Col. C.C. Mitchell (the famous silver-haired 'Mad Mitch'). With them he was part of a spearhead battalion which went to Cyprus in 1969, to be placed thereafter in charge of catering for the officers' mess at Montgomery Barracks, Berlin, fifty yards from the Communist border, where the new commanding officer was Lt.-Col. 'Sandy' Boswell.

In Berlin, fast retrieving its pre-war reputation for licence, Nilsen frequently found himself waking up in a strange bed next to an anonymous German civilian, with little in the way of satisfaction to boast of. He once went out on the town with a group of other soldiers and paid for a few minutes with a female prostitute. 'I was amazed at how easy it all was, but apart from the wonderful shock of ejaculation I found the whole experience over-rated and depressing.'[12]

At the beginning of 1970, Dennis Nilsen was selected to cater for the ski-training parties at Bodenmais, Bavaria. The idea was that the Argyll and Sutherland Highlanders, by report the best infantry battalion in the British army, should train to fight under any conditions, even on ski-slopes. So they left Berlin, drove through East Germany, and settled themselves in for two joyous months in Bavaria. Their accommodation was at an old mountain farmhouse, converted into the Kottinghammer Ski-farm, where Nilsen was required to cook for two officers and thirty N.C.O.s and soldiers every day.

I felt it was important that everyone should get a full English breakfast fry-up every morning. There is nothing more uplifting to a soldier's morale on a freezing inhospitable morning than fried egg on fried bread, bacon and sausage with baked beans and tomatoes, toast and butter with a steaming hot mug of tea or coffee. My efforts in catering (and my comradeship in drinking) made me the best friend of all ranks who attended the ski-ing school.[13]

Incidentally, it is worth mentioning, in view of the

'slaughtering skills' with which Nilsen was later credited at his trial, that his work did not involve killing animals, but only cutting them up for food. Only once did he kill a goose, for Christmas.

Dennis especially enjoyed the free ambience of equality, which accorded well with his rapidly developing sense of idealism in political matters. His Aden period had left him with a stern refusal to be seduced by the partisan view ('Arabs die, soldiers die, and bloody governments just shuffle their feet'[14]), and he was now careful to avoid both press and army propaganda from any side. In Berlin he was as resistant to Soviet exaggerations as he was to the American variety, and saw it as his duty to protect an independent attitude based upon evidence. At Bodenmais, he flirted briefly with fascism. Noticing that the war memorial in the town square bore the date 1946 as marking the end of the war, he soon found that the Bavarians, or some of them, had fought what they regarded as the 'American occupation' for some months after the official cessation of hostilities, and had been sturdy supporters of Hitler. The attractions of fascism were not at all difficult to discern. 'A stable order, national pride, military strength, full employment, unity and the achieving of national greatness'; there were old men in Bodenmais still willing to sing the same song, and Dennis Nilsen was an eager audience. But only for a moment — his radicalism would never again be tempted into such an extreme path.

The two months in Bodenmais coincided with a local beer festival and dance, for which Corporal Nilsen was dressed in lederhosen provided by the garage owner, 'Mad Hans'. Under the influence of a rollicking band and far too many beers, Nilsen was drawn to the company of a pretty eighteen-year-old local girl, with whom he danced continuously, taking her eventually by the hand to the verandah where they kissed. Her relations intervened and pulled them apart. There were shouts and tears. Dennis returned to the dance, but found that he could not stop thinking about her. A brief episode of potential romance (nothing more) led nowhere.

After returning to Aldershot to pass the Intermediate Management Course examination, Nilsen was sent, still with the Argyll and Sutherland Highlanders, to Fort George in Inverness-shire. Thus he went back to his Scottish roots, not many miles from his Aberdeenshire childhood. He was profoundly affected by Culloden Moor, where Charles Fraser from Inverallochy had fought and died so pointlessly centuries before, and where now he could stand and absorb the vast natural beauties around, seemingly contemptuous of the human follies and braveries they had witnessed. It was, he wrote, 'one of the holiest and most sacred pieces of ground I have ever stood at. I could almost hear the sounds of battle and action around me. I would always walk from that site in a state of shock.'[15]

In August of 1970, Nilsen was selected to be in charge of the N.C.O. kitchen for the Queen's Royal Guard at Ballater, during the period of the Queen's annual holiday in Balmoral. He was by now an accomplished cook whose range of skills, from English nursery food to elaborate Escoffier concoctions (which he had been required to provide for visiting foreign dignitaries in Berlin), was much appreciated by the officers. At Ballater (Victoria Barracks) the guards, when not on ceremonial parade, would act as grouse beaters for the royal party, and soldiers of all ranks were expected to attend the Gillies Ball at Balmoral.

Early the following year, the battalion was reduced to company strength, to be known thenceforth as the Queen's Company. There was a strenuous 'Save the Argylls' campaign in which Dennis Nilsen took part, but to no avail. When postings were announced, he was instructed to join 242 Signals at Aces High Station in the Shetland Islands, and so he set off on the evening of 24 January 1971 on what would turn out to be the final lap of his army career, and a turning-point in his emotional life.

Social life for 242 Signals centred on the Maybury Club, where soldiers and their wives mixed with local people, some romances flourished, and uncomplicated friendliness prevailed in a corner of the world where people still left their doors open and their cars unlocked. Soldiers took it in turns to run the bar. The evening would start decorously enough, with people turning up in their 'Sunday best' and chatting amiably, but alcohol and music soon banished inhibition, and by the end of the evening the Maybury was shaking with Scottish reels and country dancing. The party never degenerated into an ill-tempered rough-and-tumble, which would have insulted the peaceable nature and polite manners of the Shetlanders and embarrassed the offenders themselves. Corporal Nilsen was a regular participant in Maybury Club dances: 'I would drink a lot of brandy and coke and be dragged from my solitude into the mêlée of the dance. I was quite good at country dancing and we would have good boisterous times while the wind and weather howled loudly outside.'[16]

That the enjoyment was superficial is suggested by a verse he wrote at the time, one stanza of which reads:

> More and more retracting
> From the Maybury social scene,
> I brood
> At night
> Behind my iron screen.

The beauty of the location encouraged Dennis to pursue a hobby he had long contemplated. He had been fascinated by the idea of film-making since 1969, and regularly operated the film projector on recreational evenings. With the army's blessing he took a film projectionist course at Beaconsfield, and when he returned to the Shetlands he was equipped to record on film the land and seascapes which were the scenes of his constant wanderings at every available hour off-duty. The Shetlanders are proud of their Viking ancestry, which they celebrate yearly in the Viking festival, an evening pageant illuminated by a hundred torches. This occurred shortly after Nilsen's arrival, suggesting to him that his own Norwegian blood might ally him in kinship with these friendly people. The combination of uncontaminated natural beauty and a sense that perhaps he belonged there more definitely than anywhere else, provoked an affective response with deep subconscious currents that he barely understood:

I had found great beauty, sadness and poetry in the Shetlands, and a wild desolation nearly untouched by man and his civilisation . . . I felt at one with heaven and its gods and all the earth and its peoples. For one moment in my life I really had roots and I had a warming identity with all things past, present, and future . . . My feelings were such that I knelt and took some wet island soil in my hand and smeared it all over my face. Was this the earth from which I had sprung? It was cold, harsh and soothing. I had a strange tingling feeling of being, somehow, home.

This is a disquieting passage of recollection for a variety of reasons. To call the earth which he rubbed on his face 'cold, harsh and soothing' is an unusual combination of epithets; that which is cold and harsh cannot easily be soothing as well, unless one has already decided that warmth and gentleness are for other people and that coldness and harshness befit one's scarred nature. Furthermore, the sensation of being 'home' appears to be suggested less by the landscape than by the cold earth. Was this worship of the soil a manifestation of his latent idea that death was a going home, a returning to nature and transcendent reality to which mortal life was but an illusory interruption? The same morbid fancies had afflicted his mind as a boy in Fraserburgh, when he imagined himself drowning, swallowed by natural forces and carried back to his source down among the dead men. For a man overtly distrustful of all religions, these are strange metaphysical conceits. His scepticism had by now effectively crushed whatever religious inclinations he may have had and he looked with contempt upon the Church and its doings. That was the result of rational reflection. But there churned well below the surface a primitive religiosity which he forbore to acknowledge and which was alarming in its implications. For Dennis Nilsen's God was beginning to look like the measureless cycle of life and death, a cycle which had long ago claimed his grandfather and left him stranded on the beach.

A poem which he wrote about this time serves to reinforce suspicions of a morbid sensitivity. Entitled 'Fitful Head' after a spot on the Shetland coast to which he repaired frequently, it ends in lines which sound uncomfortably inappropriate for a man who professed to be happy there:

> Lives of sorrow,
> Bones of the dead,
> Given by the sea
> To Fitful Head.
> A million sea-birds,
> White with despair,
> Screaming above
> In the crisp new air . . .
> A hand, a smooth and empty hand
> Always out of reach.
> Life, like a sailor's body
> Drowned upon the beach.

An earlier line has 'flawless' hand instead of 'empty' hand, but it is the couplet hidden in the centre of the poem which strikes alarm, suggesting yet again that, in this man's mind, the concepts of death and love are entangled:

> There is no magic on this earth
> But love and death to balance birth.[17]

To stand on the cliffs at Fitful Head is to feel one is on the edge of the world, and that no feet have stood there before you. R.L. Stevenson had written about it, and it was so far beyond the easy track of the tourist that it was disturbed only by birds. If Dennis Nilsen's response to this desolate spot was melancholic in the extreme, it may have had something to do with the seismic effect of an unexpected personal event.

In the summer of 1972, during the last few months of Nilsen's army service, there came on to his staff an eighteen-year-old private named Terry Finch.* Nilsen was just finishing lunch at Maybury when he first saw Finch. 'As he walked in the door he had the effect upon me of an electric shock.' In

---

* The identity of this man is protected by a pseudonym.

the following weeks the two men became good friends, going for long walks together on the bleak, treeless, rocky terrain, recounting their lives, filming. Finch shared Nilsen's enthusiasm for film-making, and helped him to plan his films, cut and edit them, and project them. Many of them were footage of each other at Fitful Head, where they sometimes lay exhausted and chatting. All the time Nilsen was reeling with emotions which he dared not divulge. 'I loved him so much,' he writes, 'that it was a source of extreme pain to me when he was not around or when he would go off anywhere without me.' He trained Finch to use the cinema projection equipment for the regular movie show, thus giving a more professional excuse for their companionship. If they exchanged glances at the dinner-table or the bar, they would make strenuous efforts to avert their eyes, Nilsen because he felt guilty, Finch because he was confused. One of the younger man's duties was to wake Nilsen in the morning. Nilsen invariably woke before his arrival, and pretended to slumber so that he might feel a hand on his shoulder.

In many of the films they made together, Nilsen was the director and Finch the actor. Nilsen now says that the best scenes are those in which Finch was made to lie still and 'play dead', and that he was stimulated by this vision more than by any other. Perhaps he enjoyed the sense of being in control of someone, even if it was only feigned. He also says he masturbated when subsequently watching these scenes. As the films no longer exist, it is impossible to determine how much fantasy may have intruded into these recollections.

Terry Finch was not homosexual, but he was young enough and homesick enough to welcome affection from the corporal, an affection which grew more intense the longer it remained undeclared and unexplored. Nilsen was convinced that the boy was frightened of his own emotions as the friendship developed, and he was probably right. At all events, no overt attempt was ever made to give physical expression to their affection, which would certainly have proved disastrous. On two occasions their muddled sensitivity came close to collapse. After a social dinner in the local guest house the two of them went to the club for a drink.

Finch disappeared and Dennis went to look for him. He found him lying on the grass outside, weeping, and brought him back in and helped to get him safely to his accommodation. He said he had been drinking too much, and the matter was left there. On the second occasion Dennis was sitting in an armchair at the club with a late-night drink long after the bar had closed. When the stragglers had all gone, Finch was left alone. He walked over to join Nilsen and began crying, talking of homesickness and isolation. Nilsen comforted him, and for a short moment their hands clasped.

They then drifted apart. Nilsen thought that the boy had made 'a massive effort against his innermost feelings', but it is more than likely that these 'feelings' were largely in his own imagination. It was when Finch realised the intensity of his friend's attraction to him that he moved away, knowing well enough that he could not reciprocate. As for Nilsen, there was no doubt that he was entirely overwhelmed. 'I would have given my life for Terry Finch,' he wrote, and now as he watched him recede into the distance he became deeply depressed. 'I knew I was leaving the army in a few weeks and would probably not see him ever again. Every kind of deep emotional pain in those last weeks sorely afflicted me. I wished I were dead.' He went alone to the high overhang at Fitful Head and thought of throwing himself over, to the sound of the ever-present screeching birds. Then he walked back to base, finally dejected and hopeless.

Dennis Nilsen's last act in the Shetlands the night before he left amazed his colleagues. All the films which he had made with such care and pride over the last year he threw into the incinerator and destroyed. They included, naturally, the films he and Finch had made together — 15,000 feet of them. The projector he gave to Finch as a farewell gesture. It was an impulsive and dramatic act, and it demonstrated Nilsen's ability to erase memories by demolishing the evidence which could recall them. The films no longer existed; neither would the misery.

Or so he thought. The following day, Nilsen's mind was still preoccupied:

As the Viscount roared off the tarmac at Sumburgh I could see the face of Terry Finch superimposed on the flames of my imprisoned life. I imagined his lone figure standing on the dunes on Quendale Bay looking up at my passage as I flew past, out of his life, and disappeared into those high distant clouds. I never saw him again.

He was, he says, in utter despair, and nearly two years would have to pass before he could consider himself recovered. The account he gives may sound melodramatic to those whose emotional life follows a steadier path, but one cannot resist the suspicion that had he been fortunate enough to choose someone more accessible, his descent towards the ghastly events which began six years later might have been diverted.

Terry Finch married shortly afterwards. Dennis Nilsen went home to Strichen from Aberdeen airport, visualising the inscription on his own tombstone: BORN 1945, DIED 1972 AGED 26. 'A lifetime of suppressed emotion had suddenly been released, smashed completely, and left me for dead.'[18]

5

POLICE AND CIVIL SERVICE

Dennis Nilsen had been eleven years and eighty-four days in the army, almost half his life. He was one month from his twenty-seventh birthday when he completed his military career with the rank of corporal and a decoration, the General Service Medal (South Arabia). His conduct as per record book was listed as 'exemplary'. To this day, he remains a life member of the Army Catering Corps Regimental Association. If asked why he decided not to sign on again, he said that at his age he thought he was still young enough to attempt a career outside, which was true but evasive. He had gradually become more disenchanted with the military mind, particularly as it expressed itself in dealing with the troubles in Ireland (about which there was much solid information as well as gossip at the Maybury), and had felt increasingly uncomfortable on the side of the 'oppressors'. He felt, crudely, that he was hired to feed those whose job it was to kill on government orders, a role he found at first distasteful, then immoral. The one central ethic of which the army was most proud, that of obeying orders without question, was the very one which most rankled with Corporal Nilsen; how could any intelligent and sensitive man kill another merely because he had been instructed to do so by a superior officer?

The final straw was the Bloody Sunday of 1972, when elements of the British army mowed down demonstrators in Londonderry. Dennis Nilsen was horrified to discover that the side of law and order could behave with the same lack of moral scruple as the terrorists, and he felt betrayed, robbed of honour. The consequent practice of 'internment', that is imprisonment without charge or trial, and the rumours of torture, convinced Nilsen that he did not belong in the army. He enjoyed the comradeship but was dismayed by the mentality.

Dennis spent about five weeks at home in Strichen between October and December 1972, wondering what to do next. Nagging doubts about the future assailed him. The army resettlement officer had suggested he stay in catering or join the police or prison service. His mother was rather more concerned by his apparent lack of interest in the idea of marriage. If she raised the subject, he would shrug and dismiss it. She remembered that, as a boy, if he had been required to take a girl with him to a local dance, it was invariably his sister Sylvia that he chose. There had once been an occasion when he had received forms from an agency which arranged meetings between strangers for 'dating', and had asked his mother how he should describe himself. 'Good-looking,' she had said, and he had been frankly astonished that he could be so described. The forms were sent off, and a photograph of a suitable girl received in reply, but nothing had come of it.

Relations with his elder brother Olav had never been cordial. There now occurred an incident which broke their relationship completely. Dennis went to visit Olav and his wife and another couple at home in Fraserburgh, and they all sat around watching television and drinking. The film being shown was *Victim*, in which Dirk Bogarde played a married man who had to declare to his wife that he was involved in a sexual liaison with another man. It was a courageous and honest film, the first ever to deal with the subject in the British cinema, but it was treated with derision that evening. Dennis was infuriated; he felt the scorn as keenly as if it had been a personal attack. At the Station Hotel later, a row ensued in which Dennis insulted his brother and was hustled outside. Someone hit him, leaving him bruised and bleeding. When he eventually got home to Strichen in the middle of the night, he remained for two hours in the garden shed, refusing to come indoors, although Adam and Betty Scott knew he was there and entreated him. He never did tell them what had happened; Betty, as usual, respected his desire to keep things to himself. Shortly afterwards, Olav told her that he suspected his brother was homosexual. Nilsen wrote: 'I never spoke to him ever again. He represented everything that existed to put me down (especially my emotions). He was the only member of the family to guess at the scandalous aspects of bisexuality and gave me the power to hate him in his knowledge.'[1]

Dennis began to be troubled by nightmares prompted by memories of his Arabian experience. The nightmare was generally induced by a combination of drink and soaring classical music. His mother recalls that he would stay up late listening to music and writing poetry. He was a moody uncommunicative stranger in the house.

It was clear that Nilsen could not stay in Strichen for long; he simply did not fit. In an anxious condition, he decided that it would be a traditional and natural progression for him to exchange one uniform for another and become a prison officer or a policeman. He elected the latter, and in December 1972 joined the Metropolitan Police Training School at Hendon, North London. Having passed the sixteen-week course, he was posted to Q Division and attached to Willesden Green Police Station with the designation Police Constable Q287. There he was to remain for exactly a year.

The choice of a career in the police can only have been *faute de mieux* for a man who was more and more disgruntled with the exercise of authoritarian power. His left-wing propensities were more emphatic than ever, and were quickly confirmed by what he perceived as the dangerous aggression exhibited by some police officers who were all too eager to subdue a suspect while resisting arrest, especially if it offered an excuse for violence. As for himself, he claimed that 'in my year in the police I never once drew my truncheon, or assaulted any officer, prisoner or member of the public.'[2] It has to be said that he never had much excuse to do so, since his duties as a junior constable were not exacting, though he made a number of arrests and grew accustomed to appearing in court. On the other hand, he was well aware that policemen had so often to deal with messes created by incompetent or innocent politicians and were sometimes blamed for being the instruments of an ill-conceived law. It was little wonder that many an honest copper sank rapidly into miserable dejection, exhausted by all-consuming work.

Nilsen's colleague at Hendon Training School, Ian Johnson, was posted to Willesden Green at the same time, and the two of them were taken in April 1973 to look at the mortuary behind Brent Town Hall with their 'parent' copper, Peter Wellstead, responsible for supervising their initiation into the working force:

We enter a shabby little room which displayed all the disarray of an army butchers' shop behind the scenes. A couple of metal trolleys were lying around with opened bodies upon them. Mostly old men with a wooden block supporting the head with a variety of grotesque facial expressions. Each one cut from neck to navel with the breast/rib bones sawn out so that the examiner could get at the heart and lungs. The back of the head was open to give access to the brain . . . on one of the trolleys containing an old man's uncut corpse was the contrasting body of a young girl with a label attached to her left wrist. Ian felt a bit pale. I felt a bit fascinated . . . We walked out into the fresh air. Our faces were pale and serious and Ian wasn't feeling too well. Pete knew we were affected and laughed it off. 'You'll see a lot more of this in the police,' he said. He was right.[3]

Peter Wellstead liked the new recruit and enjoyed talking to him, but he noticed that an indeterminate sense of dissatisfaction clung to him like an extra skin. Nilsen admitted that he was disappointed not to find the same kind of comradeship in the police force as he had been used to in the army, a consequence of anonymous London life; soldiers had perforce to spend all their leisure hours more or less together, policemen went off in different directions to their homes and wives. Dennis Nilsen was left to his own resources, which were few. The big cosmopolitan city did not line up friends for you to choose from; you had to ferret them out. Nilsen knew no one in London and began to feel the awkwardness of isolation in a crowd, a sensation which would deepen as the years progressed. His solution was the common escape of many young men in London; he frequented the pubs, and discovered the huge subterranean homosexual fraternity which eddies around certain public houses in the metropolitan area. To call it a 'fraternity' is in reality a cruel misnomer, for the majority of men who congregate in these pubs are not interested in each other except as potential sexual encounters, which they strive hard to keep separate from their normal social lives. They go to look and to display themselves, to parade with a glance that promises orgasm and positively warns that expectations of anything further are to be discounted. The most famous of these pubs is the crowded Coleherne in Earl's Court, the first that Dennis Nilsen discovered and the crucible of his initiation into an arid homosexual sub-culture. He met a man there at the beginning of 1973 and smuggled him into the Hendon Training School. It was an unsatisfactory and belittling experience.

In August of that year he met another man, a few years younger than himself and the son of an ex-colonel, in the King William IV pub at Hampstead. They went together to Nilsen's room at the Police Section House and anal sex took place for the first time in Nilsen's life (and then only once). More importantly, he felt a renewal of the romantic attachment which had bound him to Terry Finch in the last months of his army career. He was ready to commit himself totally and thought he saw the chance of a permanent relationship. But again, his choice had fallen upon the wrong person. Derek Collins* showed no interest in Dennis Nilsen and had no intention of trying to reciprocate his affection. On the

* A pseudonym.

contrary, he was quite happy to 'sleep around' with different partners, and although he saw Nilsen on several occasions later, theirs was never anything like an exclusive friendship. 'He wanted everyone and nobody,' says Nilsen, who soon realised that his hopes were still-born. In fairness, Collins did not encourage him to think otherwise; the impetus for his emotional surrender was entirely self-generated. Nilsen resigned himself to the inevitable and sought refuge in a growing number of casual encounters:

> I was left with an endless search through the soul-destroying pub scene and its resulting one-night stands . . . passing faces and bodies the unfulfilled tokens of an empty life. A house is not a home and sex is not a relationship. We would only lend each other our bodies in a vain search for inner peace.[4]

The Derek Collins episode and consequent promiscuity convinced Nilsen that he could not remain in the police force, with any semblance of propriety. He resigned in December 1973 to the amazement of his colleagues, who could not understand why he should want to leave. P.C. Wellstead said he had performed his duties well and appeared to enjoy the work; certainly he never shirked it. He left with a moderate report and with no complaints having been lodged against him. Nobody knew that he had once shone his torch into a car parked in Exeter Road and found two men 'behaving indecently'. He could not bring himself to arrest them.

For the first four months of 1974 Nilsen was at a loose end and measurably poor. He was also without a home, a novel condition for a man who had thus far been provided with accommodation. He took a room at 9 Manstone Road, London NW8, and sold his General Service Medal for £8 to help pay for it. His employment in these months of limbo was as a security guard at various Crown properties, including the Ministry of Defence Building in Whitehall, the Parliamentary Offices in Bridge Street, and the Old Admiralty Building.

I could gather my thoughts in the quiet evenings and unwind from the hectic life of a policeman. I could even take time to browse through some exhibits at the Tate Gallery depository at Gorst Road, NW10 (I remember it was full of stuffed animals and huge tortoises from the Galapagos Islands).[5]

There was nothing but a paralysing boredom in the work of a security guard, especially after a career which had been highly active, eventful, even creative. In May 1974 he resigned from P.S.A. Security and after a week summoned the courage to sign on for unemployment benefit. It was an embarrassing and humiliating moment when he presented himself at the Department of Employment Office in Harlesden High Road, NW10; the descent into uselessness had been rapid and total.

Nilsen was interviewed by an executive officer who submitted him for a job in the civil service. On 20 May, he went for interview before a panel at the Regional Office in Hanway House, Red Lion Square, to determine whether he should be offered a post as clerical officer in the Department of Employment itself. His application was successful, and in view of his experience in the Army Catering Corps, it was thought that he would serve best at the Jobcentre in Denmark Street, in the heart of London's West End, just off Charing Cross Road. Jobcentres, run by the Manpower Services Commission, advertise vacancies in the metropolitan area, mostly low-paid and unskilled, and help to alleviate the chronic unemployment problem in the city. People may walk in off the street, see what is available, and be sent by a clerical officer for interview. Jobcentres are scattered all over London, and the large Denmark Street branch specialises in supplying labour for the hotel and catering trade, a task for which its central position makes it suitable. Many of the staff it places are foreign.

Dennis Nilsen turned up at the hotel and catering employment office in Denmark Street with a letter for Mrs Hawkins, and thought he would 'give it a try'. He stayed for the next eight years, and was still at the Department of Employment when he was arrested on 9 February 1983.

> I warmed to the creative and positive community service
> aspects of placing an unemployed person in a job vacancy.
> The number of these 'placings' each week gave a genuine
> feeling of achievement and job satisfaction.[6]

From the very beginning there was a certain amount of
friction in the office, as Nilsen was impatient of bureaucracy
and yearned to see results, while many of those he was
working with were markedly less aggressive in their approach;
his direct manner (the Buchan bluntness surging up) did not
fit well with their soft acceptance of the rules. Nevertheless,
he threw himself into learning the profession in all its aspects
and soon developed his own technique of front-line interviewing, which, to his frustration, he was not called upon
often to put to use, being relegated to the telephone most of
the time.

In these early stages, Nilsen steered clear of union activities, not wishing to draw attention to himself while 'on
probation' as it were, but he watched and learned from the
enthusiasm of the two activists, Andy Power and Ian Watson,
who between them bore most of the union work for their
branch on their shoulders. The rest of his colleagues tended
to be indifferent. His social life virtually non-existent, he
attended meetings held by various left-wing groups and was
pressed to join the International Socialists, a move he resisted because he was not attracted to dogma. He says he
remained politically independent throughout his civil service
career, and it is true that he never joined a party. On the other
hand, he did not attend any conservative or right-wing meetings. There was never any doubt where his sympathies lay.

What little social life he had was restricted to inconsequen-
tial encounters with a flow of 'pick-ups' found in various
pubs. All were anonymous and never seen again. Sometimes
Nilsen would accompany the man to his house or flat, sometimes he would bring him home to his own tiny room. When
the landlady at Manstone Road objected to these mysterious
nightly visitors and asked Nilsen to leave, he took a slightly

larger room at 80 Teignmouth Road, where the landlady was more accommodating. The years 1974 and 1975 were promiscuous and depressing. Having reached the age of twenty-eight with almost no sexual experience, Nilsen made up for the loss in wilful abandon. All his encounters were made in pubs, especially the William IV in Hampstead and the Salisbury in St Martin's Lane; of the others, many were known to be exclusively homosexual, while some took on that character on certain days or at specific hours. They included the Black Cap in Camden Town; the Golden Lion in Dean Street, Soho; the Champion in Bayswater Road, and of course the Coleherne in Earl's Court. In addition, the Pig and Whistle (now closed) in Belgravia was particularly pleasant at Sunday lunchtime, and there Dennis Nilsen met quite a number of people well known to the public.

The danger of entertaining strangers has always been the possibility of assault or blackmail, and when one is finally aware of the risk it is always too late. Blackmail was not threatened against Nilsen, who after all did not represent the promise of attractive bounty, but he did have his share of nasty moments. And he was himself the author of an unpleasant incident which should have been a portent of things to come.

A young man called David Painter called at the Jobcentre where Nilsen worked, looking for casual employment. He was seventeen, and, unknown to Nilsen, had been reported missing by his worried parents. There were no suitable jobs, so Painter left. Quite by chance, Nilsen bumped into him in the street some hours later, and they struck up a conversation, which led to the boy going home with Nilsen to 80 Teignmouth Road. They drank a little and watched a western film on Nilsen's projector. Later, David Painter went to bed, and Nilsen followed. Nilsen made sexual advances, which Painter discouraged then fell asleep. When he woke to find his host pointing a camera at his face, he panicked, tore his clothes, threw them about the room, screamed and yelled, until at last, when he smashed his arm against a glass partition, Nilsen surrendered his efforts to control the boy and called the police and an ambulance. At Willesden Green

Police Station, where he had himself served eighteen months before, Nilsen was closely interrogated, and it was not until the hospital confirmed that the boy had not been seriously molested that the police released him. Painter's parents were reluctant to press charges for fear of the ordeal of a court appearance, so the incident was filed away and forgotten. Nilsen's own recollection of the incident was that Painter went berserk for no clear reason, but there can be no doubt that he had been frightened by something in Nilsen's conduct.

It was less the dangers inherent in a life of casual encounters which were depressing, than the mortifying ephemerality of it all. Nilsen was fast coming to believe that he would forever remain alone. Colleagues at work found him talkative and articulate, but occasionally boring, and he lacked the sense to recognise when he had said enough (even when other people held newspapers in front of their faces) and went on talking as if the most profound interest had been shown. He might have alleviated his isolation by forging friendships with his colleagues after hours, but apart from sharing a drink with a few people in the early evening, after which he would always wander off alone, he kept himself essentially private. So the endless search for companionship continued, with people who did not know him and did not want to. 'The trouble with "the scene" was that everything was transitory and everyone kept walking away.'

Though promiscuous, he was surprisingly puritanical and prudish about his sexual activities. Unlike many men in his position, he could not bear the idea of sex in public (lavatories and cinemas), and he berated the very life he was leading. Anonymous sex, he wrote, 'only deepens one's sense of loneliness and solves nothing. Promiscuity is a disease. It's like compulsive gambling; you know what you will lose, but you go on nevertheless.'[8] Or again, 'Sex in its natural place is like the signature at the end of a letter. Written on its own, it is less than nothing. Signatures are easy to sign, good letters far more difficult.'[9]

Nilsen continually placed himself in circumstances where he was bound to be disappointed — as if, indeed, his self-esteem was so low that he felt intuitively, though not overtly, that he deserved no better. Meanwhile, his fantasies with the mirror in his room developed more bizarre qualities; he could explore these fantasies without fear of being misunderstood or undervalued, either by himself or by others:

> In the lonely years I became more and more 'into myself' and expressed my fantasies of physical love on my own body. I would jealously not allow others to enter that body. Only I would enter that body. My most fulfilling sexual feasts were savoured with the image of myself in the mirror. To detach this image for identifying it directly with me, it evolved from being an unconscious body into a dead body. I was constantly frequented by the dead image and body of Des Nilsen. The dead Des Nilsen seemed right as the dead Andrew Whyte seemed right all those years ago.[10]

Only thus, he says, did he reach a state of 'emotional and physical perfection'. Even more perversely, the fantasy would sometimes depict him hanging by the wrists or strapped to the wall and violated. It was by no means clear how the imaginary violator could be anyone but himself.

If this unhealthy state of mind seems to suggest a confusion of identity and a distortion of the narcissistic impulse, they were not assisted by a shattering piece of news which Nilsen received from Norway. The probate officer in Bergen wrote to inform him that the father he had never met had died and his estate had been divided. Dennis Nilsen inherited a little over £1,000 from a stranger who had married three times since he divorced Betty Whyte and who had ended his days in Ghana. Dennis suddenly realised he had half-brothers and sisters scattered who knew where, whom he would probably never see. More important than this, however, was the revelation that the dead man's name was Olav Magnus Moksheim, alias Nilsen. Moksheim is a very rare name in Norway, borne by only a few families in and around Haugesund. It was not explained why Olav Magnus had felt obliged to invent for himself a new identity, but the effect of the news upon Dennis was fundamental; already uncertain where he belonged or why his private imaginings were so peculiar, he felt he was now not even the man he had thought himself to be. His one certainty evaporated overnight, and he found that his name should have been Dennis Moksheim.

The legacy from his father had nevertheless a beneficial effect upon his material circumstances. He was tired of living in one shabby room, and longed for a self-contained flat with a garden. Now perhaps he would have the wherewithal to indulge this ambition. At the same time, he found someone who was more than ready to share it. One evening in November 1975, outside the Champion pub in Bayswater Road, he saw a young man being pestered by two older men, intervened, and took the man home with him by taxi to 80 Teignmouth Road. The young man's name was David Gallichan, and he was aged about twenty, blond, with earrings and a hint of make-up. He was living in a hostel in Earl's Court and had spent much of his young life wandering aimlessly from one person to another. His home was Weston-super-Mare. Gallichan was unemployed and totally without ambition. He stayed that evening with Nilsen, and they agreed the next morning that they would try a permanent relationship together. After one night's acquaintance it was an excessively stupid move, but Nilsen was full of his plans to have a 'home' and more or less kidnapped the first person he thought would fit inside it. As for Gallichan, anything was better than the hostel; he passively allowed himself to be persuaded. Nilsen did not stop to think that they were totally unsuited.

The landlady had no objection to David Gallichan staying a couple of nights while they looked for a flat. Nilsen contacted the accommodation agency opposite Willesden Green underground station, and was told that a ground floor flat with garden was available at 195 Melrose Avenue on payment of one month's rent in advance. Both men went to see the flat and decided to take it on the spot, although it was supposed to be furnished and was in fact merely scattered with a few bits and pieces. With the legacy from Norway, Dennis would supplement this bare minimum and try to build a domestic décor. They brought their few belongings to Melrose Avenue and settled in. As Gallichan was receiving additional benefit, an inspector from the Department of Health and Social Security was sent to inspect and approve the accommodation.

The most attractive part of the flat was the long garden at the back, which was then little more than a vacant patch of ground piled high with rubbish. They set about removing tons of debris and throwing it over into the wasteland far to the rear of the house, building a fence, laying a stone path, planting trees and shrubs and vegetables. Almost all the work had to be done by Gallichan, as Dennis was at the office in Denmark Street five days a week. Nilsen agreed with the landlord's agent that they should have exclusive use of the garden, as it was they and only they who had paid any attention to it. The other tenants of the house showed not the slightest interest or inclination to help, until the garden began to take shape and look decent, with apple and plum trees in blossom (as they still are to this day), at which point they voiced their resentment that they should be excluded. Nilsen blocked off the alley at the side of the house to make sure no one could get through (his own access was through french windows in the flat). This private use of an extensive garden would later prove to be simultaneously a crucial advantage and a devastating liability.

From the Palace in Wonderland pet shop in Willesden High Road, Nilsen bought a kidney-shaped plastic fish pond for £10, and sank this into the garden one weekend. From another pet shop in Willesden Green, David Gallichan bought a tiny black and white bitch puppy, or more precisely asked Nilsen to buy it. Nilsen was cautious, telling Gallichan that a dog was a responsibility and could not be cast aside at will, but Gallichan would not be deflected and proudly carried the dog home tucked into his jacket. On hearing the noises emerging from within the jacket, Dennis christened the animal 'Bleep'. It became 'their' dog, and together with the garden helped to cement a fragile domestic relationship.

From Teignmouth Road, Nilsen had brought a budgerigar called 'Hamish' (whose only words were 'piss off'), and the menagerie was made complete by the acquisition of a female cat whom Gallichan discovered outside the house as a kitten and then adopted. She was called 'D.D.', presumably after Dennis and David. Gallichan not only worked on the garden, but painted the interior of the flat, which, when the walls were hung with reproduction Canalettos, a large fridge was installed and comfortable armchairs were added, made a warm and cosy abode. There is a film taken of 195 Melrose Avenue at this time which shows how pleasant it was and how starkly it differed from the squalor of Cranley Gardens where Nilsen was arrested years later. The contrast is not merely a trivial one of domestic decor, but a fundamental expression of psychological health; the happy atmosphere of the Melrose Avenue film dates from a time (1976) before Nilsen's personality finally disintegrated, while the shabby, neglected flat which police discovered at Cranley Gardens was the home of a man who had in the meantime become a habitual murderer.

While he shared a flat with David Gallichan, Nilsen did not wander through the pubs of the West End. He spent almost all his spare time at home. He bought a small typewriter on which to do his union work in the evenings, and they had a large and comprehensive record collection, a film projector and a screen. With the animals, they constituted a 'family'.

The relationship was none the less fragile because it was relentlessly artificial; Nilsen had invented it, and Gallichan, now nicknamed 'Twinkle', passively allowed himself to be part of the invention. There was no deep bond of affection between them, and though sexual relations did take place on occasion, Twinkle was remote and uninterested. (They had separate single beds.) Probably his very passivity was a subconscious attraction to Nilsen, or the relationship could not have lasted the two years that it did. Meanwhile, Twinkle continued to find partners elsewhere, and to take his friendship lightly. Nilsen paid most of the bills and made all the decisions, even after Twinkle found himself a job as a buffet assistant at the Traveller's Fare in Paddington Station, spending his own earned income touring the homosexual bars in the evening. Gallichan's parents drove up from Weston-super-Mare one Sunday to have dinner, and expressed satisfaction that their son had apparently stopped roaming and settled down. Also Nilsen's half-brother Andrew Scott dropped in once with his German wife. These were agreeable signs of normality, but they never penetrated below the surface. Similarly, when Nilsen took Twinkle to the office Christmas party in Denmark Street, it was a demonstration that he was no longer alone, that he too, contrary to everyone's belief, had someone to bring with him. The personal appearance of young Twinkle predictably raised a few eyebrows, particularly with management personnel, which increased Nilsen's defiance proportionately; he was not the sort to apologise for a man's right to dress as he wished. After that, there were many who divined for the first time that Nilsen might be at least bisexual; if he was asked directly, he confirmed it, then went on to talk about something else.

In April 1976, Nilsen suffered from acute stomach pains. Investigation indicated probable gall-bladder trouble, but he would have to wait two months for an operation. During those two months of discomfort, Nilsen became increasingly irritable, berating Gallichan for his stupidity, and many rows flared up over trifles. He was operated on by Dr Kirk at Willesden General Hospital on 16 June 1976, and a gallstone was removed. In the week and a half that he stayed in hospital he was visited once by Gallichan, and that was after a telephone call to summon him. Nilsen's hopes that their commitment might endure began to fade. Gallichan's gentle and shy nature was not equal to bridging the chasm which existed between them on every level of intellect and interest, and he grew tired of Nilsen's arrogant nagging.

Both men started to bring home strangers, causing resentment to hang in the air. A youth of seventeen whom Twinkle brought back ended up, after excessive drinking, in Nilsen's bed, and was left there by both of them when they went their separate ways to work the next day. The boy then forced the gas and electric meters and took the cash.

One incident deserves mention for its uniqueness. Nilsen

met a Swiss girl called Elisabeth whom he took back to 195 Melrose Avenue for sex. Their love-making proved entirely satisfactory and confirmed Nilsen's belief that he could perform the sexual act with a woman just as pleasurably as with a man. To be actively bisexual, rather than homosexual, did not set one so much apart from one's fellows, and he did not go out of his way to disguise the love-bites he had as trophies to show at work the next day.

Tensions at home multiplied to such an extent that it was clear the relationship must come to an end. Nilsen in a fit of anger demanded that Gallichan should leave, whereupon, in the summer of 1977, Twinkle packed his bags and moved off in search of a new protector. Gallichan's version is that he left spontaneously, which would certainly have offended Nilsen to the core, as he considered Gallichan his inferior intellectually and his dependant socially. To be 'deserted' by such a man would be the deepest insult. At any rate, Nilsen's one attempt at a sustained relationship had failed, and he was left with the conviction that he was probably unfit to live with. He thereupon channelled all his affection into caring for Bleep, all his lust into anonymous late-night meetings, all his self-pity down the neck of a bottle, and all his abundant energies into work. Work became an obsessive substitute for an empty life, and since he seemed unable to convey his concern for individuals in any way which they understood or could accept, he would devote his concern to the nebulous concept of mankind in general.[11]

Nilsen claims that he became involved in trade union politics by accident, 'through shame and embarrassment of my colleagues when, while all the machinery of democracy was given to them, they remained largely apathetic.'[12] At the Annual General Meeting of the Denmark Street branch of C.P.S.A. no one would consent to stand for the post of branch organiser, so Nilsen volunteered. Motivated by a strong social conscience, he quickly became immersed in the task and it was not long before he was branch secretary.

Working at the hotel and catering Jobcentre it was not difficult to grow indignant at the blatant exploitation of waiters and kitchen assistants by restaurants and hotels alike.

The profession is notoriously underpaid, and few proprietors resist the temptation to employ foreigners, many without work permits, who are content to work long hours for a pittance rather than be exposed and deported. In other words, the Denmark Street branch came into contact regularly with some of the lowest-income workers in London, and their plight could not fail to influence anyone who was already predisposed to think that society reserved its harshest treatment for the downtrodden. Nilsen's enthusiasm did not endear him to the management, who looked askance at the anti-government badges he sometimes wore, and though he sought to maintain 'total freedom to judge each issue on its merits, according to conscience and experience',[13] they could not help noticing that his conscience invariably found in favour of the workers.

Nilsen was furiously active in many disputes at the end of the 1970s, an involvement which effectively delayed his chances of promotion. His constant presence on picket lines was an embarrassment, his call to arms offensive to those who prized caution, including many other union officials. He was altogether too keen, too impulsive, too angry; they wondered what deep irritations fed his manic eagerness.

The Garners Steak House dispute of 1977, provoked by the unceremonious dismissal of black and immigrant workers, was the first to excite Nilsen's commitment. He was photographed on the picket line in Oxford Street and verbally assaulted by a lady who had the misfortune to advise him that a couple of years in the army would do him good. Capital Radio contacted him for an interview (word of his vigour in argument had already spread) and he arranged to do a broadcast with Jane Walmsley. But the management intervened and forbade any identities to be disclosed; it was against the Department of Employment's policy to permit any of its employees to speak *qua* employees. But Nilsen's influence prevailed in so far as Denmark Street refused to fill vacancies at Garners Steak House until the dispute was resolved, which it was after some months, though not to the advantage of the dismissed workers. Nilsen thought they had been betrayed by the apathy of people prepared only to fight for themselves, not for others.

In September 1978 Nilsen applied to attend the C.P.S.A. Branch Chairman's School at Surrey University and was accepted. This was a heady time, mixing with highly-placed union officials in the bar (Kate Losinska, Penny Judge, Len Lever) with the delicious freedom to express contentious views in the knowledge that they would be heeded (no newspapers held in front of the face here!). The established union officials at the top of the hierarchy were less to Nilsen's taste than the revolutionary radical young people who converged upon Guildford. Nilsen was now thirty-three, but the army had delayed his maturity with the result that he was now experiencing that rush of uncompromising idealistic excitement that normally assails one at the age of twenty. He had found his place; he knew where he belonged; he stayed with the youngsters and disdained the elderly moderates.

A long series of industrial disputes not directly involving the civil service union (such as, for instance, the Talk of the Town dispute) brought Nilsen out in a supportive role, distributing leaflets, picketing, persuading with his increasingly dogmatic rhetoric. It was remarkable how unable he was to see any aspect of a question other than the one he supported. Compromise and consensus were anathema to him, and in this he displayed both the Buchan gene of stubbornness and his own gloss of dangerously simplistic rigour. Fudging the issues and 'making do' would no longer be admitted; 1978 saw the birth of the 'monochrome man', the man of extremes and opposites, the Manichaean double-headed monster.

The ultimate dispute was the one which concerned the civil service itself. On 25 November 1980 the Conservative government scrapped the 1974 Civil Service Pay Agreement, provoking fury throughout the country. All the unions called for an afternoon walk-out and march to demonstrate feelings. Coincidentally on the same day the Denmark Street branch was celebrating its golden anniversary (fifty years) with a party attended by Members of Parliament, top hoteliers and other dignitaries, munching canapés and giving speeches. Dennis Nilsen caused consternation by leading a walk-out of eleven staff members in protest against government policy.

The civil service pay dispute aroused Nilsen to the point where he came perilously close to antagonising even his supporters. In a circular to all members, he appealed for the strength of character to stand against 'the gutter principles and practices of a totally discredited employer' (i.e. the Conservative government), and while his zeal was applauded, some resented the implication that if they disagreed they must lack essential 'strength of character'. Dennis Nilsen was no diplomat; he was impatient of the strategy whereby an important objective was attained by subtle means. In another circular designed to galvanise the entire workforce into the right attitude to win the campaign, he made the mistake of criticising those employees who continued to co-operate with management. 'These are the parasites', he wrote, 'who are amongst the first in the line to grab the wage benefits which have been hard won on the personal principles and sacrifice of trades unionists whose financial commitment is for the good of all staff.' This was not far removed from saying, 'I have given you my all, don't let me down,' a disguised plea for personal affection which had quite the opposite effect. When the 'parasites' did not come flocking to his side, he could not understand why.

The Council of Civil Service Unions co-ordinating committee asked Nilsen to appear on Robin Day's programme 'Question Time' with a prepared question on the subject of government cash limits. At the coffee and sandwiches reception before the show the producer indicated that he wanted Nilsen's question to be put forward, but in the event it was not called, and Nilsen's raised hand was lost in the forest. Although he is in the programme, he is uncharacteristically mute.

Nilsen was a delegate at the C.P.S.A. National Conference, held for one week in Southport in May 1980. He stayed, along with everyone else, at the Queen's Hotel, having first made arrangements for his dog, Bleep (from whom he was now rarely separated), to be cared for by a colleague in Orpington, only to discover to his chagrin that guests at the Queen's Hotel were allowed to keep dogs after all. The conference was the usual mixture of drink, talk, and bed-swapping, and Nilsen was noticed for his contribution to the first two and his scrupulous avoidance of the last.

Dennis Nilsen had made a mark, but it was not the kind of reputation which pleased those in authority. In their view, he was volatile and excitable, and although they could not fault his work (indeed, he worked harder than most) they discreetly decided that his time for promotion would be passed by and unaccountably forgotten. They may well have been influenced by his strident union activities; on one occasion, the Metropolitan Police catering office had sent to Denmark Street an urgent request for sixty casual catering workers, which alerted Nilsen to the possibility of a substantial turn-out of police to counter a mass picket by steelworkers. His response was to warn the steelworkers' union, claiming that on an issue of principle he could not, as a trade unionist, simply sit on the fence.[14]

The question of Nilsen's promotion had first arisen in 1978, after four years of service, at which point his Job Appraisal Review had reported that he 'was considered unsuitable for promotion because of personality and attitude, and that his basic ability was not in question.' Nilsen's response to this was to point out that the civil service was afraid of intellectual initiative and enterprise: 'Sometimes a personal submissiveness can provide an opportunity for advancement in the face of limited personal ability.' He was not, and never would consent to be, submissive.

On the contrary, he fought with ever-increasing vigour to break, bend, or divert the rules which he seemed to think were being applied for his personal chastisement. In June 1981 he asked to be present at a District Manpower Committee meeting to observe, in his capacity as a union official, management decisions in the making. The committee secretary, Mr J.C. Cole, refused the request without giving reasons. Nilsen wrote back immediately demanding to see the minutes of the meeting which had denied his request. In the same month, he applied to be transferred to the Overseas Workers Section at Denmark Street (otherwise known as the Aliens Section), as it was the only department in which he had not so far served. This, too, was refused, in a letter signed by the manager, Iain Mackinnon, which stated 'your manner in relationships with your colleagues is usually outspoken and often overbearing. I am concerned that — despite your undoubted desire to provide an effective service to our customers — your manner with the public on Overseas Workers Section might cause offence.' The remark infuriated Nilsen. To the district manager he wrote, 'I challenge the validity of this smear and libel against my record,' and went on to say, quite correctly, that in seven years of public service at the Jobcentre he had not been the subject of a single complaint from a member of the public. He could not see that to deal with the sensitive issue of employment for foreigners not only commitment would be called for, but great tact as well. In this he was deficient.

Meanwhile, the time had again come round for his appearance before a promotion panel. He wrote to the area personnel manager, Mr T.A. Jones, asking to know 'what there is about me which prevents you from recommending me, as my recommending officer, for an opportunity to present myself before an Executive Officer Promotion Panel', adding the postscript that he, Jones, might as well admit that responsibility lay with the secret annual staff reports which had consistently slandered his reputation. These reports, he maintained, placed overriding emphasis on the loyalty of a civil servant, interpreting 'disloyalty' as any dissidence from officially accepted views and any vocal adherence to union policy. Invited to appeal, he declined with some petulance, saying that 'principles are of more lifelong value to personal progress and development than promotion or financial gain.' Once more, he added a sting of sarcasm which revealed how deeply emotional were his reactions to ostensibly professional matters. 'I must admit', he said, 'that official attitudes and treatment of me over the years have not left my health unaffected.'

Nilsen took some pride in his unpopularity with managers, a small price to pay, he thought, for his integrity. The man he blamed most was the district manager, Mr Cole, who, he suspected, interpreted his controversial union activity as a 'defect in attitude', and his homosexuality (which was not unknown at the office though never flaunted) as a 'defect in personality'. He further intimated that enthusiasm and an inquiring mind were officially deemed dangerous qualities in a civil servant. A passage in a revolutionist's handbook earned his especial approbation and was circled in red: 'The reasonable man adapts himself to the world; the unreasonable one persists in trying to adapt the world to himself. Therefore all progress depends upon the unreasonable man.'

Nevertheless, Nilsen relented enough eventually to appeal against the decision of the promotion panel, and at his interview he managed to convince the personnel officers without being submissive and without curbing his sour anger. To the question, what had he done best in the year, he replied, 'I repelled the temptation to resign the service.' What had he done least well? 'Maintaining the will to survive (mentally) after seven years of continuous, monotonous clerical tedium, i.e. being kept employed in the most basic trainee duties.' He admitted that his character contained a nonconformist element and suggested that this would lie dormant if he were given more demanding duties. When asked what improvement might be expected from his senior officers, he said, 'It is idealistic to expect some managers to deflect their energies from serving self, their careers and cosy world and start serving the spirit and aims of this public service.' As for improvements in himself, he thought that he should 'try not to seem to belittle others in response to their opinions on all matters'.[15]

Those at least were the written answers to be completed before interview. One must assume that he was more amenable in discussion. A measure of his conspicuous gracelessness as well as the qualities which it concealed is attested by a personal letter which Mr Mackinnon sent to Nilsen before his appearance. 'We've had our differences in the past', he wrote, 'and we've had our differences this week, but I stand by my belief that you are "fitted for promotion". I hope you do yourself the justice of making a real go of it.' He continued:

Think what the panel knows of you, and how to counteract it. They will have quite serious doubts about your ability, but if you can show them your enthusiasm, your desire to help and to provide a good service, your intelligence, your concern for efficiency and your good ideas, you will impress them, and at the very least make them look critically at the evidence of the Annual Reports.

If, at the end of the day, you are unsuccessful, you will at least have the satisfaction of knowing that you did your best ('within the confines of the system', if you like). Unless you do that much you cannot seriously claim to have been 'thwarted by the system'.

I wish you luck (the best of us needs luck!) and hope that you succeed.

The letter was signed 'Iain' and was obviously sincere, though it looks as if Nilsen was expected to fail yet again.

In the end he did not. The promotion panel was impressed by his honesty, frankly eager to rid itself of this troublesome thorn, and doubtless aware that it could not reasonably delay Nilsen's promotion any longer in view of his evident ability. They raised him to the status of an executive officer after a probation of nearly eight years.

Nilsen made a desultory application to be appointed chief clerk at the Opposition Whips Office in the House of Commons (without of course telling anyone at the Jobcentre). This was refused in a one-sentence reply. On leaving Denmark Street, he was presented with a gold pen and cigarette lighter by colleagues who remembered his sense of fun and ignored his bossiness.

On 28 June 1982, he was posted to the Kentish Town Jobcentre where his superior officer was a young woman of charm and elegance, Janet Leaman. He and Miss Leaman quickly formed a close professional relationship which was the most satisfactory of his civil service career, based upon mutual trust and respect. In order to learn his new responsibilities in the shortest time, he declined to take leave that year, and threw himself into the work with a relish which surprised the people at Kentish Town. He was a finance supervisor, a post supervisor, an accommodation and premises officer, and much else besides. It was the busiest period of his career so far, and the one which held most promise for the future. His quick temper was on the whole forgiven in view of his obvious eagerness to do well and his constant willingness to stay after hours. When a flood occurred at Kentish Town, he was the only member of staff to volunteer to stay behind with Miss Leaman to mop up the damage. The next day she gave him a packet of cigarettes as a gesture of gratitude. He was totally astonished.

Nilsen had both purpose and respect and one would have thought that his meandering progress towards the age of thirty-seven had at last found direction. It is interesting, however, that Miss Leaman felt sorry for him as soon as she saw him, although she could not exactly say why, and she naturally never told him. Neither she nor anyone else knew that his life had long since been engulfed by a nightmare.

Even before he moved to Kentish Town, colleagues had noticed that Nilsen was working to a degree which implied that he dared not allow himself the luxury of time on his hands. He was meticulously efficient. If he was required to take leave, he would do casual work at Dinah's Diner in Endell Street, helping in the kitchen. Or, on a day off, he would turn up at the office with his dog. It seemed he could not keep away. His demeanour was confusing; he could be abrupt, short-tempered, impatient, and driven by a need to talk without pause, or even better to argue. He was passionate in debate. When aroused, he could be woundingly sarcastic. On the other hand, he was at times docile, generous and kind. He brought into the office a birthday cake for a colleague whom none thought he liked, not through any desire to attach himself to a celebration (on the contrary, no one else realised there *was* a birthday), but because he sensed the man was a 'loner'. There was also the time when he displayed unsuspected compassion by bringing into the office an injured bird which he kept for three days until it was well enough to fly off. There were plenty of occasions when he generated real laughter. On two points everyone was agreed: he was secretive, and he was erratic.

When he went home to 195 Melrose Avenue, Dennis Nilsen's world shifted focus. First of all, there was the dog, Bleep, to attend to. At least twice a day he would walk the length of Melrose Avenue, with its stunted, pollarded trees scarcely able to hide the sky, and take a brisk walk in Gladstone Park, exchanging small talk with the other dog-owners on like journeys. Occasionally, there would be instead an excursion to the enticing wildness of Hampstead Heath. Back home, he would pour himself a drink and watch a great deal of television lying on the floor with the French windows open and the burgundy red curtains billowing in. The stereo system played a large role in the evening's entertainment as well; with headphones, Nilsen would listen for hours to Elgar, Mahler, Britten, Grieg, Tchaikovsky, Sibelius, or some sophisticated pop music (Rick Wakeman, Mike Oldfield, and the strange hypnotic 'Oh Superman'). When the weather permitted, he would spend a lot of time keeping the garden tidy, weeding and mending fences.

There were some visitors and there were some lovers. The original pair of bunk beds had been converted by Nilsen into one large platform bed, up near the ceiling, where strangers or acquaintances would collapse after too much rum, with some mild sexual activity perhaps in the early morning. A sporadic visitor who was neither a lover nor just an acquaintance, but someone who made a point of calling in at intervals over a number of years and therefore represents one of the only friends who did not eventually drift away, was Martin Hunter-Craig. Nilsen trusted him and allowed his aggressive self-confident exterior to melt in his presence. The bombast and the garrulity subsided, Nilsen mellowed. Another who kept in touch with frequent chatty letters was Alan Knox, in Aberdeen, who stayed with Nilsen whenever he was in London.

Nilsen made one final attempt to introduce some kind of permanence into his chaotic emotional life. Steven Martin, picked up at the Golden Lion where many 'rent boys' hang out, came to live with him for about four months. A good loving relationship developed which expressed itself not only in sexual intimacy but in little domestic gestures, as when

Martin fixed a light in the dog-kennel for Bleep's puppies. The friendship could not endure, as Martin was yet another young man without roots or responsibilities who would not curb his wanderlust. Nilsen was deeply hurt when Martin was unfaithful, and he asked him to leave. 'I always sadly regretted his leaving. He could perhaps do better elsewhere. I had nothing much by way of luxury to give. Just me.'[16]

Another man who stayed for a while was Barry Pett, followed by a succession of short-term flat-mates who never showed any wish to linger. Stephen Barrier was contacted through an advertisement in the Adam Bureau, and stayed for ten days. In September 1978, when Nilsen went to attend the Branch Chairman's School at Guildford for a week, he foolishly gave his keys to a man from Liverpool who was living in West Hampstead and whom he had met at a pub. The idea was that this man should go to the flat once a day to feed the dog in its kennel, change its water, and so on. Nilsen did not feel he could ask the neighbours upstairs because there was much ill-feeling consequent upon his having barricaded the access to the garden, which he continued to keep for his exclusive use. When he came back from Guildford, he found that the dog had been well fed but that his film camera and projector had been stolen and his meters forced and emptied. The experience left him morally dejected.

More and more, Nilsen took refuge in the private fantasies of his mirror fetish, which in the course of 1978 developed sinister refinements:

I put talc on my face to erase the living colour. I smear charcoal under my eyes to accentuate a hollow dark look. I put pale blue on my lips. I rub my eyes to make them bloodshot. I have put three holes in my old tee-shirt. I make a mixture of cochineal and saffron to synthesise blood. I soak the 'blood' into the holes and the liquid stains my shirt and runs down my body. I lie, staring-eyed, on the bed in front of the mirror and let my saliva foam and drip from my mouth. I stare in fascination at the shot body of me in the mirror. I step outside myself in detached imagination. There is another imaginary person in the room who finds my body out in the woods. I have been executed and left there by the S.S. I am a French dissident student. The other person, an old hermit who lives in the woods, drags my dead body back to his old shack. He is wearing rags and he decides that I have no further use for clothes and begins to strip my limp body. He is speaking to me as though I were still alive. He pulls my now naked body off the bed on to the floor. He washes me. He ties my penis and puts some wadding in my anus. He sits me on a chair then he puts me over his shoulder and carries me back into the woods and buries me. Later he returns and digs me up and takes me back to the shack. He masturbates me and my penis comes to life and I ejaculate. It is over. I tidy up the room, replace the mirror and have a bath. I turn on the T.V. and call the dog over to me. She wags her tail unsure of her reception. I reassure her and she jumps on to the bed and makes herself comfortable. I watch T.V. She goes to sleep. I must be in love with my own dead body. I am quite sober — it worries me.[17]

One night he met three young men in Kilburn High Road and took them home for a drink. All three stayed the night. When they had all fallen asleep, Nilsen got up, closed all the doors and windows, and placed a jacket over the oil-stove. Having sprinkled the jacket with water, he lit the stove and stood back as the room filled with smoke. He then nonchalantly took the dog into the garden. One of the men woke up, whereupon Nilsen sprang into action, flung open all the windows and assumed the role of gallant rescuer. It was an odd but not an isolated incident. Martin Hunter-Craig had similarly woken up one night to find the room full of dense smoke.

The last person to stay at 195 Melrose Avenue before fantasy exploded into reality was Paul Dermody, who spent two weeks with Nilsen in November 1978. Nilsen's compulsion to talk was edged with panic — 'He talked at me not to me,' says Dermody, who added that he thought the only real friend Nilsen had was his black scruffy mongrel dog.[18] Nilsen himself confirms this. He loved the dog and treated her like his child; 'as soon as I reach for her metal chained lead Bleep becomes frantic with excitement'.[19] They even went together on demonstrations and on the picket line. Once a week she was given raw egg in a bowl. There was a day when she drank from his beer and showed signs of intoxication, an adventure she never repeated. Over the years she produced scores of puppies and had been known to kidnap kittens in response to their cries. In Gladstone Park one day she carried in her jaws a tiny sparrow which had fallen from its nest, and presented it to Nilsen; he tried to keep it alive with an eye-dropper, but it was far too young to survive, and was buried in the garden in a band-aid tin with a little note. Many of Bleep's dispatched pups were also lying in that garden.

The demoralisation of Dennis Nilsen reached crisis point at the end of 1978. 'I felt defeated on all fronts.' Career prospects were stunted by his union activities. The apathy of those work-mates who had elected him to be their front man and then would not support him with enthusiasm added a deepening depression. And the loneliness threatened to overwhelm him. In the days before Christmas there were plenty of social occasions with heavy drinking, but in the morning there would be just himself, the dog, and a hangover. If he vanished, he thought, no one would notice.

Loneliness is a long unbearable pain. I felt that I had achieved nothing of importance or of help to anyone in my entire life. I would think that if I drank myself to death my body would not be discovered until at least a week after (or longer). There was no one I felt I could call upon for real help. I was in daily contact with so many people but quite alone in myself . . .[20]

. . . I was becoming depressed and conditioned to a belief that I was impossible to live with. This feeling of despair reached its peak when I spent Christmas of 1978 alone with the mutt. I would find comfort in music and the bottle. I was in a fit of drunken desolation by the time New Year approached.[21]

The thought that he might meet someone who would then,

like all the others, walk away, caused him to view himself with extreme self-pity. On 30 December he decided he must at all costs get out of the flat and seek some company. Instead of going to one of his usual haunts, he went to the Crickle-wood Arms, a rough Irish bar on Cricklewood Broadway, where he drank pint after pint of draught Guinness. He spied the local police constable across the room but did not speak to him. He did however engage in desultory conversation with a number of other people in groups until he found himself chatting to an Irish youth who was, like himself, alone. 'That night things began to go terribly and horribly wrong.'22

6

VICTIMS

They walked from the Cricklewood Arms to 195 Melrose Avenue, where they stayed up late drinking themselves insensible. Eventually they both undressed and crawled into bed together, but no sexual activity took place. Dennis Nilsen woke up a couple of hours later, as first light was dawning, and looked at him lying there.

> I was afraid to wake him in case he left me. Trembling with fear I strangled his struggling body and when he was dead I took his young body back to bed with me and it was the beginning of the end of my life as I had known it. I had started down the avenue of death and possession of a new kind of flat-mate.[1]

When the police asked him what had started him off on his murderous career in 1978, Nilsen said that he had never stopped asking himself the same question and had not yet found a reply. Later, after the trial, he wrote a more detailed account of the first killing which offers some insight into his state of mind at the time (assessed retrospectively), and into his disastrously contorted emotions:

The fire had been on all night so it was quite warm. I snuggled up to him and put my arm around him. He was still fast asleep. Still lying there I pulled the blanket off us and half-way down our bodies. He was on his side turned away from me. I ran my hand over him exploring him. I remember thinking that because it was morning he would wake and leave me. I became extremely aroused and I could feel my heart pounding and I began to sweat. He was still sound asleep. I looked down on the floor where our clothes lay and my eyes fixed on my tie. I remember thinking that I wanted him to stay with me over the New Year whether he wanted to or not. I reached out and got the neck tie. I raised myself and slipped it on under his neck. I quickly straddled him and pulled tight for all I was worth. His body came alive immediately. We struggled off the bed on to the floor. 'What the . . . ' he said, but I retightened my grip on the tie. Pushing himself with his feet (with me on top of him) we moved along the carpeted floor . . . We had moved about three yards from the bed and so doing had knocked over the coffee-table, ashtray and glasses. His head was now up against the wall. After about half a minute I felt him slowly going limp. His arms flopped on to the carpet. I stood up trembling with tension and exhaustion. Then I noticed he had resumed breathing in rasping breaths. He was still unconscious. I wondered what to do. I ran into the kitchen and filled a plastic bucket with water. I returned to the main room and placed it on the floor. 'I'd better drown him,' I thought. I got hold of him under his armpits and pulled him up and draped him head down over the seat of a dining-chair. I placed the bucket near and grabbing him by the hair raised his head, which I pushed into the bucket of water. Excess water splashed all over the carpet. I held his head in there and he did not struggle. After a few minutes the bubbles stopped coming. I lifted him up and sat him in the armchair, the water was dripping from his short brown curly hair. I just sat there shaking, trying to think clearly about what I had just done. It was still early in the morning. The room was in a bit of a mess. I kept looking at him and a multitude of thoughts kept pounding through my head. I smoked a lot and made myself a cup of coffee to help the shaking.

Having cleaned the room up to some extent, the dog came in from the garden and sniffed the dead man's leg. Nilsen took her by the scruff of the neck and harshly told her to leave, after which she kept out of the way. Then began a ritualistic second stage to the crime. For a long period he sat down, shocked. If anyone had walked in at that moment, he would not have stirred a muscle. He took the tie from the corpse's neck as if that would make everything better.

I sat opposite the dead youth and just stared at him. I went into the bathroom and ran a bath. When it was nearly full I put a towel over the curtainless window and returned to my room. I knelt down in front of the armchair and pulled the body forward over my right shoulder. Supporting it around the thighs I hoisted it over my shoulder and carried it to the bathroom. I lowered him on to the rim of the bath and slid him into the water . . . With washing-up liquid I washed him and his hair. He was very limp and floppy. Getting him out of the bath wasn't easy as his wet skin made it difficult to hold him. I pulled him out by the wrists and sat him on the lavatory seat. I towelled him dry. I hoisted him over my shoulder again, carried him into the room and laid him on the bed. I cleaned myself up and went over to take a closer look at him. His face was slightly discoloured (pinkish) and his eyes were half open. His face seemed to be slightly puffed up and his lips (bluish) slightly parted . . . I turned him over on the bed and ran my fingers down the length of him . . . he was still warm to the touch. His wet hair left a mark on the pillow. I straightened him up (on his back) on the bed and pulled the bedclothes up to his chin. I sat down thinking what I was going to do. I expected a knock on the front door in a few hours when he didn't come home. I had lost all interest in him over the New Year, my mind was concentrated on how to get rid of him. I left the house and walked down Willesden High Road to clear my mind.

In a local ironmongers he bought a cooking pot and an electric knife, but when he returned home he thought the idea which had occurred to him was ridiculous, and put them away. (The electric knife was to be used a year later to carve turkey at the office Christmas party and was eventually given to one of the staff; it was never used in the pursuit of Nilsen's crimes.)

I couldn't think what to do at all — at that stage. I was now feeling the full tired effects of a hangover. I pulled the bedclothes off the youth's body. I went to the wardrobe and took out some underwear and socks (still in their cellophane packets from Woolworth's). I dressed the youth in the white Y-fronts, vest, and socks, and put back the bedclothes. I had a bath myself and got into bed with him. I held him close to me with my arms around him, and I began to remove his pants and explore his body under the blankets. (I had an erection all this time.) When I tried to enter him my erection automatically subsided, I could feel that his body temperature was cooling. I got up and lifted him into my arms, laid him on the floor and covered him with an old curtain. I went back into bed and fell instantly asleep.

Nilsen slept soundly all that day. In the evening, he let Bleep in, made himself something to eat and watched the television. The shrouded body was still lying on the floor. He determined that he would prise up some floorboards and put the body beneath them, with bricks from the garden and some earth, but rigor mortis had set in and when he pushed the body under, feet first, it got stuck and he had to take it out again. He stood the body up against the wall. 'I heard somewhere that rigor mortis soon passes, so I could wait.'

The next day he was still standing against the wall. I laid him on the floor and worked his limbs loose. I examined closely and systematically every part of him from his toes to his hair . . . I eased him into his new bed and covered him up. It was very cold under the floorboards. The cat got in there and I spent ten minutes coaxing her out. I replaced the boards and the carpet. I ripped up all his clothing and put it with his boots into the dustbin. A week later I wondered if his body had changed at all or had started to decompose. I disinterred him and pulled the dirt-stained youth up on to the floor. His skin was very dirty. I stripped myself naked and carried him into the bathroom and washed the body. There was practically no discolouration and he was pale white. His limbs were more limp and relaxed than when I had put him down. I got him out of the bath and washed myself clean in the water. I carried the still wet youth into the room and laid him on the carpet. Under the orange side-lights his body aroused me sexually. I knelt over him and masturbated on to his bare stomach. Before I went to bed I suspended him by the ankles from the high wooden platform. He hung there all night, his fingers just touching the carpet. The next day while he was still hanging there upside down I stood beside him and masturbated again. I wiped him and took him down. I laid him on the kitchen floor and decided to cut him up, but I just couldn't do anything to spoil that marvellous body.[2]

Nilsen replaced the body under the floorboards, where it stayed unmolested for the next seven and a half months. On 11 August 1979, he brought the body up and burnt it on a bonfire in the garden which he had constructed the day before. It was not dismembered but wrapped in bags and tied with string. With a seven-foot-high fence and a derelict house next door, Nilsen knew he could not be seen, and he added rubber to the fire to cancel out any smell of burning flesh. 'I pounded the ashes to powder and raked them into the ground.' Thus the Irish youth disappeared without trace, his existence obliterated for no clear reason by a man who did not know him. He has never been identified and probably never can be; indeed, we have only Nilsen's own confession to indicate that this murder ever took place.

Nilsen went about his work in a thoroughly normal way in the months before the burning, and for the rest of that year.

He was able to forget about what lay beneath the floor, the more so as time passed and nobody came to investigate. It seemed astonishing to him that such a thing should happen and pass unnoticed. If anyone had missed the boy there was nothing whatever to link him with 195 Melrose Avenue. At times Nilsen thought he should present himself for arrest, but his instinct to survive was stronger than this impulse and was reinforced by the lack of any inquiry at his home or work. Gradually he realised that this appalling episode need never be discovered, and he might continue his life in an equable way. He could not bear to think of the moral implications. He had no reason, he thought, to believe it would ever happen again. He continued occasionally to spend an evening or a night with a stranger without anything going wrong, although, oddly, no sexual activity took place for nearly two years. It looked as if he was safe with his one dreadful secret and would not commit murder again. But he was wrong.

An incident occurred in October 1979 which served to remind him of what he was capable. He met a young Chinese student, Andrew Ho, who accompanied him home. There the man started talking of bondage and wanted either to tie Nilsen up or be tied up himself. He also said he was short of money. Nilsen offered him a sum for his company, but did not want to indulge in any intimacy. The man wondered what on earth he had come for, in that case, and Nilsen tied his feet together to keep him quiet. He thought Ho might have wanted to rob him, and told him he was leading a dangerous life. He put a tie round his neck and pulled it, saying that this was the sort of thing that could happen to him. Ho panicked and Nilsen released his grip. He threw a candlestick at him and rushed out. Half an hour later the police called, but no charges were brought because Mr Ho was reluctant to proceed and Nilsen denied that there had been any attempt at strangulation, which was strictly true. Nevertheless, he had placed the tie around the man's neck, whether to frighten him or to teach him a lesson and then get rid of him, and that gesture alone must have sounded an echo in his mind. He said later (in 1983) that it was a pity that he was not arrested there and then.

Before he moved from Melrose Avenue in September 1981, Nilsen killed a total of twelve men, of whom four have been identified; they are Kenneth Ockendon, Martyn Duffey, Billy Sutherland, and Malcolm Barlow. The other eight remain nameless. At Cranley Gardens in 1982 he killed another two men, John Howlett and Graham Allan, and the last, Stephen Sinclair, at the end of January 1983. In addition to these fifteen deaths there are, by Nilsen's own account, seven attempts at murder, in which either he was fought off, or he himself managed to 'snap out' of the killing trance before it was too late. One man he actually saved from death after he had almost succeeded in killing him. There is no unifying thread of behaviour either during the murders or after them; similarities occur between some of them, and are not repeated in others. With the exception of Kenneth Ockendon, who was a Canadian tourist on holiday in London, they all had the most slender connections with their origins. Some were in trouble with the police, some were drug-addicts or 'punks', some (but not all) were homosexual, many were homeless and jobless, and many drifted through the crowds of London without aim or purpose, their disappearance being such a regular event that their few acquaintances were neither surprised nor alarmed. Kenneth Ockendon was the only one whose disappearance was noted in the national newspapers.

The world of the young, single, unemployed homeless people of London is invisible. It is impossible to say how many there are, or where they all come from. If you have nowhere to live, no job to occupy you, and no close family ties, you will come to London simply because it is the capital and it must offer more opportunities. If you have an acquaintance there, you may sleep on his floor for a while before you move on. Then you may very easily vanish.

There are a number of hostels and organisations in central London devoted to giving help to young people who are drifting — advice, care, a bed for the night. Centrepoint Nightshelter in Shaftesbury Avenue offers emergency accommodation for short periods; every day residents are

sent on their way with a list of addresses for employment,
medical attention, and housing, and have to report back with
their belongings in the evening. The system encourages
initiative and responsibility, but it makes scant allowance for
a man who is inadequate to these demands. City Roads deals
with youngsters who have been trapped in the whirlpool of
drugs. The Soho Project offers help on all levels, and it is
frequently there that a young man who has given up or who
does not know where else to turn makes his first appeal. None
of these organisations is able to keep track of what happens to
a man after he has passed through their hands. If he signs on
with the Department of Health and Social Security there will
be a card recording his existence, but if he ceases to claim
then the D.H.S.S. does not initiate inquiries to find out what
has happened to him. He may be on a doctor's list, but if he
moves about from one district to another he will not stay on
the list for long, and anyway doctors discourage the sort of
young 'drop-out' who most needs help; he does not look good
in the surgery. The man may well end up as a piece of
flotsam, anchored nowhere, belonging to no one, stranded
on the streets of central London hoping for a chance meeting
which may provide a meal or a bed. Even if his family wishes
to trace him, the task has by now become hopeless.

Every year the Soho Project sees two thousand young
people at their top-floor office in Charing Cross Road. With
patience, tolerance, and a determined absence of moral
preaching, they counsel runaways and often gradually effect
a reconciliation with their families. But many are so damaged
by their home life that the 'instant' community of the streets
of London is preferable, despite its instability, to a return to
parents or to being 'in care'. Some have been discharged from
care on reaching a certain age and thus, in effect, abandoned
to the winds. The workers of the Soho Project spend almost
every evening touring the streets and amusement arcades of
Soho, Leicester Square and Piccadilly Circus, talking to
youngsters who may need help but who either do not know
where to go or are too distrustful to follow advice. These
young people congregate in coffee-bars, hoping to make a
cup last all night, or offer themselves for prostitution. The

116

Soho Project is able to provide some help, but not for long. They well know that their organisation is engaged essentially in 'first aid', though their work is no less vital for that. They are campaigners, tirelessly passionate in their efforts to provide a harbour for young people in crisis and, incidentally, to protect them from men like Dennis Nilsen.

It happened that the second victim, who died almost a year after the first, was not typical of the young men so far described.

On 3 December 1979, Kenneth Ockendon had breakfast at the Central Hotel in Argyle Street, London WC1, and left for the day with his camera. He had been staying there at a rate of £7 a night, on a tour of England looking up relations, and was due to fly back home to Canada in the near future. He never returned to the hotel for his belongings. At lunchtime, he met Dennis Nilsen in a West End pub, Nilsen having leave from work for the afternoon. They chatted amiably until three in the afternoon, each buying a round of drinks, then went off to see the sights of London and take photographs. They fed the pigeons in Trafalgar Square, then went to Horseguards Parade and on to Downing Street and Westminster Abbey. At the end of the afternoon, they agreed to go to Nilsen's flat and have something to eat, then perhaps go out for a drink later in the evening. After a meal of ham, eggs and chips, their plans changed and they went together to the off-licence next to Willesden Green underground station and filled a carrier bag with rum, whisky and beer, Ockendon insisting on sharing the bill. Back at the flat, they put drinks on the table and sat down to watch television and listen to music. They seemed to enjoy each other's company, having been together for nine hours. They were friends already. Ockendon reminded Nilsen of Derek Collins. It was for Nilsen the happiest evening of the year, and Ockendon, too, was relaxed. But Nilsen could not get out of his mind the fact that Ken would be flying back to Canada the next day. In the following weeks, newspapers carried stories of the disappearance of a Canadian tourist.

Nilsen's recollection of Ockendon's last night is as follows:

It must have been well after midnight — maybe one or two in the morning. I was dragging him across the floor with the flex around his neck. The flex was round his throat. I was saying, 'Let me listen to the music as well.' He didn't struggle. I was dragging him across the floor. The dog was barking frantically in the kitchen trying to get in the door and I opened the kitchen door to put the dog out in the garden and said, 'Get out, this is fuck all to do with you.' He was lying on the floor. I untangled the earphones. I must have put half a glass of Bacardi in the glass. I put the earphones on, sat down, and listened to the whole sequence of records. He was dead. I kept on drinking. With the music and the drinking I could get away from what was around me. In the morning the record player was still going round.

Going back, I don't actually remember putting the cord around his neck but I remember pulling him with the cord around his neck and dragging him.[3]

After I had killed him with the headphones cable I stripped him naked, finding that he had completely messed himself. I cleaned him up a bit with a long piece of paper kitchen towel and hoisted him over my shoulder . . . I bathed his body and laid him on the bed. I kept him in the bed with me for the rest of the night. No sex, only caressing, etc. When I awoke in the morning he was hanging half out of the bed and to touch he was much colder. I pulled him back in beside me and straightened him up. I got up and cleaned the mess. I ditched all his things. I put him in the cupboard as I was going to work. That night I checked him in the cupboard where he was doubled up and he was rigid in that approximate position. The next day I bought a cheap polaroid colour camera. That evening I took his body from the cupboard and straightened him. While he was crouched in the cupboard a brown liquid had been dripping from his nose on to his chest and arms, so I washed him over with a wet paper towel.

I sat him on a kitchen chair and dressed him in socks, briefs and vest. His face was a little bit puffy and slightly reddish. I put body colour on his face to remove the colour. I arranged the body in various positions and took several photos (which I destroyed with the last burning). I lay in bed fully clothed with him lying spreadeagled on top of me as I watched television. I would sometimes speak to him as though he were still listening. I would compliment him on his looks and anatomy. By crossing his legs I had sex between his bare thighs (although no penetration of the body occurred). I wrapped him well before putting him under the floorboards.

I took him up on about four occasions in the next two weeks. It was cold down there and he was still very fresh. I always stripped him before wrapping him. I would sit him in the other armchair next to me as I watched an evening's T.V., drinking. I thought that his body and skin were very beautiful, a sight that almost brought me to tears after a couple of drinks. He had not a mark on him save for red lines on his neck. Before he returned to his 'bed' I would sit him on my knee and strip off the underwear and socks, wrap him in curtain material and put him down (actually saying, 'Good night, Ken'). I destroyed the records which reminded me of him afterwards, smashed them with a spade and put them in the dustbin.[4]

Martyn Duffey came from the Merseyside area. He had had a troubled childhood with marked signs of instability: theft, running away from home, threatening behaviour. When he was fifteen, he had walked out of his parents' house saying that he was going to the library, hitch-hiked to London, and after a week of sleeping rough had been directed to the Soho Project, which paid his return fare to Birkenhead. His father committed him into care, and he attended a school for maladjusted children. More than once he was seen by psychiatrists. He returned home on discharge from the school and was for a short time employed as a junior salesman.

In many ways, Martyn was no different from thousands of other youngsters who experience a difficult adolescence and emerge from it battered but mature. He frequented homosexual clubs in Liverpool and often stayed out all night (becoming addicted to valium tablets), but he kept up a correspondence with a social worker in London which gave growing evidence of touching sensitivity and intelligence. Heeding his correspondent's advice to keep away from London, he took a catering course and formed a deep attachment to a girlfriend. For the first time, his future held promise of stability. He was visibly and hearteningly overcoming his problems, but he relapsed after he was questioned by police for evading his train fare. In May 1980 he packed a suitcase, including the kitchen knives he had acquired on his catering course, and informed his family that he was going to live in New Brighton. They never saw him again after 13 May. Somehow he turned up in London. Had he contacted a social worker, all might have been well; but he didn't. He slept in stations, then a few days later met Dennis Nilson on the day that Nilsen returned from the union conference in Southport. He was not quite seventeen.

Nilsen recalls that Martyn Duffey drank only two cans of beer on their evening together. After that, the boy crawled into bed.

> I remember sitting astride him (his arms must have been trapped by the quilt). I strangled him with great force in the almost pitch darkness with just one side-light on underneath. As I sat on him I could feel my bottom becoming wet. His urine had come through the bedding and my jeans. When he was quite limp I pulled him by the ankles to the edge of the platform and stepped on the ladder. I pulled him over my shoulder and carried him down. He was unconscious but still alive. I put him down, filled the kitchen sink up with water, draped him into it, and held him there, his head under the water. I must have held him there for about three or four minutes. I then lifted him into my arms and took him into the room. I laid him on the floor and took off his socks, jeans, shirt and underpants. I carried him into the bathroom. I got into the bath myself this time and he lay in the water on top of me. I washed his body. Both of us dripping wet, I somehow managed to hoist this slipping burden on to my shoulders

and took him into the room. I sat him on the kitchen chair and dried us both. I put him on the bed but left the bedclothes off. He was still very warm. I talked to him and mentioned that his body was the youngest looking I had ever seen. I kissed him all over and held him close to me. I sat on his stomach and masturbated. I kept him temporarily in the cupboard. Two days later I found him bloated in the cupboard. He went straight under the floorboards.[5]

Nilsen threw Duffey's knives away, but allowed them to rust first.

Billy Sutherland was a heavy drinker from Edinburgh who had been to an approved school and to prison. He was covered in tattoos on his arms, hands and chest. The fingers of his hands were tattooed with the words LOVE and HATE. In Scotland he had had a girlfriend and fathered a child, but in London his style was that of a gypsy, never staying long in one place, and sleeping with men for money. He would steal when necessity demanded. He was known to the Soho Project. Wherever he was, he would keep in touch with his mother in Scotland, and it was she who reported him as a missing person to the police and the Salvation Army when he abruptly ceased contact with her. (The missing persons list included forty men named Billy Sutherland.) He met Dennis Nilsen in a pub near Piccadilly Circus and they started an evening of pub-crawling, finishing up in Charing Cross Road. Nilsen said he was fed up with walking and wanted to go home. He walked down the stairs into Leicester Square underground station and bought himself a ticket, then turned to find Billy Sutherland standing behind him. He said he had nowhere to go, and Nilsen, rather reluctantly, bought him a ticket and took him to Melrose Avenue. Sutherland was then twenty-seven years old.

Nilsen has no precise recollection of the killing of this man, only that he strangled him from the front, and that there was a dead body in the morning.

Malcolm Barlow was about twenty-four but looked much younger. He had spent most of his life in care or in hospitals for the mentally handicapped. His parents were dead and he was totally friendless. He suffered from epilepsy and could, when occasion demanded, induce a fit to extract sympathy. Another method he used to gain attention was to tell heavy lies. He was disruptive, extremely difficult to handle, and no one who spent any time with him could stand him for long. He would do anything for money, including sleeping with men and attempting blackmail. He would live in hostels or with anyone who picked him up off the street. Originally from Sheffield, where he had a probation officer with whom he kept in touch sporadically, he would turn up in all parts of the country. Although of low intelligence, Malcolm Barlow understood the D.H.S.S. system like a professional, and never missed a date to sign on. In September 1981 he was claiming from a London office.

On 17 September, Dennis Nilsen left his flat at 195 Melrose Avenue at 7.30 a.m. to go to work. On the pavement, his back against a garden wall a few houses away, was Malcolm Barlow. Nilsen asked him if he was all right, had he fallen down or something? Barlow said it was the pills he was taking (for epilepsy), and that his legs had given way. Nilsen told him he should be in hospital and, half supporting him, took him back to the flat and made him a cup of coffee. Nilsen then went to a telephone kiosk in Kendal Avenue (leaving Barlow in the flat to keep an eye on the dog) and dialled 999, asking for an ambulance immediately. It arrived within ten minutes and took Barlow away to Park Royal Hospital.

The next day, 18 September, Malcolm Barlow was released, and signed on as usual with the D.H.S.S. He then went to 195 Melrose Avenue and sat down on the doorstep waiting for Nilsen to come home. He had had some difficulty in finding the house as he had mistakenly taken the address as Number 295. When Nilsen saw him there he said, 'You're supposed to be in hospital,' to which Barlow replied that he was all right now and had been discharged. 'Well, you'd better come in, then,' said Nilsen.

Dennis Nilsen cooked him a meal and sat with him to watch television. Nilsen started drinking, and Barlow asked for a drink himself, which Nilsen initially refused on the grounds that alcohol should not be mixed with the pills he was taking. But Barlow was insistent that one or two drinks would not do him any harm, so Nilsen relented. 'Be it on your own head,' he said. Barlow had at least two Bacardi and cokes, then went to sleep on the sofa. After about an hour Nilsen went to wake him, slapping his face, but there was no shifting him from a deep slumber. Nilsen thought he might have to call the ambulance again, and sat for twenty minutes before deciding what to do. 'I'm sorry that he managed to find me again,' he later wrote.[6]

The decision to kill Barlow, after sober reflection, proved to be one of the most intractable problems which Nilsen's defence psychiatrists faced, for it showed a cool deliberation for which no excuse could be found. Barlow was murdered because his presence was a nuisance:

> Putting my hands around his throat I squeezed tightly. I held that position for about two or three minutes and released my hold. I didn't check but I believed him to be now dead . . . I finished my drinks, switched T.V. off and climbed back into bed. The next morning, not feeling much like prising up the floorboards, I dragged him through into the kitchen and put him under the sink and closed the door. I went to work.[7]

Malcolm Barlow was the last person to die at Melrose Avenue. There were half a dozen bodies already awaiting final disposal. A total of seven men died between September 1980 and September 1981, most of whom are identified only by a stray physical characteristic recalled by the murderer, such as the skinhead with the words CUT HERE tattooed around his neck (not easy to trace — there are hundreds of men with similar tattoos in London), the long-haired hippy, and the emaciated young man whose legs rose in cycling motions as he died.

The skinhead's body was hung up by the wrists, the clothes cut away with a knife, and a basin of warm soapy water placed beneath him. Nilsen washed the body down, dried it clean, and took it to bed with him, where intercrural sex took place.

One other anonymous victim was remembered in detail by Nilsen, and the incident needs to be related here for the light this memory sheds upon the murderer's state of mind, his motives, and his calm after the event:

We climbed our drunken way naked up to the wooden platform bed. Later I remember being straddled over him, my knees each side of him with the back of my head pressed against the ceiling. I was squeezing his neck and remember wanting to see more clearly what he looked like. I felt no struggling. I got up shaking and nearly fell down the ladder. I put all the room lights on and comforted Bleep to go back to sleep. I put a chair beside the ladder and climbed up. I pulled aside the bedding and pulled his ankles until he half hung off the platform. I got on to the chair and pulled his warm, limp, naked body into my arms. I got down from the chair and saw my reflection in a full-length mirror. I just stood there and looked at myself with the lad's naked body in my arms. His head, arms and legs hung limply and he looked asleep. I could feel his warmth against my skin. I began to have an erection and my heart began to beat fast, my armpits were sweating. I put his legs on the floor and changing my hold on him I hoisted the inert youth on to my shoulder. I washed him in the bath and sat him dripping wet on the loo, and bathed myself in the water. It was an act to purify him and apparently (with hindsight) me also. I carried him into the room and sat his wet body on a dining-chair. His head lay right back. I dried his body carefully with a bath towel and the steam rose from him in the cold air. (When I moved or carried him a deep sigh would come from his throat.) His hair was still damp. Putting him again over my shoulder I carried him up the ladder and laid him on the bed. I dressed him in his socks and my tee-shirt and underpants. I tucked the body into bed and lay beside him naked on top of the bedclothes. I smoked and fetched a stiff drink. A tape was playing of Copeland's 'Fanfare for the Common Man'. I was crying. I got into bed and held him close to me. I was whispering to him, 'Don't worry, everything's fine, sleep.' The music subsided. I explored his body in simulated seduction. I held him so close in my arms that my erect penis was held between his thighs. I stripped off his pants and pulled the bedding back. I took his genitals in my hand and masturbated myself with the other hand . . . I wiped him clean with a paper towel and lay with him asleep in my arms. I remember first thing in the morning thinking 'This is absolutely ridiculous,' and pushed his cold body from me. (I kept him for a week before putting him under the floorboards.) Getting up in the morning I put him sitting naked in the cupboard and went to work. I never thought of him again at work until I came home that evening. I got dressed into my jeans, ate and turned on the T.V. I fed Bleep and the cat. I opened the cupboard and lifted out the body. I cleaned him up. I dressed him and sat him in front of the T.V. in the armchair next to mine. I took his hand and talked to him my comments for the day with cynical remarks about the T.V. programmes. Bleep would find a cosy corner and behave as if he were not even there. Perhaps life to a dog means something warm. I would also take him [the body] on to the armchair with me and hold him safe and secure. I placed him on the table and slowly stripped him. I would always remove his socks last. I would closely examine (slowly) every part of his anatomy. I would roll him on to his stomach and do likewise to his back. His naked body fascinated me. I remember being thrilled that I had full control and ownership of this beautiful body. I would fondle his buttocks and it amazed me that there was no reaction from him to this . . . I was fascinated by the mystery of death. I whispered to him because I believed he was still really in there. I ran my fingers all over his body and marvelled at its smooth beauty. If he were in there alive it was obvious that his penis was irrevocably dead. It looked so small and insignificant. I would hold him towards me standing up and view in the full length mirror (my arms around him). I would hold him close often, and think that he had never been so appreciated in his life before . . . After a week I stuck him under the floor. Three days later I removed him

(only once). I wanted him to lie there underneath in a bed
of white roses.[8]

Three murders took place at 23 Cranley Gardens. The first
was John Howlett, a ne'er-do-well constantly in trouble with
the police, who had been virtually evicted by his family at the
age of thirteen and had done nothing much since. He had
lived at times in houses for backward children, had been
imprisoned for stealing, and was a chronic liar. As he boasted
of being an ex-Grenadier guardsman (and Dennis Nilsen did
not know his surname) John the Guardsman is the nickname
which police investigators used. He and Nilsen met twice.
On the first occasion, they had a long conversation in a West
End pub in December 1981, about two months after Nilsen
had moved to Cranley Gardens; they drank for a couple of
hours, then parted company. In March 1982, Nilsen was
drinking in the Salisbury in St Martin's Lane when John the
Guardsman walked in. He recognised Nilsen immediately
and went up to join him at the bar. He explained that he was
down from High Wycombe for the day and would return
there later. He grew impatient at the slow service and suggested they go together somewhere else. They walked to an
off-licence and stocked up, then on to Charing Cross underground station where they took the Northern Line to
Highgate. From there they walked to 23 Cranley Gardens.
Nilsen cooked a meal for them both, and they settled down
to watch television, drinking continuously. The late film
started (towards midnight) and John the Guardsman said he
wouldn't mind getting his head down; Nilsen muttered
assent and continued to watch the film, while John disappeared into the front room (at that stage the bed was kept
in the front room). About 1 a.m. Nilsen put the lights out and
went to the other room, where he found John asleep in bed. 'I
thought you were getting your head down, I didn't know you
were moving in,' he said. He roused him and told him that he
would call for a taxi to take him home, but John said he didn't
feel much like moving. Nilsen went back to the kitchen and
poured himself another rum, then sat on the edge of the bed.
He noticed that John the Guardsman had taken most of his

clothes off, but he did not feel like getting into bed with him. In fact, he did not want him there at all:

I went to the armchair and under the cushion there was a length of loose upholstery strap. I approached to where he was lying in bed under the blankets. I wound this material round his neck. I think I said, 'It's about time you went.' I was astride him and I tightened my grip on the material. He fought back furiously and partially raised himself up. I thought I'd be overpowered. Summoning up all my strength I forced him back down and his head struck the rim of the headrest on the bed. He still struggled fiercely so that now he was half off the bed. In about a minute he had gone limp. There was blood on the bedding. I assumed it was from his head. I checked and he was still breathing deep rasping breaths. I tightened my grip on him again around his neck for another minute or so. I let go my grip again and he appeared to be dead. I stood up. The dog was barking in the next room. I went through to pacify it. I was shaking all over with the stress of the struggle. I really thought he was going to get the better of me. I returned and was shocked to see that he had started breathing again. I looped the material round his neck again, pulled it as tight as I could and held on for what must have been two or three minutes. When I released my grip he had stopped breathing. But I noticed as he lay there on his back and I checked afterwards his heart was still beating quite strongly. I couldn't believe it. I dragged him through to the bathroom. I pulled him over the rim of the bath so his head was hanging over the bath, put the plug in still holding him and ran the cold water full on. His head was right at the bottom of the bath. In a minute or so the water reached his nose, the rasping breath came on again. The water rose higher and I held him under. He was struggling against it. The bath continued to fill up. There were bubbles coming from his mouth or nose and he stopped struggling. I held him in that position for four or five minutes. The water had become bloody and a substance as well as particles of food was coming from his mouth. I left him there all night. I washed my hands and went through to the bedroom and pulled off the sheets and soiled parts of the bedding . . . I placed a clean blanket on top of the under-blanket and went to bed. I was smoking and shaking in bed. I called the dog and it came through looking a bit sheepish. I tapped the bed saying, 'Come up here,' and it curled up by my feet and put its head down trying to keep as quiet as possible. I must have gone to sleep quickly induced by the alcohol — I was completely exhausted . . . For a week afterwards, I had his finger marks on my neck.[9]

Graham Allen was referred to in court as the 'omelette' death:

The thing he wanted more than anything else was something to eat. I had very little supply in but I had a whole tray of eggs. So I whipped up a huge omelette and cooked it in the large frying-pan, put it on a plate and gave it to him. He started to eat the omelette. He must have eaten three-quarters of the omelette. I noticed he was sitting there and suddenly he appeared to be asleep or unconscious with a large piece of omelette hanging out of his mouth. I thought he must have been choking on it but I didn't hear him choking — he was indeed deeply unconscious. I sat down and had a drink. I approached him, I can't remember what I had in my hands now — I don't remember whether he was breathing or not but the omelette was still protruding from his mouth. The plate was still on his lap — I removed that. I bent forward and I think I strangled him. I can't remember at this moment what I used . . . I remember going forward and I remember he was dead . . . If the omelette killed him I don't know, but anyway in going forward I intended to kill him. An omelette doesn't leave red marks on a neck. I suppose it must have been me.[10]

Stephen Sinclair was a 'punk' aged twenty, often to be seen loitering in Leicester Square. He was from Perth in Scotland, and his real name was Stephen Guild, but this name was never used as he had been adopted by the Sinclair family. He had severe personality problems. Not only did he take drugs whenever he could lay his hands on them, injecting himself with 'speed' — a stimulant — but he suffered from the habit of slashing his arms, for no apparent reason except to hurt himself. His arms were covered in scars as a result, and he might make an attempt to injure himself at any time of day, impulsively. He was known to welfare workers in the area, who usually tried to deal with him on street level, where his unpredictability might cause less harm. He once arrived with a can of petrol, which he threatened to pour over himself and ignite. He lived in 'squats', derelict houses, or Salvation Army hostels, stole, burgled, was generally a nuisance and had been imprisoned more than once. His ravaged body was riddled with hepatitis B. Yet there were times when Stephen contrived a degree of self-control, and then he could be a sensitive and agreeable companion. He had plenty of 'mates' in the West End streets, whom he knew only by their first names. On 26 January 1983 some of these saw him go off with a strange man, but did not disturb him in case he was 'tapping' for money, as was his custom.

Nilsen said he could walk with him to the underground station; he was going to stop at McDonald's in Oxford Street on the way. 'I haven't eaten all day,' said Sinclair, so Nilsen offered to buy him a hamburger. They stopped at an off-licence on Shaftesbury Avenue to buy spirits (for Nilsen) and six lagers (for Sinclair). Sinclair walked down to Centrepoint to talk to his friends, asking Nilsen to wait. After ten minutes, they took the tube to Highgate and walked to Cranley Gardens. It was some time after 9 p.m.

During the evening, Sinclair disappeared into the lavatory, causing Nilsen to assume that he was injecting himself. He then dozed off in the armchair, while Nilsen sat in the other chair wearing his stereo headphones and listening to the rock opera *Tommy*.

At the end of this book there is a long account of the death of Stephen Sinclair, written after his killer had begun his sentence. For the moment, we shall restrict ourselves to the versions which Nilsen gave the police and which he wrote for the present author while on remand, awaiting trial:

> I remember nothing else until I woke up the next morn-
> ing. He was still in the armchair and he was dead. On the
> floor was a piece of string with a tie attached to it.[11]
>
> . . . I entertained no thoughts of harming him, only
> concern and affection for his future and the pain and plight
> of his life. I saw him in the early hours of the morning at
> peace in my armchair, through a drugged haze. I remem-
> ber wishing he could stay in peace like that forever. I had a
> feeling of easing his burden with my strength. He lay
> there. I later became aware of him still there, and I felt
> relieved that his troubles were now over. I noticed that his
> jeans were soaking wet with urine. I wanted to wash him
> clean. As if he were somehow breakable and still alive, I
> gently undressed him and carried him naked into the
> bathroom. I washed him carefully all over in the bath and
> sitting his limp body on the edge I towelled him dry. I laid
> him on my bed and put talc on him to make him look
> cleaner. I just sat there and watched him. He looked really
> beautiful like one of those Michelangelo sculptures. It
> seemed that for the first time in his life he was really feeling
> and looking the best he ever did in his whole life. I wanted
> to touch and stroke him, but did not. I placed two mirrors
> around the bed, one at the end and one at the side. I lay
> naked beside him but only looked at the two bodies in the
> mirror. I just lay there and a great peace came over me. I
> felt that this was it, the meaning of life, death, everything.
> No fear, no pain, no guilt. I could only caress and fondle
> the image in the mirror. I never looked at him. No sex, just
> a feeling of oneness. I had an erection but felt he was far
> too perfect and beautiful for the pathetic ritual of com-
> monplace sex. Afterwards I dressed him in my clothes
> which remained on him until many days later.[12]

Of the other victims Nilsen has the haziest recollection. 'I
remember next day he was dead and I had probably strangled
him'; 'Next morning there was another body'; 'My impression was that I'd strangled him because he had marks on his

neck.' It is not surprising that the one he recalls most vividly is the first, when he discovered that he was a murderer, and his degree of recollection of subsequent murders seems to depend upon the amount of alcohol consumed at the time, and/or the level of his attraction towards the person concerned. Not the least baffling of the many inconsistencies in this squalid saga is why he should have killed both people he liked and others for whom he cared not a jot, a question which makes the search for an emotional trigger all the harder. There was a break of nearly a year between the first and second killings, then a period of dense activity for eighteen months in 1980 and 1981, when ten people died, the last three victims falling in the eleven months preceding his arrest. It is significant that these three last occurred at the new address in Cranley Gardens, where Nilsen lived from 3 October 1981, and where the problems attached to the disposal of the bodies were, as we shall see, very much greater than at his previous address and may have acted as an impediment to further killings. But that presupposes a degree of conscious thought which the evidence does not always support. A fuller analysis of motive and psychiatric condition must await consideration in a later chapter, but there are three elements repeated often enough to be regarded as fairly consistent: alcohol as a means of breaking the inhibiting mechanism; music as an agent of emotional exhilaration; and loneliness as a prospect to be fought against. For the rest, the reader is invited to bear in mind some fundamental questions and relevant facts:

(a) There are minor contradictions in the murderer's narrative, for example as to whether a victim was on the bed or on the floor. Are these to be attributed to the rush of memories brimming over and seeking release after a long silence, or does fantasy occasionally intrude as the events are relived, embellishing and confusing the strict truth? We already know that Nilsen's imagination had travelled into dark, mysterious areas. On the other hand, his professional training and personal inclination both engendered a deep respect for accuracy.

131

(b) It seems incredible that he should so fiercely resent the 'House of Horrors' publicity which followed his arrest. Is his grip on reality so slight that he does not find it revolting that a man's life should be squeezed out of him? Does he feel that in some way it was 'another person' who committed these acts, leaving Des Nilsen, the union branch secretary and responsible civil servant, inviolate? Does he confuse his *feeling* of doing good with the *fact* of doing ill? He told the author that he knew the killings were monstrous, but that he did not feel like a monster.

(c) There were sexual relations of a limited sort with six of the victims, and none at all with the other nine. The sexual element took the form of masturbation over the body, or intercrural sex, but never penetration. These are not, therefore, strictly homosexual murders. The sexual act did not take place before, during, or after death with any of them, unless intercrural sex is regarded as a hesitant variation of anal sex. He intended penetration with the first victim after death but did not persevere. Why, then, did he fondle six and ignore the rest? Were they those with whom he could most readily identify himself? Did he imagine himself as victim? The mirror fetish he had evolved was brought into play with these six men. 'They had to be dead like my corpse in the mirror before we were fully in communion,' Nilsen writes. 'As my mirror fantasy developed I would whiten my face, have blue lips and staring eyes in the mirror and I would enact these things alone using my own corpse (myself) as the object of my attentions.'[13] If the other nine men did not arouse him sexually, nor serve to feed his appetite for identifying himself with death, why were they killed?

(d) With some victims he does not recall the act of killing, only having noticed later that they were dead. When he does remember the act of murder, he told the police that it felt like a compulsion. 'My sole reason for existence was to carry out that act at that moment.' Enlarging on this, he has since written: 'I could feel the power and the struggles of death — a series of impressions — of absolute compulsion to *do*, at that moment, suddenly.' At other times he seems to imply that he is performing a charitable deed, helping the victim, giving succour and comfort, releasing him from a miserable life. He felt keenly, for instance, that he wanted to help Stephen Sinclair, whom nobody else could tolerate. 'He seemed a total symbol of failure and defeat, miserably ruined.' This, too, might suggest that he is transferring his own unhappiness on to the victim. His whispering words of solace to the victim after death might well be addressed to himself.

(e) Music is frequently the catalyst for death, the creator of illusions, the exciter, and ultimately culpable as an accessory in the murderer's mind. One victim was actually listening through headphones to the London Symphony Orchestra's medley of classical tunes to a disco beat as he was being throttled.

(f) Alcohol is another stimulant often cited by Nilsen. Can one summon the energy to kill when one is intoxicated to such a degree? Some victims fought back and there was an almighty struggle in which Nilsen might have found it difficult to win if he had been very drunk. The first man, at least, was killed in the early hours of the morning after some sleep, when the worst effects (though not all) of alcoholic intoxication would have worn off. Has Nilsen exaggerated the power of alcohol to affect his behaviour? Following his arrest, he was examined by Dr Mendoza at Hornsey Police Station and declared to show no symptoms of alcoholic withdrawal.

(g) What, finally, was the significance of the ritual whereby the body was washed and dried? Nilsen talks of purification, and even uses words like 'sacred' and 'holy', not the usual vocabulary one might expect from a professed sceptic. Are we dealing with a corrupted religious instinct? In short, was Dennis Nilsen 'possessed'? And if so, what is there in his life, as related in earlier chapters, which made him ripe for possession? Are there clues which might have indicated that his personality was likely to disintegrate and open the doors to some objective force of evil? If not, is he just like the rest of us?

Possible answers to these questions might be offered by psychiatry, by philosophy, or by intuition. They might also be suggested by Nilsen himself if we observe the way in which he coped with this new dimension to his life; how he adjusted (if he ever did) to a recognition of himself as a killer, and what thoughts assailed him from New Year's Day 1979 to 9 February 1983 and beyond. One of the most astonishing aspects of the case is Nilsen's ability to go about his daily work with energy and enthusiasm, to go out for drinks, walk the dog, and even entertain people peaceably at his flat, while all the time there was a collection of bodies under his floor or in his cupboard. Eventually, he would have to deal with their disposal. Does this ability display callousness and indifference, or merely a practical grasp of what had to be done? Most murderers are ordinary, banal people faced with the consequences of an extraordinary event. Is Dennis Nilsen one of them, or does his story set him apart as an unfeeling creature of scarcely human dimensions? Merely to consider the question is to inquire into an aspect of the human predicament, with its decisions, its catastrophes, and its responsibilities. The first step is to listen to Nilsen's own account of how he saw himself during those years when he and he only knew that he had the hands of a killer.

7

DISPOSAL

'I cannot judge or see myself in any of it.'[1] During the course of 1980, when Nilsen had already killed two people and was forced to recognise that the initial event could no longer be dismissed as an isolated incident whose detection he had been lucky to escape, he felt bewildered and apprehensive. He now knew that what had happened before was likely to happen again, and by the end of the year there were several more bodies to confirm his worst fears. Should he give himself up? He told the police that one side of him was 'talking about survival, shame, exposure, position, the future — even the dog, what's going to happen to the dog. There was always this battle between doing the right thing and surviving and escaping the consequences of these actions. It's a perfectly natural side of someone to want to survive and avoid detection.'[2] He went so far as to say that if it had not been for the dog he might well have surrendered himself to the police, a possibility that the investigating officers treated with the greatest scepticism. After the third killing in May 1980 he says he was growing less and less 'emotional' about it and was simply resigned to the knowledge that he was a compulsive killer. But in moments of introspection, resignation gave way to confused disbelief:

135

Hanging would have been no deterrent in my case. I was not even thinking clearly about what I was exactly doing. Power of responsibility was nil at these times. There was fear afterwards, with a massive and suppressed remorse. I looked at a photo of Martyn Duffey today and it shocked me seeing him so lifelike in that photo and dead, gone, destroyed by *me*. I can't stop thinking about it. I am not full of self-pity, just amazed that all this — from beginning to end — could ever happen. I should feel like some two-headed monster — all I see in the mirror is me, just the same old respectable, friendly, helpful, responsible me. I do not feel mentally ill. I have no headaches, pressures or voices, nothing in my thoughts or actions to suggest insanity. Madness, as Quixote would say, is seeing life as it is and not as it should be; to seek treasure where there is only trash; to surrender dreams to be what you are not.[3]

The above lines were written while Nilsen was on remand in Brixton Prison. He does not say whether the spectre of insanity ever splintered his consciousness before arrest, but there were times when he was brutally reminded of the dark mad new life which now ran parallel to his visibly perceived existence and which he strove mostly to forget: 'A fly buzzing around would sometimes remind me of another dimension under the floor. I would dismiss these intrusive thoughts as though these events had happened to someone else other than me.'[4] But at least twice a day he could not avoid being reminded, for he sprayed the flat, morning and evening, to kill the flies as they emerged from their pupas, or put deodorant sticks under the floor. A tenant in the house, Miss Adler, mentioned the pervasive smell, which Nilsen attributed to general decay of the building. He felt that both parts of his life were continually 'spying on each other', and developed the ability to step into and out of either world. He even found it exciting to reflect that he might be arrested any day.

Various items scattered around the flat also pricked the memory — a watch, a St Christopher medallion, a carving fork, a tobacco tin, pieces of a camera — but they seem not to have disturbed Nilsen unduly: 'The small objects belonging to the dead became part of the household. I did not feel that it was theft as their owners hadn't really gone away.' So indifferent was he to the suggestive power of objects that he wore a watch taken from one victim and gave another away to a rent boy on the game. Clothing he generally threw into the dustbin.

Music, on the other hand, did have the power to frighten him as nothing else could; hence his destruction of records. At Christmas in 1979 he organised the office party, supervising the catering, cooking for eighty people, costing and planning. As usual he put all his energies into the task, and there is a card of gratitude signed by about fifty staff members in affectionate terms which testifies to its success. But he made the mistake of taking along some of his tapes from Melrose Avenue and leaving it to somebody else to play them:

The music started, I was frozen in shock. It was the classical rock track — his and my music. My mind raced. A few days before he had been killed and I had him under the floorboards. I couldn't touch another drop all evening. Here were two different and opposite worlds in collision.[5]

Back home he found it difficult to sleep, the music still running through his head. Then he shouted out loud, 'Right, if you want to listen to the music then damn well come out and listen to it.' Taking the body from under the boards, he sat it on a dining-chair, but left the carrier bag over its head as he did not want to look at the face. He put on a tape, poured himself a drink, and stood naked and trembling for many hours. The next day he tried to busy himself cleaning up the office after the party, to prevent his thoughts from returning to Melrose Avenue. 'He was back there waiting for me.'[6]

It was established at the trial that the second victim, killed in December 1979, was the Canadian Kenneth Ockendon. A whole year had passed since the first murder, and Nilsen was confident, at that stage, that the nightmare would not be repeated. 'The shock, grief and horror which followed the death of Ken Ockendon hit me like an "A" bomb,' he says.

'He was my friend. I liked him a lot. His music still haunted me. When I heard classical rock [L.S.O.] one night, I think I raised the floorboards and begged his forgiveness.'

The office Christmas party, on 14 December, took place less than two weeks after the death of Kenneth Ockendon.

There were other times when the reality of his deeds overwhelmed him and he could not maintain the fiction that they had been committed by 'someone else' who inhabited him:

Long-haired hippy, why did I bring you back? I tremble at your death and permanent presence. I brush the hair from your eyes. I try to shake you alive. I want to say that I'm sorry and see you walk away. I try to inflate your lungs, hopelessly, but nothing of you is working at all.

He then took a knife, sat in the armchair, and contemplated suicide, but Bleep came in, wagging her tail, and he sank to his knees, sobbing. He got up, made coffee and smoked, and spat at his image in the mirror to obliterate it.

I undress the man's body and wash it there on the floor. I look at the pale naked corpse and hold out my hands and stare at these instruments of death. I wipe the body clean and dry and put the clothing back on it (except his under-pants soiled in death). When he is under the floor my shaking hands reach for the bottle and headphones.

This account, written with hindsight, sounds melodramatic and totally out of tune with the bland, emotionless statements he gave to the police. Nilsen's explanation for this is that the statements were purely factual, designed to give evidence which would secure his conviction, whereas his private sufferings would be of no use to them; his civil service training made him stick to the point under questioning. On the other hand this latter account, told in the present tense years after the event, may indicate his vision of how he would have *liked* to have felt, or *ought* to have felt, for his moral sense remained alive in spite of his immoral actions. (He told the police that he was amazed he had no tears for the victims, implying that he knew perfectly well that tears would be expected from a 'normal' man.) But we also know that he did once succeed in bringing back to life a man whom he had tried to kill, a fact which lends weight to his contention that he was often besieged with the emotions of fear, horror and remorse, and kept them to himself. 'I feel a personal remorse not open to public expression.'

Another similar memory is told with the conviction and force of authentic truth:

The domestic debris of the night before litters the back room of my flat at 195 Melrose Avenue, NW2. My skull seems shrunk by the pressure of last night's drinking. Sitting on the chair I survey the chaotic scene in fuddled concentration. There is a dead body on the floor and it is still quite early in the morning. Bleep comes up to me and I give her the assurance that all is well to keep her happy. I kneel beside the body and my hands are shaking. I undo the neck-tie from the neck of the body and the face is puffed out and red. I turn him over on to his back and a sigh escapes from his lungs. I stand and stare down at my unbelievable result. I sit and stare, with shaking hands, and draw deeply on my cigarette. 'Hell, fucking hell, how long can this go on and on and on?' I think. I take Bleep up into my arms and say out loud, 'Bleep, what's going to become of us, who will look after you when they come for me? They're all gone, one after the other, it was me, me, nobody else but me. This is all my work. I must be mad, insane. They're dead forever by these hands.' I hold Bleep to me and cry and my tears turn to rage. I overturn the coffee table containing all the glasses, cans, ashtrays, mugs and things and bury my head in my hands. I take up a plastic folder containing my union correspondence and throw it across the room. It strikes the top of the music centre and the playing arm is dislodged on to an L.P. which had been turning all night on the turntable . . . I'm drifting away from all my present problems with my thoughts crowded out by the music. The applause at the end of the music track greets me as I stand dazed in the centre of the room in black recognition of the wreckage strewn around me. I sit down and work myself up to cleaning up the mess and seeing to the dead man on the floor. I don't care what they think upstairs about the noise.[7]

Nilsen could never tell when another murder might occur. He naively and rather desperately hoped that the latest would remain the last. He claimed that he never went out pub-crawling to look for a victim, a proposition that the police were happy to accept. What he did do was to go out and look for company, and it is important to remember that there were more people who accompanied him back to his flat and were left unharmed than there were those who died. 'I could never beforehand make a deliberate choice to kill,' he says. The crucial word here is 'beforehand'; how far in advance of the event is 'beforehand'? Sinclair was throttled with a tie with a piece of string attached to it; they were knotted together. Nilsen woke up on the morning of 27 January 1983 to find a dead man in the armchair and on the floor a piece of string with tie attached. Recognising the significance of this, D.C.S. Chambers questioned him closely:

Q. Where do you keep this piece of string?
A. I must have made it up that night.
Q. When?
A. That night. It must have been that night.
Q. I'm going to show you exhibit BL/8. Is that what you're talking about?
A. Yes.
Q. Did he struggle?
A. I don't know. I thought it would be quick. In the morning you can tell if there was a struggle because things would be in disarray, but there was nothing. Nothing was knocked over.
Q. Are you saying that you made up this string solely for the purpose of killing the man?

A. I don't remember making it up. There's a bit of the tie missing.

Q. Where's the other bit?

A. I don't know.

Q. Yesterday you told us that you had killed three people in the flat and that Sinclair was the last one. Did you use this piece of string to kill the first two?

A. No, because that combination of string and tie could not have been in existence. The morning I met Sinclair that tie was hanging up in the wardrobe.

Q. What did you kill the other two with?

A. A belt or a sock, something like that. I'm not really sure.[8]

Chambers was trying to establish that some degree of premeditation was necessary in order to put together the instrument of murder, to make a knot of the string and tie; at some point before the attack Nilsen must have known it was going to take place and so prepared for it. How long before? He would not say, and claimed it was not until the next day that he could tell whether or not there had been a struggle. Other murders were committed with an ordinary tie, with the hands, or with whatever was near, such as a cord or a piece of upholstery. None of these would have needed time to assemble, so that the moment of murder could have been a sudden impulse without preparation.

Did he not worry that the drinking might provoke another attack? 'While drinking, the previous killings had gone completely from my memory.'[9] What, then, was the motive which made victims of some and left others unscathed, bearing in mind that none of them, while living, were the object of sexual attraction or activity, and that only six of them became so after death? 'I can't think of any slot to place myself in!' he writes. 'I can't begin to grasp it.'[10]

Why, if violence is so alien to Nilsen's principles, instinct and nature, did he kill? He was, he says, the most unlikely killer he could think of. It happened as if by 'casual whim of nature'.

141

I wish there was a clear view on motive, conventionally speaking, then I could come to grips with the problem. Sex maniac? (I suppose I could lie and say they refused to have sex and I killed them.) No, that's not true. Robbery? No, impossible. Sadism? No, the thought of receiving or inflicting pain is abhorrent to me. Necrophiliac? The thought of sex within the sacredness of a dead body turns me right off.* Hate or vengeance? No, I can't remember any hateful feeling to any one of them. Insanity? No, I don't feel insane. Temporary insanity? Perhaps, but drink-induced temporary 'anything' cannot be an excuse for not keeping off the stuff. What I am is totally irresponsible.[11]

Another of the disquieting aspects of this case is the emergence of a motive which seems so bizarre, so incongruous, so unequal to the enormity of murder itself that it is almost insulting. We have already seen that Nilsen would often place a body on a chair in front of the television days after the death and then conduct a weirdly commonplace conversation with it, and also that he would carefully wash and dry the body to make it clean and comfortable. The stark, unpalatable fact is that Nilsen killed for company, to have someone to talk to, someone to care for. Nilsen's own explanation of his feelings runs as follows:

In none of these cases am I conscious of feeling any hate towards any of the victims . . . I remember going out to seek company and companionship, which perhaps would lead to a personal sexual and social relationship being established. On these excursions I cannot remember thinking about death, killing, or past events. I was living for that moment only, and for the future. I would invite some people back with me, others would invite themselves. Sex was always a secondary consideration. I wanted a warm relationship and someone to talk to. Also I

* He had thought that he might make the attempt with the first victim, but found that he was not aroused.

wanted to be a material provider and give hospitality. Because of the effects of drinking sex would (or would not) happen the next morning. Through the night it is a nice relaxing feeling to have someone warm beside you in bed. I would never plan to kill anyone. In a sudden inexplicable act, I would be a bit dazed, shocked and shaking all over afterwards. I had a feeling of hopelessness, grief, and a sense of emptiness, and even if I knew the body to be dead I felt that the personality was still within, aware and listening to me. I was the forlorn seeker after a relationship which was always beyond my reach. I felt somehow in- adequate as a human being . . . Sex was not a factor of continuity with the victims (looking back and trying to work it out). The only similarity was a need not to be alone. It was to have someone to talk to and be with. They were not all homeless tramps, etc. Not all young homeless men who came to my flat were attacked or killed. Not all were even homosexual or bisexual. The reason that some were homosexual was mainly because they would come to the pubs which I frequented. I was approached marginally more times by those liaisons than I approached them . . . I sometimes imagine that I may have felt that I applied a relieving pressure on a life as a benevolent act, in that the subjects were ultimately free from life's pain.[12]

One is bound to ask, whose life was being relieved, the victim's or the killer's? The confusion is inherent in this killer's mind. He told the police that at the time of murder he felt that his only reason for existing was to carry out that act at that moment. More revealing is the passage which follows, wherein confusion of identity is patent: 'I never sensed the feeling of *killing* as such, only a feeling of stopping *something terrible from happening*, a compulsion to squeeze the person by the throat to relieve and absolve him and me from some- thing terrible.'[13] Nilsen himself underlined these words, but others might feel that the words 'and me' could be empha- sised more tellingly. He found the interviews with a psychi- atrist painful because they forced him to relive the details of each murder. It was bad enough, he wrote, when he had to

143

keep control during the sessions at Hornsey Police Station:

> I cannot bring myself to keep remembering these inci-
> dents over and over again. These are ugly images totally
> alien to me. I seem to have not participated in them,
> merely stood by and watched them happen — enacted by
> two other players — like a central camera.[14]

The significance of this is, once again, the detachment, the
distance, the implication that the identity of the actors is
uncertain. Is he killer, victim, or producer? The roles are
malleable, not fixed and finite. Nilsen's identity floats in and
out of reality.

There is not only confusion of role in the killer's mind, but
a potentially significant confusion of meaning. Back in the
Shetlands Islands many years before, we noticed that Nilsen's
concept of death was strangely intertwined with his concept
of love, an amalgamation further manifested in his mirror
fantasies, wherein narcissistic love could only be expressed if
the image of himself was still enough to appear dead and,
later, was made pallid to simulate a corpse. How to interpret
his attitude towards Sinclair at the moment of killing ('I had a
feeling of easing his burden with my strength') unless it is
seen as a grotesquely distorted version of the act of giving
love? The desire to ease suffering, the care lavished upon
victims after death, the wish to cherish and possess, the
posthumous admiration bestowed in front of the mirror ('He
had never been so appreciated in his life before'), all point to
the almost inconceivable and unpalatable possibility that the
act of murder was, in this case, a diabolical corruption of the
act of love.

Of course, this reading of events cannot hold true for those
murders in which there was little or no element of love, as
with the emaciated stranger whom Nilsen did not even wish
to look at after death, though there might still be a confusion
of role at the moment of murder. But to pursue further the
theme of love and death being hopelessly muddled, there is
an interesting poem written by Nilsen on remand, in which
the words 'evil' and 'love' change places in the course of the

writing, and 'killing' in the first stanza becomes 'loving' in the last:`

> Confusion in the fact of being evil,
> 'Born into evil, all the time?'
> When evil is the produce
> Can there be a doubt?
> When killing men has always been a crime.
>
> What can I say in septic mitigation
> When innocents bear heavily on my soul.
> Living like a coward
> Safe behind the Crown,
> Guilty of a devastating toll.
>
> There is honour in killing the enemy,
> There is glory in a fighting, bloody end.
> But violent extirpation
> On a sacred trust,
> To squeeze the very life from a friend?
>
> Sentencing the fact of being evil,
> Dying of evil all the time.
> When love is the produce
> Can there be a doubt?
> When loving men has always been a crime.[15]

I have omitted three stanzas, but they do not alter the drift of the poem. (Nilsen denies there is confusion. He is guilty of 'killing men', but has all his life been regarded as guilty of 'loving men'. His poem muses on the contrast.) Another poem that he wrote after having read Oscar Wilde's *The Ballad of Reading Gaol*, whose metric rhythm he echoes, conveys similar ideas:

> It's now the turning tide of time
> When all will ask me, why?
> I sleep, the only company
> Forever with me lie;
> And is there love in such a thing
> When everything must die?[16]

Nilsen found that murder was the route which his disturbed emotions chose to express their purpose and their need. 'Do they not know that I have lost the things I love?' he asks. 'That I have killed everything of love that I need? Do they really think that I enjoyed any of it?' To summarise, then, Nilsen went to pubs to search for company which might relieve his loneliness; he found some temporary companions who came and went; he found others, less fortunate, whom he wanted to keep and to care for; and these died before they could refuse his attention by walking away. But, 'in place of love I had only made death . . .[17] I had cared for them to such a bizarre degree that I had sacrificed their lives and ultimately my own in an unbalanced obsession.'[18]

Disposal of the bodies was a problem which Nilsen solved after much deliberation. Having corpses in the flat caused him no distress, and he only bothered to get rid of them when lack of space dictated the necessity. After seven and a half months under the floor, the first victim was burnt whole in a bonfire at the bottom of the garden at 195 Melrose Avenue on 11 August 1979. By the following summer there were two more bodies under the floor, and one of them was decomposing so badly that it caused a constant smell. At this point Nilsen decided they would have to be removed. In the cupboard under the stairs there were some old suitcases. Nilsen brought the bodies up and laid them on the kitchen floor, dissected them into several parts, placed the parts in various bags and stuffed the suitcases with these bags. He then put the suitcases in the garden shed (originally constructed for Bleep), built a low brick wall round them, put in a few deodorant sticks, and covered the lot with piles of newspaper and more bricks. The door to the shed was always unlocked, and the suitcases remained there, with their grisly contents, for the next six months.

In September, October and November of 1980, three more men died and were placed under the floorboards. At one point there were two whole bodies beneath the floor, and one dismembered. If Nilsen forgot to put a body to rest out of sight (yes, he could forget), he might be suddenly reminded when he opened the cupboard; 'two bare legs fell out on me and I snapped back into the reality of my situation.'[19]

By the end of 1980, Nilsen had six corpses on his hands, some in pieces in the garden shed and some under the floor, plus the arms and hands of one victim which he put down a hole by the bush outside the French windows, having found that the torsos and severed heads filled the suitcases and left no more room. These arms and hands remained under the bush for over a year. The rest of the bodies were burnt in a bonfire on waste ground a few feet beyond the garden fence. But first he had to complete the dissection.

'I dreaded pulling up those floorboards and getting the kitchen floor prepared,' wrote Nilsen. He would put the dog and cat out in to the garden, and strip naked or to his underpants. He wore no protective clothing and used an ordinary kitchen knife. The pot he used on three occasions* for the head 'was used for boiling the flesh from the skulls and the term "cooking" is totally misplaced'. This was the same pot as he had taken to the Denmark Street staff party, but at that stage it had not yet served its additional purpose. (It had also served as a provisional home for goldfish.) He would never allow the dog anywhere near him when dissecting, and never fed it any human flesh. 'The flesh looked like just any meat one would see in a butcher's shop and having been trained in butchery I was not subject to any traumatic shocks.'[20] Traumatic or not, the business of dissection was acutely distressing. Cutting up bodies held no fascination for him, he says. The body was 'a relic of mood' which had to be destroyed. The years he had spent in the Army Catering Corps gave him all the experience he needed to decide where to cut most effectively; his knowledge of anatomy was now put to the most diabolical use.

Some bodies were in better condition than others, but Nilsen dealt with them all in the same way, kneeling beside them on the stone kitchen floor. The manner in which he set about the task is best described in the murderer's own words; it makes unpleasant reading:

*Later at Cranley Gardens.

I prised up the floorboards. I uncovered the body and took it by the ankles. I pulled it up through the gap in the floor and along the floor into the kitchen on to a piece of plastic sheeting. There were other bodies and parts of bodies under the floor. I got ready a small bowl of water, a kitchen knife, some paper tissues and plastic bags. I had had to have a couple of drinks before I could start. I removed the vest and undershorts from the body. With the knife I cut the head from the body. There was very little blood. I put the head in the kitchen sink, washed it, and put it in a carrier bag. I then cut off the hands, and then the feet. I washed them in the sink and dried them. I wrapped each one in paper towelling and put them in plastic carrier bags. I made a cut from the body's navel to the breast bone. I removed all the intestines, stomach, kidneys and liver. I would break through the diaphragm and remove the heart and lungs. I put all these organs into a plastic carrier bag. I then separated the top half of the body from the bottom half. I removed the arms and then the legs below the knee. I put the parts in large black carrier bags. I put the chest and rib-cage in a large bag and the thigh/buttock/private parts (in one piece) in another. I stored the packages back under the floorboards. I would leave the bag with the entrails/organs out. I uncovered the next body which had been there longer. I pulled it out by the ankles on to the kitchen floor. There were maggots on the surface of the body. I poured salt on these and brushed them off. The body was a bit discoloured. I was violently sick. I drank a few more glasses of spirits and finished the job as with the other. I got a bit drunk that afternoon. The French windows were open and I had to go out every so often. I was naked to save soiling my clothes. After I replaced the packages under the floor I had a bath. To carry out these dissections I only used a kitchen knife — no saws or power-cutting tools. Afterwards I would listen to music on the headphones and get really drunk, and perhaps take the 'weed' [his dog] out to Gladstone Park. (Bleep was always a bit apprehensive and stayed in the garden while I carried out these tasks.)[21]

148

The messiest part of dissection came with the removal of the internal organs, which inevitably involved liquids and an overpowering smell. Yet they were the quickest to dispose of. Nilsen would put the liver, intestines and so on in the gap between the double fencing at the side of the garden, and within a day or two they would have disappeared, devoured by minute creatures of the earth during the night.

Nilsen realised that he would have to build a second bonfire to consume the remains in suitcases in the garden shed and under the floor; he could delay no longer, and the last four murders had occurred in such rapid succession that he could foresee himself being overwhelmed by corpses if they continued. Still, nobody appeared to notice, nobody knocked at the door with a warrant, nobody was aware of what he was doing. Seven men had walked through the front door at 195 Melrose Avenue and not walked out again. Nilsen himself thought it incredible that he was able to carry on, and dispose of what he called 'my tragic products' in his own way, unmolested.

One very cold day at the beginning of December 1980, Nilsen prepared a huge bonfire on the waste land beyond the garden. The base was built of large sections of tree trunk from an old poplar which had been felled months before and left there. On and around these he stacked pieces of wood from unwanted furniture dumped by neighbours, leaving a sizeable hole in the centre. When he had finished, the bonfire stood about five feet high. Then he went to bed.

At 6.45 a.m. the next day, Nilsen went out into the garden to make sure no one was about. He then pulled up the floorboards, and wrapped the two bundles which were kept there in large amounts of carpeting, tied and secured. He dragged these one after the other down the garden path to the back fence, paused to remove four palings from the fence to squeeze through, and dragged the bundles across the ground to the bonfire. He removed some of the wood to expose the hollow in the centre and managed to push the bundles through into the very heart of the construction. With each movement he looked around nervously, but it was still early and no one appeared to be abroad, besides which the bonfire was strategically placed to obscure the view between it and the fence.

The shed was in a convenient place at the bottom corner of the garden just inside the fence, a couple of feet from the missing palings. He lifted the door off and began pushing the suitcases one by one through the fence. The ones on top were heavy but intact, whereas those at the bottom of the pile had been crushed almost to papier-mâché and fell to pieces when he lifted them. Pieces of brown-coloured bone and flesh fell out, leaving a trail of human debris. The shed was awash with dead flies and fly chrysalises as well as maggots. He threw the carrier bags containing heads* into the centre of the bonfire, and went back several times to pick up bits strewn along the way. When he had concealed everything in the bonfire, he tidied up the shed and put all the magazines and newspapers around the pile, closing the gap with more wood. On the top he placed an old car tyre to disguise whatever smells there might be. Periodically he checked the garden next door to see if anyone was about, but there was no sign of movement. Then he sprinkled lighter fuel on to the newspaper around the base, and set it alight.

The fire burned all day long. Nilsen watched it constantly, throwing on some extra wood whenever necessary. Children from the neighbourhood came to watch, and Nilsen warned them to keep their distance:

The large bonfire is blazing fiercely while I stand near, stone cold and in a nervous sweat. Three neighbourhood kids are gathered and it would seem in order if they danced around it. The devilish purity and innocence of children dancing around a mass funeral pyre would have a simple and solemn grandeur beyond the most empty and formally garish State funeral. The sparks, heat, hot air, smoke and energy of life arrowing skywards in a great visual display of living natural forces. Like some Viking ship glowing west-wards to Valhalla. I thought on those who now magnified

---

*One of them was the very bag he and Kenneth Ockendon had used to carry home their shopping. Remnants were not recognisable.

my empty life seeing their sweetness pervading the London air. I stood like an obedient usher, silenced by them and their powerful consuming presence. Through the open French windows of 195 the two large speakers rang out their 'Tubular Bells'. I remembered them and knew that they were not in the flames but in me, an integral part of me. Not for them the insulting monotony of a uniform and anonymous corporation cemetery. A mixing of flesh in a common flame and a single unity of ashes. The children turn away to resume their lives. The sun is setting on the glowing embers and I, weeping, drink the bottle dry.[22]

'I stood there amazed,' he later wrote, 'trying to comprehend what I had just done. I found it all hard to believe, that I, Des Nilsen, had actually done all that. It all seemed like some bad dream from which I would soon awaken or at best forget forever.'

As the fire died down, Nilsen returned occasionally to see if anything was visible. Spotting a skull in the centre, he crushed it into powder with a garden rake and smoothed the surface over. When there was nothing left but ashes, he placed some of the bricks which had been in the shed on to the ashes, to discourage any casual observer from scratching around. Then he washed the floor of the shed with disinfectant, allowed it to dry out and replaced the door. Finally he put the fence palings back into place and retreated indoors, comforting Bleep. 'It's all right,' he murmured, 'everything's all right now.' It had taken one complete day to vanish from the earth all traces, or as it turned out almost all traces, of six people.

Afterwards, Nilsen took a bath, dressed, and went by underground to Tottenham Court Road station. He wandered down to the Salisbury pub in St Martin's Lane, where he met a young man and took him back to Melrose Avenue in a taxi. They had satisfying sexual contact and slept soundly together. The next morning they walked to Willesden underground station and said their farewells. Nilsen never saw the young man again. He felt, perhaps, that the past was finally behind him and would never again intrude on the present.

This, he says, was the first overtly sexual encounter he had permitted himself since the murders had started two years before. Why? The long series of casual bedmates who had filled the years before Christmas 1978 had suddenly ceased with the first murder and were not resumed until the next six victims had disappeared once and for all. Why did Nilsen feel the need for normal sex, and the freedom to enjoy it, immediately after this ritual burning? Did the bonfire represent a release from imprisonment, the shedding of an irksome personality? Could he not hope to retrieve what was left of his former self as long as bodies remained on the premises as physical evidence of his new, murderous identity? And why deny himself sex during the period when those murderous impulses threatened to well up at any time? It cannot have been to protect people from himself, for he did not have sex with any of the men who subsequently died, and could hardly, therefore, regard sex as the trigger. Was it that sex was guilty and murder pure? Sex dirty, murder clean? Or was it the other way round, that he could not give himself sexually until he had exorcised in fire the demon he harboured within him?

But the demon was not exorcised. The nightmare continued, with five more people dying in 1981, often indiscriminately in so far as few of them held any interest for Nilsen. In fact, 1981 was a year of growing crisis in many respects, building towards a crescendo which was not subdued until his departure from 195 Melrose Avenue.

In the first place, Nilsen's continued neglect by the promotion panel at Denmark Street depressed and angered him. At the same time, he had been subjected to a series of petty robberies (often through his own carelessness) culminating in an attack in the street as he staggered back drunk from the Cricklewood Arms. He was overpowered, his jacket and shoes taken, and was left to lie in someone's front garden. Worse, there was one month's wages in the jacket, rather in excess of £300; he had to apply for money from the Department of Employment Benevolent Fund to tide him over. After that, he learnt not to take with him any more than he could afford to lose in one evening. His camera and projector had already been stolen in a previous incident. 'I became more and more depressed with the callousness of life,' he writes, adding that he was so debilitated and demoralised that he once collapsed in the street, and himself summoned an ambulance to take him to Park Royal Hospital. This combination of defeats was compounded by his self-imposed workload of dealing with union matters in the evening, for which he felt, rightly or wrongly, that he received scant regard. He threw himself into work, he says, 'believing each hour to be my last', and to avoid concentrating on the explosive cargo accumulating out of sight. He sometimes wondered how his colleagues would react if they knew all the things he had done. No matter how seriously he took his duties at the Jobcentre, they were insufficient to deflect his murderous impulses. 'God knows what I was going to do with all those bodies which were happening . . . It became like a disease.'

The final straw was an acute exacerbation of his always strained relations with the landlords.

Nilsen had never been an easy tenant. Irritatingly aware of what was and was not permitted by law, he resisted any scheme the landlords might propose which disregarded their legal obligations. From their point of view, he was not only uncooperative but obstructive. They wanted to know why the electric meters were empty, and why his rent was delayed. There had been occasions when Nilsen had returned home to find Asian men about to enter his flat, and they would then issue grave hints that they intended to 'modernise' the house and would need to have vacant possession. He had once written to the landlords' agents that 'I will not be intimidated into giving up my rights as a tenant no matter what kind of tactics this company adopts.'

One day in June he discovered that his entire flat had been vandalised. The television and record-player were smashed, as was the mirror. His clothes, bedding, chairs and carpets were covered in creosote to the point where they were completely unusable. Even the records were smothered in it. Everything he owned apart from the suit he was wearing was utterly destroyed, and he learnt that another flat upstairs had been accorded the same treatment. He contacted the police, who sent detectives to investigate and make a report (unaware that bodies were lying beneath the floor on which they were standing), but those responsible were never caught. It took Nilsen two weeks to restore any kind of order to the flat, but he was left with virtually nothing, and all wooden furniture was chucked into the garden, to await its later destiny as the basis of another bonfire. There was, however, one pleasant consequence of this incident. Nilsen had told the story at work, and was astonished when, a few weeks later, he was presented with a cheque for £85 which his colleagues had collected for him to rebuild his home. He wrote to them a letter which was displayed; it was one of the few expressions in gentle prose which he had ever committed to paper:

Dear Friends and Colleagues,

I am humbled by the quiet dignity and unsung qualities of support and encouragement I have received from all my colleagues at Denmark Street. A cynic like myself seems to know the price of everything and the value of nothing.

It is with a little half-guilt and humility that I gratefully accept this kind gift from fellow workers whose own personal financial situations are never 'overcomfortable'.

It is at times like this that I fail to fully articulate my feelings for your generous and caring response. Emerson (from his Journal of 1836) can express it better than I: 'Sympathy is a supporting atmosphere, and in it we all unfold easily and well.'[23]

Yours faithfully,
Des Nilsen

He could hardly have chosen a more ironic quotation, for Nilsen's personality at that very time was unfolding with the most profound unease. He had murdered four more people since the bonfire, and placed all of them under the floor. In August, the smell persisted in spite of his spraying disinfectant daily, and so one Friday evening he set about dealing with the problem.

I sat and deliberated this task reluctantly. I fortified myself with about half a bottle of drink before lifting up the floorboards. I removed the intact bundles one at a time, placed them on the kitchen stone floor and un-wrapped the bundles one at a time. I put the wrapping to one side. I removed the clothing from the bodies and set about dissecting them. The smell was grossly unpleasant and in some cases there existed large colonies of maggots. I dissected the bodies and wrapped the parts in white paper kitchen towel rolls of which I had an adequate supply. I tightly re-wrapped the parts in smaller compact bundles and put them to one side. I treated the three bodies in this fashion until all was complete and a number of bundles lay on the kitchen floor. I re-packed the bundles in the space under the floorboards, packed them with earth and deodorant tablets.[24]

As before, the internal organs were placed in separate bags and not consigned to the space under the floor, where only bones and flesh were to be stored from now on. These bags were taken to the bottom right-hand side of the garden and the contents spilled in the gap between the two fences. There was quite a lot, but it all disappeared in time, feeding the earth and its varied population.

The problem had been shifted, but not solved, and it was to be disastrously magnified within a month by the murder of Nilsen's twelfth victim. According to his own account, he still did not know when these killings were likely to occur, nor indeed if they were ever to occur again. It was only at the moment of strangulation that he 'knew' what was happening, and then nothing, not even a bomb-blast, would have stopped him. 'What I was doing had to be done — my eyes must have been staring.'[25] There was no room under the floorboards for the twelfth victim, so he had to be stuffed in the cupboard under the sink, where he obviously could not remain for long. Besides, the landlords had finally given up their efforts to prise Nilsen out of his flat, and had decided that he might go if they were to be conciliatory, even generous. The agent acting for the landlords commiserated with Nilsen for the trouble caused over the past year, and made a proposition on their behalf. There was a nice self-contained flat at 23 Cranley Gardens which he could have, and he would also receive £1,000 in compensation for the difficulties endured. In effect, of course, he was being bought out, and one might have expected his attachment to principle to raise some objection. But it was a fair offer, and he had more pressing reasons to get out of Melrose Avenue than the agent could ever divine. He was driven round to Cranley Gardens, accepted on the spot, and made arrangements to move at the beginning of October.

First, he had to get rid of the evidence which still littered the flat. Two days before he left, Nilsen built his third bonfire; on his last day of residence, it burned; the day he drove away in the removal van, it was reduced to cinders, the past once more incinerated, denied, renewed. This is how he told the police what he did:

I made a huge well-constructed bonfire using furnishings, cabinets and things from the house, and left a sizeable hollow at the centre of the structure. This I did the day before. Early in the morning, I lifted the floorboards and started to pack the packages into the centre of the wooden structure, the base of which was two large doors on house bricks. I did not replace the floorboards at this time. Going to the kitchen I opened the doors of the cupboard under the sink. I noticed that the body had become bloated. I removed the body and dragged it through the house and laid it inside the structure. I covered the entire structure with more wooden posts and palings, and all the bundles of paper from under the floorboards were pushed inside. The opening was sealed with more wood and the bonfire set alight. It was positioned about fifteen feet from a point exactly halfway between the french window and the kitchen windows. The fire burned fiercely, extraordinarily fiercely. The fire started early morning. There were spurts, bangs, cracks and hisses, a continual hissing and sizzling coming from the fire. This was what I took to be fat and other parts of the bodies burning.[26]

Any rubbish from the flat that he wanted to throw out was consigned to the flames, including the high platform bed he had constructed. One curious neighbour from the same house came to see what was going on. Nilsen told him that he was moving out the next day and was burning rubbish before he went. The neighbour was perfectly satisfied with this explanation, if he was ever really interested, and went on his way.

The next morning, as he waited for the removal van to transport his few belongings in a couple of tea-chests (the £1,000 would be useful perhaps to buy some more furniture), he sat and wondered whether he had left anything behind which a new tenant, or decorators, would notice.

I checked under the floorboards. I could see one or two bits and pieces of clothing maybe, but it was dark. I replaced the floorboards and nailed them up. I checked inside the house and there was nothing I could think of. I went out into the garden. I checked the bottom shed. There was nothing in there, except for damaged items from earlier. I went to the site of the recent fire and became aware of a large pile of ashes. Some of it looked like bone splinters or even small pieces of skull, probably not identifiable as skull to the casual observer. I took the garden roller and rolled it over the site several times hoping to crush yet further any bone fragments there might be. I stood back and had another think. It was then I remembered I had placed the hands and arms of Malcolm Barlow in a small hole next to the bush outside the window.

The larger bones he broke as best he could with a shovel, and flung them over into the waste ground behind the bottom fence. At least one of these turned up in the jaws of a neighbourhood dog some time later. Into the hole by the bush he shovelled several piles of ash. 'Driving away from 195 Melrose was a great relief.' It was 5 October 1981.

Sixteen months later, police officers searched the garden at various points indicated by Nilsen, and recovered over a thousand items of bone.

157

Perhaps it was bound to be a vain and forlorn hope, but as Nilsen settled into his attic flat he nursed the belief that his new conditions would conspire to prevent his criminal activities being repeated. At 23 Cranley Gardens there were no floorboards that could be prised up, nor was there a garden for his exclusive use; ease of disposal no longer existed. Two months after he moved in, there was an incident which greatly encouraged him. In the West End one evening he found a young man, paralysed through drink, lying in the street. He hailed a cab and took the man home to Cranley Gardens, cared for him, gave him his bed and made sure that he slept on his stomach in case he vomited during the night. The next morning he fed him a decent breakfast and went with him to the underground station to see him safely on his way. This was in December 1981. It was, Nilsen says, an act of kindness with no hideous consequences, an interpretation entirely corroborated by the young man, Kevin Sylvester, who declared that he was grateful for Nilsen's assistance that evening; he had indeed been rescued by a stranger whom he had no reason to regard as anything but benevolent. 'I felt elated and happy,' says Nilsen. 'He was alive and I had not been beyond control or anything. I felt really good and that the past was well behind me.'[27]

But it was not to be. Three men were strangled by Nilsen at Cranley Gardens, in March and September 1982 and in January 1983, and the methods used for disposing of the bodies were even more repugnant than before. After the first murder occurred, Nilsen placed the body in the wardrobe for a few days while he pondered what to do. The problem required urgent attention as he had a friend, Alan Knox, coming to stay for a short time. He decided that the safest course would be to dissect the body into small pieces and flush it down the lavatory. He carried the body into the bathroom and carried out the dissection in the bath itself. First he opened the stomach area and concentrated on the organs, chopping them on a cutting-board into small two-inch pieces and putting them down the lavatory in loads of about half a pound in weight each time. At this rate it threatened to be a long and laborious business, so he began cutting off large pieces which he boiled on the kitchen stove to make them disintegrate. The boiling could continue while he dealt with further dissection. The head was boiled in the large cooking pot, followed by the hands and feet, and the ribs, cut from the body one by one. Once boiled free of flesh, the bones were separated into smaller fragments and simply thrown in the dustbin, to be removed in the normal way by the council's refuse collectors. Meanwhile, flesh, hair and organs were sent down into the sewage. Nilsen was then left with some large bones which still had some flesh attached. The shoulder blades he hurled over the back garden fence into waste ground, while the skull, arm-bones, leg-bones and pelvis he placed in several bags, sprinkled with a large amount of salt, in the tea-chest in the corner of the room. He packed the tea-chest with material, and covered it with the red curtain he had salvaged from Melrose Avenue. There it stayed while Alan Knox was visiting, and there it remained until police removed the tea-chest and its contents eleven months later. (In the summer of 1982 he entertained an Irish youth for a weekend, without thinking once of the tea-chest in the corner.)

A similar procedure was followed with the next victim, except that he was put straight in the bath the day after the crime. He stayed in the bath for three days, Nilsen periodically changing the cold water in which he lay and, of course, still going to work every day (he had by now been posted to Kentish Town). On the fourth day he dissected the body in the bath, boiling the head, hands and feet and putting the rest into black plastic bags. One bag was hidden in a cubbyhole at the end of the bath (removed by Nilsen and placed in the wardrobe the day of his arrest), the other joined the remains in the tea-chest. Some flesh and organs were flushed down the lavatory,* but it appears likely that Nilsen took some larger pieces out of the flat in a bag and dumped them. In December 1982 Fred Bearman saw a black plastic bag lying on its side next to his allotment in Roundwood Park,

---

*It was these which eventually blocked the drains and led to Nilsen's arrest.

Willesden. It was open and had been, he thought, ravaged by dogs. The contents were spilling out. He saw what he thought was a rib-cage with a central spinal column, but he had no idea what kind of animal it could have come from. It looked quite horrific and revolting. Later that day he took his flat-mate, David Anfam, to have a look. Anfam thought it might have been the remains of a Christmas dinner, but he had never seen anything quite like it. Neither man touched the bag or reported it. Four days later it had gone, presumably collected by dustmen. What Bearman found was, however, too far away from Nilsen's flat to be positively connected with him, even with hindsight. Much more significant was the bag of entrails found by Robert Wilson and reported to the police in the summer of 1981 (see Appendix). They were in Dollis Hill Lane by Gladstone Park, where Nilsen frequently walked his dog. When asked about this, Nilsen thought it 'impossible' that he could have had a hand in it, but he now concedes that in a drunken condition he may well have discarded parts of a victim in this way. All that remained of this man were 'a bunch of keys, a digital watch, legs and pelvis, arms and a head.'

The last man to be murdered, Stephen Sinclair, was in the process of being butchered in much the same way as the previous two when Nilsen was arrested on 9 February 1983. The crepe bandages on Sinclair's arms were used to tie the bags into which he was placed. Dismemberment had not proceeded very far, and police were able to assemble the parts in the mortuary of Hornsey Police Station.

Dennis Nilsen's response to the outrage felt by most people who know how he disposed of the bodies is one of frank incomprehension. 'I can never quite understand a traditional and largely superstitious fear of the dead and corpses,' he writes.[28] Even when he was overwhelmed with remorse for his crimes in the months following his arrest, he saw no need to apologise for having 'desecrated' the bodies, except once when he acknowledged that he had denied the families of his victims the right to a gravestone. Other remand prisoners at Brixton pointed out to him that while they, as possible criminals, could conceive the act of murder without too

Wedding photograph
of Olav Nilsen and
Betty Whyte, Dennis
Nilsen's parents,
2 May, 1942.
(*Mrs Elizabeth Scott*)

Nilsen's class at
Fraserburgh Primary
School. Dennis
Nilsen, aged seven, is
in the centre of the
back row.
(*Mrs Elizabeth Scott*)

Dennis Nilsen at the age of six.
(*Mrs Elizabeth Scott*)

Aged fifteen, in army uniform, shortly after he joined the Junior Leaders' Regiment at Aldershot.
(*Mrs Elizabeth Scott*)

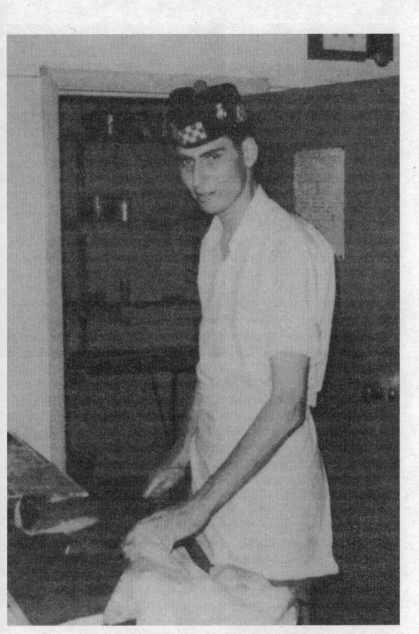

Nilsen acquired his skills as a butcher in the Army Catering Corps, where he was chef to several regiments in succession. (*Mrs Elizabeth Scott*)

Nilsen was Police Constable Q287 at Willesden Green Police Station between 1972 and 1973.
(*Mrs Elizabeth Scott*)

The mongrel bitch Bleep, who was Dennis Nilsen's companion from 1976 until his arrest in February 1983, and who shared two flats where fifteen murders were committed. It was Bleep who alerted Nilsen to the fact that Carl Stottor was still alive. She died under anaesthetic a few days after Nilsen's arrest.
(*Press Association*)

Above left, The manhole at the side of 23 Cranley Gardens. Plumbers discovered human flesh on its floor; *above right*, the tea-chest in the corner of the front room of Nilsen's flat. Under a thick velvet curtain, police found bags containing a torso, a skull and various bones. *Below*, the bathroom at 23 Cranley Gardens. In the bath Nilsen had dissected the bodies of John Howlett and Graham Allen. (*Metropolitan Police*)

Police photographs of Nilsen's wardrobe containing two plastic sacks. When these sacks were opened, their contents included two torsos, four arms, one boiled head, one partly boiled head, and a shopping-bag of internal organs. (*Metropolitan Police*)

23 Cranley Gardens, Muswell Hill, in north London. Nilsen occupied the attic flat from October 1981 until February 1983. Neighbours noticed that the front window at the top was always left wide open. Three people died in this flat, the bodies of two of them cut into small pieces and flushed down the lavatory. Blocked drains led to Nilsen's arrest. (*Metropolitan Police*)

The official police photograph of Dennis Nilsen, taken in February 1983. (*Metropolitan Police*)

much trembling, they could not understand, let alone forgive, the violation of dismemberment. It is this aspect of his
crimes which has caused the most public revulsion, but to
Nilsen it appears to be the least important. He was faced with
a problem, he says, which he had to resolve somehow. He
regards the murders themselves as unpardonable and disgusting, but the disposal of remains as merely the inevitable
consequence that flowed from them. In a much-quoted
sentence, written in the cell at Hornsey Police Station,
Nilsen said, 'The victim is the dirty platter after the feast
and the washing-up is a clinically ordinary task.' This is an
attitude not altogether unfamiliar to psychiatrists who have
had dealings with murderers, and some maintain that it
shows an innate grasp of logic which a feeling of outrage
would distort. The wrongful act, in their view, is to kill; once
a victim is dead, no amount of grotesque behaviour towards
the body should be allowed to divert one's horror from the
murder itself. One cannot hurt a corpse, after all, and if one
is more outraged by dissection of the dead than by extinction
of the living then one's moral priorities have gone awry.
Murderers do not generally suffer from this confusion.
Nilsen's attitude towards the dead is catastrophically confused in many other respects.

Nilsen took refuge in work with ever-growing commitment. Miss Leaman was grateful that he seemed happy to
take work home, including the drawing of graphs and charts
which most people avoid, and that he took pains with them.

Before Christmas of 1982, he received a telephone call
from his mother in Scotland. It was the first time they had
spoken in years. Mrs Scott regularly wrote Dennis a letter on
his birthday, and sent a Christmas card every year, but he
replied to neither. Her last letter had been typical of her usual
style. 'Dear Dennis,' she had written, 'Well, you'll be another
year older on the 23rd and I still don't know how you are
getting on. It will be seven years come Christmas since you
have been home.' She had said that she was enjoying herself
at last, after bringing up seven children, and wondered if
Dennis was ever thinking of marriage. This plea for news, like
the others, had been ignored. Now here she was suddenly

on the telephone. Janet Leaman remembers that he flew into her office and talked about the call for twenty minutes. While declaring indifference to his mother, his very garrulity on the subject betrayed him. He was pleased. It was a slender sign of normal human contact.

In addition to the fifteen murders admitted by Nilsen, there were a further seven attempts at murder (by his own reckoning) which failed for one reason or another. Of these, four people have been identified; the rest presumably either walk the streets today unaware that they were nearly killed, or have decided for their own purposes to keep silent.

Paul Nobbs

On 23 November 1981, Paul Nobbs, a nineteen-year-old student of Slavonic and East European Studies at the University of London, decided to miss his lecture and go instead to buy some books at Foyles. First, he thought he would have a drink at the Golden Lion in Dean Street, where he arrived about 1.30 p.m. He fell into conversation with a man who introduced himself as Des Nilsen and they chatted for about an hour. 'He wasn't the kind of run-of-the-mill Golden Lion type and seemed very intelligent,' said Nobbs. They left the pub together and spent about fifteen minutes in Foyles, when Nilsen suggested Nobbs should accompany him to his flat in Muswell Hill for something to eat. Nobbs agreed. The date was seven weeks after Nilsen's move into 23 Cranley Gardens, and a few weeks before the happy encounter with Kevin Sylvester. It was also, incidentally, Nilsen's thirty-sixth birthday.

They stopped at Sainsbury's on the way home and bought some chops, some rum and some Coca-Colas, and arrived at the flat in time for the television news at 5.45 p.m. They spent the evening, after Nilsen had cooked a meal, drinking and watching 'Panorama', at which point Nobbs telephoned his mother in Watford and said he would be home soon.

162

Later, he felt rather ill as a result of the Bacardi, and called again to say that he would not come home after all, but would stay with friends. The two men undressed and got into bed; some tentative sexual activity took place, but they were both too tired to bring it to a conclusion. They fell asleep.

At two in the morning, Paul Nobbs woke up with a throbbing headache and went to the kitchen for a glass of water. He sat on the sofa for about ten minutes, trying to contain the raging pain in his head and feeling nauseous. He had no idea why. Nilsen stood by the door. Eventually, they both went back to bed, and Nobbs fell asleep within five minutes.

At 6 a.m. he woke again, turned on the light and saw himself in the mirror above the kitchen sink. There was a deep red mark around his neck and across his throat, his face was red, bruised and sore, and the whites of his eyes had turned completely red. His throat felt sore and he was shaking. Nilsen got up and told him, 'God, you look awful,' and advised him to see a doctor. Before he left, Nilsen gave him his address and telephone number, with the information that he could find him by taking the underground to Highgate or a Number 134 bus. He hoped they might meet again.

Nobbs staggered down the street, barely able to keep his balance. He went to Malet Street and met his Polish language tutor who immediately arranged for him to be seen at the clinic of University College Hospital in Gower Street, just a walk from the building. Another student, Christopher George, accompanied Nobbs, who was shaking so badly that he knocked over a coffee cup in the waiting-room and could not light his own cigarette. Doctors gave him tranquillisers and eye ointment and confirmed that his symptoms were consistent with a classic case of strangulation. He took about five days to recuperate at home, and the mark around his neck remained for three months. He did not report the matter to the police, and told doctors he had been mugged by a stranger.

Paul Nobbs did not care to think about the incident, but he realised that if indeed someone had tried to strangle him, it must have been Des Nilsen. Yet this realisation did not conform with his impression of Nilsen: 'He seemed a fairly reasonable man and in no way strange.'

Nilsen says, 'The clearest recollection I've got is that I had a tie around his neck and he was on the bed. I was panicking. I remember trying to revive him because his heart was still beating. I must have thrown a glass of cold water in his face as well.'[29]

The two men never met again, although Paul Nobbs did spy Nilsen in the Golden Lion about a year later and avoided talking to him. 'I am very happy that he did not die,' says Nilsen now.[30]

Toshimitsu Ozawa

On the evening of New Year's Eve 1982, Vivienne McStay and Monique Van-Rutte were cooking a meal at their flat in Cranley Gardens when there was a knock at their door. It was Des Nilsen, the man who lived upstairs. He invited them to come up and watch television with him, but they declined, partly because they were busy preparing dinner, and partly because Nilsen appeared drunk, swaying from side to side. He left them with the impression that he was very annoyed by their refusal, but suggested none the less that they join him for a drink later at a local pub. Then he went back upstairs.

They heard him leave the house at about 11 p.m., and return with someone else at about 12.30 a.m. on New Year's Day. An hour later they heard a great commotion from upstairs, voices raised, banging and crashing, the dog barking furiously. They were quite afraid until they heard people rushing downstairs, someone fall, sobbing, and the front door slam. They wanted to see if Nilsen was all right and met him on the stairs, carrying a torch. He appeared very drunk.

The man who had run out of the house in terror was Toshimitsu Ozawa, who later told the police that he thought Nilsen had intended to kill him. Nilsen had approached him calmly, with a tie outstretched between his hands. At first Ozawa had thought he was joking. When the gesture was repeated, he took it seriously. When the police read out

Ozawa's statement, Nilsen commented, 'I find that frightening.'[31]

Douglas Stewart

Stewart, aged twenty-six, met Nilsen in a West End pub on the evening of 10 November 1980, and agreed to go with him to Melrose Avenue for a late-night drink. They listened to records. At about 1 a.m. Stewart said he ought to be making his way home, and Nilsen told him he could stay the night if he wished. Not being homosexual, Stewart refused the suggestion that they share a bed, which Nilsen accepted without fuss, and Stewart fell asleep in the armchair. Some time later he woke to find that his feet had been tied and that Nilsen was standing behind him pulling the tie around his neck. He fought, and managed to scratch Nilsen and draw blood. Nilsen fell and offered no resistance; he simply told Stewart to take his money and leave, but Stewart was not interested in robbery. Then he noticed that Nilsen was staring at a large bread-knife which he held in his right hand. Stewart thought he must at all costs keep him quiet, so they chatted for about ten minutes, and the knife was laid down. Stewart was convinced that the knife would have been used to attack him. He left the house at about 4 a.m., ran down the street and called the police. Two officers from Kilburn Police Station picked him up and went with him to Melrose Avenue, where Nilsen appeared surprised. They formed the impression that this had been a homosexual encounter which had gone wrong, and that neither man could be believed entirely. The incident was filed for report to C.I.D. branch. There was a red mark on Stewart's neck, but no evidence that Nilsen had been injured.

When parts of Douglas Stewart's statement were read to Nilsen he could recall nothing of the incident, though he conceded that the story was quite possibly true in essence. He denied, however, that he would ever have tied the man's legs or threatened him with a knife.

165

Carl Stottor

Carl Stottor, aged twenty-one and unemployed, met Des Nilsen at the Black Cap in Camden Town one evening in April 1982. They went back to Cranley Gardens for a drink, where Stottor consumed too much and became depressed. Eventually they went to bed, and slept straight away. No attempt at any sexual activity was made by either of them. Stottor then remembers waking up and not being able to breathe. Nilsen was behind him, and something seemed to be round his neck. He thought at first that Nilsen was trying to release or untangle whatever it was, but the pressure increased. Stottor could not see properly, could not swallow, and felt dizzy. He heard Nilsen say to him 'Keep still.' He felt his tongue had swollen up. He kept periodically falling into unconsciousness, until he was being carried into the bath-room. The next thing he knew was that he was in the bath, and was being pushed under the water. Several times his head was put under, with him swallowing water, and several times he came up again. The last time he was pushed under he could no longer resist. Then he felt Nilsen was lifting him out of the bath and placing him on the bed, where the dog was licking his face. He does not know how long he stayed in the flat, probably more than a day, as he kept falling asleep for long periods. When he saw the condition of his face in the mirror he was shocked. There was a red mark around his neck. Nilsen told him that he had got caught up in the zipper of the sleeping-bag which lay on top of the bed. He was inclined to believe this, as the alternative seemed incredible at the time. He attributed his experience in the bath to a nightmare. They left the flat together, and Nilsen hoped they would meet again. Stottor said yes, but actually had no intention of renewing the acquaintance. Stottor went to the casualty department of the London Hospital in Whitechapel where examination showed that his condition was consistent with having been strangled. Stottor denied this interpret-ation as he did not want to have dealings with the police, and in any case he would not have been able to prove the matter

166

without witnesses. A part of him still wondered whether he had dreamt it all; the distinction between conscious memory and what might have been unconscious imaginings was smudgy, to say the least.

The reason Carl Stottor has only intermittent impressions of that night is that he frequently lapsed into unconsciousness, and probably came to within seconds of death. Nilsen had strangled him from behind, had carried him to the bath, and had held him under water in the bath until he ceased struggling. At that point Stottor's ears, throat and eyes were in excruciating pain, his lungs were filling with water and his grasp of what was happening to him was unclear; he had, however, found the strength to say, 'Please, no more; please, stop.' After that, he gave up. When Nilsen lifted him out of the bath and put him on the bed, he thought he was dead. The body was cold and still. But the dog, Bleep, knew differently; it was she who saw the signs of life, and started licking Carl Stottor's face, which Stottor remembers. What he does not remember is that as soon as Nilsen realised the body was alive, he covered it with blankets and got into bed with it, spending the next several hours warming it with his own body heat, rubbing and quickening the body until Carl Stottor came totally back to life. He also put on all the bars of the electric fire.

This is a most interesting story, for it throws new light upon Nilsen's state of mind. In the case of Paul Nobbs, the murderer actually prevented himself from completing the act; he stopped wanting to kill *while* he was killing. But with Stottor, Dennis Nilsen thought the murder was over, that he had a dead body on his hands, and when alerted by his dog that the man was alive he spent hours trying to revive him. He could have finished the job pretty easily; but he had already reverted to the ordinary non-violent Des Nilsen, and it was this Des Nilsen who saved Carl Stottor from the murderer Nilsen. This incident at least shows that the killer instinct was not constant, was perhaps not conscious, and possibly not voluntary.

Incidentally, it was Nilsen's recollection of the event, scribbled down on a piece of paper headed 'Unscrambling

Behaviour' at Hornsey Police Station, which enabled the
police officers to trace Carl Stottor, who confirmed that the
dog's licking his face had been his first memory on regaining
consciousness, and that he had slept afterwards for a very
long time. Nilsen's account of that night came first and
Stottor's matched it, not the other way round.

'I am grateful for snapping out of the killing trance in the
cases of attempted murder,' writes Nilsen. Bleep, it appears,
may have saved more than one life. Whenever a cigarette was
left burning, or fell to the floor, the dog would bark furiously
and bring Nilsen sharply back into the real world. 'I could
not really have meant to kill the others at all as I successfully
pulled back, regained control of myself and did nothing
whatsoever to prevent them leaving.'[32] This sounds like *post
facto* self-justification, but it is more the result of bewildered
introspection, for whoever heard of a would-be murderer
who accompanies his victim to the bus-stop and gives him his
name and address, expecting their acquaintance to continue?
The attempted murders suggest that there were two Nilsens
at large, and that the one had only sporadic control over the
other.

Implications and suggestions such as these would henceforth be for the court to consider and for psychiatrists to
unravel. They would in the meantime be for Dennis Nilsen
to ponder during his eight months of remand, and presumably
for the rest of his life. He had, according to his own lights,
offended against his own most cherished principles and
values:

> I like to see people in happiness.
> I like to do good.
> I love democracy.
> I detest any criminal acts.
> I like kids.
> I like all animals.
> I love public and community service.
> I hate to see hunger, unemployment, oppression, war,
> aggression, ignorance, illiteracy, etc.
> I was a trades union officer.

I was a good soldier and N.C.O.
I was a fair policeman.
I was an effective civil servant.
STOP. THIS ALL COUNTS FOR NOTHING when I can kill fifteen men (without any reason) and attempt to kill about nine others — in my home and under friendly circumstances.
Am I mad? I don't feel mad. Maybe I am mad.[33]

With what can only be seen as a desperate need to reassure himself, or more, to rediscover himself, Nilsen returned time and again to a rehearsal of those qualities he could discern within him that seemed so hideously out of tune with the offences laid against him. 'I do not like the sight of blood, I despair at the very thought of people in pain, I am repelled by the idea of suffering.'[34] He wrote to his mother that he could scarcely come to terms with the fact that it was he at the centre of this notorious case, and not someone else. The period on remand would give him pause to reflect on and absorb the truth with greater honesty than he had ever done before and to prepare himself for the justice to which his responsible side wished his demonic side to submit. 'I must find the strength,' he wrote, 'to face with dignity a public vengeance for the vanished blood that dried on my hands.'[35] 'The glutinous dread of past evil is still lying sharply in my eyes.'[36]

Remand was also to show the volatility of his temperament under stress.

8

REMAND

Dennis Nilsen referred to 9 February 1983 as 'the day help arrived.' He went through the motions of work at the Job-centre in Kentish Town, his mind nailed to the contemplation of an arrest which he knew must be imminent. Before leaving the office, he turned to his assistant Don Stow and said, 'If I am not in tomorrow, I will be either ill, dead, or in jail.' They both laughed.

On the way home, he bought a tin of dog food as usual, and a few items of food for himself, these gestures of normality cushioning him against what was to come.

My heart began to beat very fast as I walked down Cranley Gardens. I approached the house and I knew instinctively that something was out of place, i.e. that nothing seemed out of place. The house was almost in total darkness. I opened the front door and stepped into the dark hallway. On my left the front room door opened and I could see three large men in plain clothes. That's it! My mind began to race in all directions.

He had rehearsed what he would say ('I'd better come down to the station and help you with your inquiries'), but there were a few more seconds of freedom to which Nilsen clung. D.C.I. Jay said, 'I've come about your drains.' Nilsen expressed surprise that the police should concern themselves with blocked drains, and wondered if the other two men were health inspectors. They all went upstairs to the attic flat, and the conversation proceeded (in Nilsen's version):

'The reason I'm interested in your drains is that they are blocked with human remains.'

'Good God, that's terrible! Where did it come from? This is a big house.'

'It could only have come from your flat. We've confirmed that.'

Then Nilsen said he would come to the station.

'I must caution you,' said D.C.I. Jay. 'I don't need to tell *you* anything about that.'

'No,' replied Nilsen. 'I will consider myself cautioned.'[1] The police had already discovered that D.A. Nilsen had once been a probationary constable, and would therefore be familiar with the procedure. But they were not prepared for the gush of unburdening which followed throughout the next week, as Nilsen, for the first time, released his ghastly secret. He could not even wait until they reached the station; he started talking in the police car, and from that moment there was no stopping him. He wanted to talk. He needed to talk. Saying it all would be the first step towards a long and seemingly endless path of introspection.

Mr Jay promised that the police would look after Nilsen's dog. From his cell at Hornsey Police Station Nilsen could hear her whining, but he declined the offer to see her, as a further parting would only distress her more. She died a week later under anaesthetic. 'I am ashamed that her last days should be so painful. She had always forgiven me everything, and nothing but me could ever break her heart. She never let me down, but in the moment of her greatest crisis I was not there.' What he would miss most about Bleep was the fact that, like all dogs, her responses were genuine, not counterfeit. In a revealing phrase, he admitted that 'her great redeeming feature was that she was not in my image'.[2]

On arrival at Brixton Prison, Dennis Nilsen was made

quickly aware of the notoriety which preceded him. 'You evil bastard, Nilsen,' shouted one prisoner through the door of the reception cell. Having put his own clothes in a cardboard box, he was issued with prison uniform (brown trousers and blue striped shirt) and marched off to the hospital wing as a Category A maximum security prisoner, Number B62006.

When he first went to Brixton, Nilsen's mood was one of resignation and relief, coupled with a determination to co-operate fully to secure his own conviction and await his fate. He assumed that, until the court heard the evidence and made its decision, he would in accordance with the law be regarded as innocent. It was his belief that he was not so treated that gradually changed his mood into one of defiance.*

He first objected to the imposition of prison uniform upon someone who was merely remanded in custody, but relented when it was made clear to him that no exception could or would be made in his case. The problem would erupt again six months later with profound consequences. Nilsen resented his Category A status because he could see no reasonable justification for it. He was not likely to escape, or to intimidate witnesses, or to commit suicide (he thought). In his view, the co-operation he had given to the police should be recognised, not punished; police officers were sympathetic to this attitude, but had no power to influence Home Office policy. It is an interesting comment on Nilsen's perception of reality that he could admit a series of ghastly acts, and be surprised if people reacted with hostility towards him.

Nilsen was placed in a cell for twenty-three and a half hours every day, with half an hour for supervised exercise with a prison officer. Every few days he and other Category A prisoners would be moved to different cells. They were allowed no association and precious little in the way of privi-

---

*The author has given a written undertaking to the governor of Brixton Prison that he will not publish details of conversations held on prison visits. Information in this chapter derives partly from letters which passed through the prison censor, partly from notes prepared by Dennis Nilsen for the author.

leges. Like other remand prisoners, Nilsen was permitted his
own money to supplement the standard 'income' of 88p a
week, as many cigarettes as he could afford, and eventually a
transistor radio in his cell. For the first three months he was
taken at regular intervals to Highgate Magistrates Court to be
further remanded in custody while the police completed their
gathering of evidence, but was sometimes not permitted to
wash and shave before a court appearance. When he was told
that there was not the staff or time available to supervise his
washing, he volunteered to sacrifice his half-hour of exercise
and use that time to wash. This was refused. Although he was
resident in the hospital wing, he had not once been medically
examined.* Dr Bowden saw him for conversations with a
view to preparing his psychiatric report for the prosecution.
Nilsen's experience as a union branch secretary and his
natural Buchan rebelliousness predisposed him towards a
seditious attitude in prison, which earned him a reputation
among warders for awkwardness and arrogance. From his
point of view, he merely wanted to see the prison rules
applied properly, and he was frustrated that his voice should
no longer be heard as it had been in the C.P.S.A.

Friendships were formed invisibly in prison. Inmates
would have long conversations through walls or shouting
down corridors, and Nilsen took to the 'comradeship' of
prison life. We do not have to rely solely on his word for this.
One man who was in the cell next to his for a time subsequent
sent him a letter. 'You did a lot for me, those ten days I was
with you. I still look back to those joke sessions we used to
have . . . Keep your chin up, and good luck for the future.'

The despair which he could perceive in the 'body language'
of other inmates excited Dennis Nilsen's latent and rarely
expressed humility. They had wives and children to worry
about, whereas he felt that 'I have the least problems of

---

*An electroencephalogram (EEG) test might have been useful.
EEG abnormalities occur four times more frequently in cases of homicide
than other cases. (*British Journal of Psychiatry*, vol. III, p. 1115, 1969.)
It is fair to add that the precise value of EEG findings is now more open to
dispute.

anyone in this prison.' Furthermore, their crimes could be blamed at least partly on poverty and unemployment – the cruel circle of deprivation. His could not. 'I feel I have no reasonable excuse . . . I must be one of the few guilty men in our block.'[3]

Trivial incidents helped bolster morale and instil in Nilsen the feeling of solidarity which he most prized. On the other hand, morale could be easily deflated. On being moved from one cell to another, he had not been given a chamber pot. In the middle of the night he rang the bell for the attendant night nurse, who told him that his cell could not be opened until the morning and that he should shit on the floor.[4]

Some inmates were so frequently on hunger-strike as their only form of protest that the event barely warranted notice. Nilsen did it twice for a few days in order to break the monotony. Besides, he wrote, 'It is perfectly feasible to eat normal rations here and still remain effectively on hunger-strike.'[5] It was a remark illustrative of his liability to mis-represent through humour.

The worst depression of his early confinement arose, strangely, from the denial of his privilege to attend a church service. He was still not a religious man and was hardly amenable to the blandishments of priests, though he enjoyed regular chats with the Methodist minister who made no attempt to impose religious content on the conversation. But the weekly service was a welcome interval, until it was suggested to Nilsen that his presence there disturbed other inmates who did not wish to be contaminated by such a monster. He wrote, 'The prison shepherd puts a strong guard on the 99 in the fold who want to get out. He goes out to seek the lost sheep and when he finds it he cuts its throat because it will not fit into the fold.'[6] Nilsen had been trying hard to foster the impression that he was one among many, that he was human and belonged with humans. The blow shattered his illusion in a moment, reminding him that the offences with which he was charged set him far beyond the pale where he was destined to remain, in a solitary confine-ment more severe than that represented by the prison cell. He wrote to his mother the shortest letter of his entire life, telling her to forget him as he was already in the tomb.

I first met Dennis Nilsen on 20 April 1983, and we had corresponded for three weeks before that. I sent a letter to Brixton Prison in March, together with a copy of one of my earlier books. On 30 March I received the first letter on lined prison notepaper, every inch of the four sides used up to avoid waste, which began, 'Dear Mr Masters, I pass the burden of my past actions on to your shoulders.'[7]

I could have had no notion, at that stage, that the flood of letters, often more than one a day, would build into an impressive archive measuring a man's mood as he contemplated his fate, and full of iconoclasm, humour, anger and despair; nor that I would be virtually Nilsen's only visitor and confidant in the coming months. I have to admit that I did not find it a burden. It would be easy and fruitless to condemn, but arduous and worthwhile to discern, if I could, the source of a tragic disturbance. It was in his second letter that Nilsen warned me I might be distressed by what I read, in notes that he was preparing for his solicitor, Ronald Moss, with specific instructions that they be passed to me after his trial. That alone, at the very outset, was revealing, for a man who knows the emotion of distress and is alive to its causes cannot be amoral. He used this very adjective himself. As he sat and thought and wrote about the past, he described himself as 'an amoral John Bunyan who is making progress backwards in all directions',[8] but the concept of morality, albeit severely crippled, was apparent in his musings on the images which filled his mind, images of the dead, images of which he knew he would never be relieved. Picturing himself on the last weekend at Cranley Gardens with the body of Stephen Sinclair before him, he wrote a poem which suggests turmoil beneath calm:

> I try to smile
> Despite the vengeance looking at me,
> Covered in your tomato paste,
> A man of many parts
> I try to forget.

Even the perfume of your passing
Lingers on.
More problems now
With all your bits and pieces.
I try to run,
And pinioned to this spot
In acres full of you,
Of dust and bones.
I try to weep,
With you looming large in my cell,
Of problems to the grave.
I try, I try
To unravel enigmas,
And each way I turn
I'm still holding you.
I try to smile
But you're not smiling now.
In April death is dead
And all the new life lives
Upon our garbled inquest.[9]

From the letters already exchanged, I expected a sensitive and introspective man. At our first meeting we sat opposite one another across a small table, and I saw an assertive man, bristling with confidence and swagger, amazingly relaxed as he slouched with an arm over the back of the chair, totally in command and behaving as if he was interviewing me for a job. He gave forth an impression of intellectual intensity, coupled with a contemptuous disregard for appearances. He was polite (he stood to shake hands, for example, and never failed to do so subsequently), but strangely casual. When the fifteen minutes allowed for visits had elapsed, he asked me to call in any time, as if it were to a local pub. Of course, the circumstances were odd, we were each sizing up the other, and there were two warders present in the room. Later, our talks were much less strained. Yet one clear inference from this first meeting remained constant throughout: the divorce between the Nilsen who wrote and the Nilsen who spoke was marked to an unusual degree. All of us conceal in conversation clues to personality which we happily reveal on paper, because the added distance of writing lends protection and encourages the risks of intimacy. Nilsen also maintained that a lifetime of public service laid on top of the inherent 'shame' of his sexuality had taught him to wear an 'official' face. Yet neither explanation quite accounts for the gulf between his reflective writing and his assertive conversation.

On 21 April, the day after this initial meeting, Nilsen surprised everyone at his routine appearance at Highgate Magistrates Court by declaring that he wished to discharge legal aid. Ronald Moss was completely taken aback and discussed with him at length what he meant. Did he intend to instruct another solicitor because he was dissatisfied with Moss? No, Nilsen was adamant that he had no complaint with his legal representation, but wanted to dispense with legal aid altogether. Henceforth he would defend himself. The magistrate was even more perplexed and seemed not quite sure what to do. Nilsen was asked three times if he realised the implications of his request, and three times he replied that he did. At root he was frustrated by his treatment at Brixton, where every application made to the governor or through his solicitor to the Home Office was ignored, and he found the notion of innocence before trial ruefully funny. The final straw had been the decision by church-going inmates that they did not wish to be soiled by his company.*
He wrote to me that he would battle on alone, and that if he were going to fail he would do so in his own way, with his 'integrity' intact. I noticed the interpretation he implied in the word 'failure', not failure to win his case, but failure to stand up to the 'system'. He was still the union branch secretary hostile to abuses of organised authority. He knew it would be difficult, but not impossible, to conduct his own defence, and he did not intend to withhold any of the truth. He was angry about what he thought were leaks to the press from within the prison and/or from the police. I noted in my

---

*In fact, though Nilsen did not know it at the time, none of the inmates had complained. The governor had made the decision as a precaution in case they might.

diary, 'It is alarming how easily he assumes conspiracy and corruption.' I further wrote, 'Though his suspicion of the venality and awfulness of all authority is perhaps exaggerated, it is rooted in a healthy distrust of any humbug. And it is perhaps right that he should be aggrieved at the denial of all his freedoms when he is only on remand.' I thought that he wanted me to know everything to test whether I should still be able to look him in the face afterwards. Could a relationship based upon trust survive the revelation of such iniquity?

Ronald Moss accepted Nilsen's decision, as he must, but wondered whether this was the right way to make his protest. He respected the man, intuited his loneliness, and wanted the best possible outcome for his former client. He let it be known that if Nilsen were to change his mind, he would be available. As it turned out, Nilsen would discharge legal aid twice more, and twice more apply for it to be renewed. Five weeks before his trial, when Moss had already written his brief for counsel and while a psychiatrist appointed by the court, Dr MacKeith, was preparing his report, he elected to instruct a new solicitor with quite a different approach to his case, Ralph Haeems. These changes of strategy were not as abrupt as they seemed. They derived both from the erratic emotional state of Nilsen himself, and from the pressures of cellular confinement at Brixton. The Nilsen who kept control, who organised, finally succumbed to the Nilsen who felt trapped and despondent. The two sides of his character, locked in perpetual disequilibrium, would not be reconciled.

On 28 April he appeared without legal representation at Highgate and complained that he was afforded no facilities to prepare his defence and that confidential papers were removed from his cell. He was told these were matters he should take up with the prison governor. By 6 May he had been granted a renewal of the legal aid order, and on 26 May he was committed for trial at the Central Criminal Court on five charges of murder and two of attempted murder. On 15 July he discharged the legal aid order again, though Mr Justice Farquharson told him frankly he thought the move unwise. Legal aid was renewed at Nilsen's request on 5 August, as the direct result of an incident at Brixton Prison.

At the end of July, Nilsen refused to wear prison uniform in accordance with his understanding of the 1964 Statutory Prison Rules. He was therefore not allowed to leave his cell to 'slop out'. On August 1 his chamber-pot was overflowing and he shouted through the window of his cell door that everyone should stand clear; he then threw the contents of the pot out, and splashes hit some prison officers. In the fracas which followed Nilsen's glasses were removed and smashed, he received a black eye and lost a tooth. He was due to appear at the Old Bailey on August 5 to announce his decision on legal aid after a week's time for reflection allowed by the court. I saw him on August 4 and he asked me to contact Ronald Moss to have him present in court in order that he might re-instruct him. Moss resumed the case on August 5. An adjudication panel heard the charges against prison discipline which were levelled at Nilsen on 9 August. He was found guilty of assaulting prison officers and given fifty-six days' punishment withdrawing all privileges, including the right to smoke cigarettes. He maintained that he had assaulted no one, but was not believed; the panel decided that he was lying.

Later in August, he tore up some of his depositions (he says in order to have something to do – he only destroyed the least important papers) and was placed in a 'strip cell' for having committed an 'irrational act'. Nilsen's response to this was that the papers were his to do with as he chose, and that anyway it was an irrational act to vote Conservative, but one was not punished for it by enforced nakedness. Finally, some autobiographical papers entitled 'Orientation in Me', which covered his sexual history, were not among the papers returned to him after his period in strip cell. The prison authorities made an internal inquiry, but the papers were not found, and were assumed to have been 'removed' by persons unknown.

Nilsen's behaviour began to show signs of paranoia. He went so far as to accuse the prison governor (in a letter to me) of stealing postage stamps from his letters, and he did not appear to be joking. His reasonable justification was that when his letters were stopped by the censor, envelopes bearing his stamps were not returned. He said the governor had called him an 'impertinent wretch' and told him he was behaving like a schoolgirl. On one of my visits, he walked out of the room when the warder said he could not smoke, and had to be coaxed back in. One of the warders had apparently told him with reference to another prisoner who might try to hang himself that he (the warder) would willingly hang on the suicide's legs. Nilsen's emotional state swung from one extreme to the other, including compassion for a cleaner who had smuggled him a roll-up cigarette, and warm feelings towards a former female colleague who visited him while she was heavily pregnant; he cherished, he said, 'the nearness of new innocent life to such a mess of guilt as I am myself'. The remark betrayed a degree of egomania of which he was himself quite unaware.

By September Nilsen's resistance had broken, and he was uncharacteristically submissive, openly indifferent to what happened to him. He was due to discharge legal aid yet again on September 19 (and request permission for me to sit with him in the dock), until another prisoner mentioned the name of Ralph Haeems, and it was this solicitor who took over his case forthwith. The judge warned that the court would tolerate no further applications from Nilsen.

Throughout this tempestuous time, his relationship with me gradually developed into real loyalty. Whatever happened to his legal representation, the one connection 'outside' which he could not envisage breaking was mine, and he frequently claimed that my visits and support gave him the will to continue when he was at his lowest. Naturally I knew well enough that part of this loyalty sprang from the knowledge that I and I alone was going to tell his story from his point of view. It was not fame that he sought; on the contrary, he felt bitter that his good work for the union went unnoticed, while (understandably) his crimes brought the spotlight of public attention burning in on him. He would have liked, he said, to make a mark in his career, not be notorious for these dark acts. So he did not rely upon me to spread his name about — that would be done anyway — but to display the clean linen as well as the dirty. I imagined also that he might be a clever manipulator using me for his own ends; he could not have escaped detection for four years without some native cunning.

I was now fast becoming his mouthpiece, his only contact with the outside world, and I should not underestimate his ability to engineer situations which might make me his moral representative.

I was especially alarmed one day when he intimated that he would need to see all the exhibits to be presented by the prosecution (this was at a time when he had no solicitor), including the photographs taken by the police photographer. I knew and he knew that these pictures included nauseating shots of skulls, a half-boiled severed head, a bag full of human entrails, and the separate limbs of Stephen Sinclair. He had not seen them, but he wanted to, and showed no sign of fear. Frankly I found this chilling, as I could only imagine that the contemplation of such photographs in a lonely prison cell would corrode the soul. But I forgot that Nilsen had gone beyond that; he had not seen photographs, but he had seen the real man, and had dismembered his body, and had looked at him afterwards.

The reasons for Nilsen's loyalty to me were born of a simple (some might say naive) reverence for principle which was elevated in his mind to the status of a god, the only god he worshipped. It was the one constant factor in his turbulent life, and it remained strong in spite of the fact that he knew his offences had violated his own most deeply-held principles as well as those of society. He clung to it with passion. Two incidents among many might serve to illustrate the point. A rumour had spread in prison that I was a fraud, a secret journalist in the employ of a tabloid newspaper. Nilsen was so angry that he refused to see his solicitor and counsel as a protest to demonstrate that he would not suffer my honour to be impugned in this way. He expected an apology from the assistant governor who had made the allegation. Once he had given his trust, he would not dilute it or allow it to be challenged. He nursed and protected it with the stubbornness of a child; to those who did not know him, these impulsive reactions might appear petulant. A similar conclusion could be drawn from the other incident I want to introduce. During a conversation between cells, an inmate launched into an attack upon Nilsen, telling him that the only reason he spoke to the rest of them was to collect material which he would then sell to newspapers. He had until then rejoiced in the small acts of comradeship in prison, and that he could be suspected of betraying his last friends for money hurt him. He withdrew into morose silence for three days.

Nilsen's moods in prison were kaleidoscope, shifting from elation to gloom, from resignation to despair, from regret about the past to hope for the future. They were rarely equable. His most robust and jubilant period followed his discovery that he was in love with another prisoner on the block. The man was David Martin, himself the object of much press attention at the time as he had been on the run prior to his arrest and was now awaiting trial on a number of serious charges.* When those newspapers more interested in scandal than news got wind of the fact that Martin and Nilsen were in the same wing at Brixton, they invented a story to the effect that the two men were enjoying a passionate love affair. This was both more than and less than the truth. Their relationship was never sexual, but it did evolve into a tie of affection and confidence which was important to them both. David Martin, habitually reticent and reluctant to talk to anyone, found himself able to chat at length to Nilsen when they walked together in the exercise yard, revealing much about his life that he withheld from others. For Nilsen, ever the 'monochrome man' incapable of compromise, the friendship reached deeper levels and engaged his emotions to the point of abandon:

> If I was sentenced to a choice of either freedom or fifty years in prison with him I would without question make the latter option. I can't fully understand why him? Why doesn't really matter. I'm really alive and vibrant and there

---

* Convicted in October 1983 of malicious wounding and other offences. Committed suicide in his cell at Parkhurst Prison, Isle of Wight, in March 1984. Another prisoner subsequently wrote to Nilsen saying, 'I am sure if you were in the same prison with him, it would not have happened because he would have told you how he was feeling and you could have talked him out of it, like you did before in Brixton.'

is no one in Britain who I would change places with now that he is here . . . If I kill myself, I will no longer be able to think about him . . . Few really beautiful and wonderful things have ever happened to me . . . This is perhaps the most glorious event of them all. Providence has not forgotten me.

Inspired by this unexpected affection (the third such in his life after Terry Finch and Derek Collins, and eclipsing them both in intensity), Nilsen wrote a poem entitled 'Danger', expressing his fear of rejection if ever he were to declare himself, as well as fear lest the relationship compromise Martin's reputation with the tabloids:

> I am at the peak of feeling
> When I shield him from me,
> And all the secret places
> Wherein sleeps my emotion.
> I have a lead-lined skin,
> Not so much to keep him out
> As keep my power in.[10]

The piece is interesting in its implication that someone needs to be 'shielded' from the 'power' of his emotions; others in the past had been less fortunate. He also intimated that it was 'perverse to be happy after lives are silent'.

So deeply did he think about this other prisoner that Nilsen hoped their trials would be concurrent and that they would pass into history together. (He was gratified to the extent that they would share the same solicitor and advocate.) The qualities and faults which he saw in the man were more often than not the qualities and faults which he wanted to possess himself. 'He is the timeless expression of me, myself. His happiness is my happiness. His misery is my misery.' It is not too much to say that he was once more engaged in an attempt to shed his identity and leave the shameful skin of Dennis Nilsen to rot upon the prison floor. Most significant of all, perhaps, was the fact that he had first seen this prisoner lying on a stretcher as he was brought to the hospital wing following a hunger strike.

Over and over again, as he lay in his cell, Nilsen ruminated on the past. 'I have led a strange life so far,' he wrote,

> schoolboy, soldier, chef, projectionist, policeman, clerical officer, executive officer, drunk, sexualist (male and female), murderer, animal lover, independent trades union officer, debater, champion of social causes, do-gooder, dissector of murder victims, grand vizier, and probably 'lifer'. If there is a god he must have a weird and jumbled sense of priorities — job finder, peace campaigner, amateur film maker, mine of useless information, administrator, pen-pusher, detained prisoner, solitary reaper, killer of the innocent, unremorseful, reformed character, enigma — now rapidly becoming a national receptacle into which all the nation will urinate, warped monster, madman, ungodly, cold and alone.[11]

On 9 May 1983, D.A. Nilsen resigned from the civil service with a formal letter addressed to his superior at Kentish Town, Janet Leaman, the resignation to take effect from midnight on 22 May. 'I have in my time tried to do the best for my colleagues,' he wrote, 'and for the greater public interest in the commissioning of my official and union duties in the M.S.C. I hope that I can be forgiven for the excesses of my professional temperament.'[12]

Meanwhile, the excesses of his emotional disorder were, beyond all else, the main preoccupation of his mind during the summer of 1983.

'Emotions are the most toxic substances known to man,' wrote Nilsen. He had, for the past four years, been reluctant to examine himself too deeply for fear of what he might discover. If his responses to stimuli were not subject to his will, but had an energy of their own which used him as a vessel, it was better to leave them alone than to engage in a struggle one was bound to lose, and whose outcome could not fail to be catastrophic to the psyche. The enforced contemplation of a remand in custody brought him to this conflict at last. 'I have now taken possession of my own emotions,' he wrote (again implying that they existed independently of him), and he emerged from the exercise battered, reduced, exhausted. The events he rehearsed in detail, and the analysis he brought to bear on them, were of a kind that in general happened to someone else, casually glimpsed in a newspaper or overheard in a bar. 'Now the someone else is me.'[13] Dennis Nilsen would have the rare and fearsome opportunity to peer into the mind of a murderer, knowing that murderer was himself. How would it be possible to absorb and digest such knowledge? What would it be like to face squarely the recognition of evil in oneself?

'I go through a personal hell each day,' wrote Nilsen from Brixton Prison. 'I know that I have no hate in me . . . what made you kill all those people? . . . Part of me was aware of what it wanted but it never took the trouble to explain *why* to my sober conscious mind.'[14] He went on to talk of 'slaying the dragon within', presumably by his efforts at self-understanding, and this idea was to be enlarged, as the weeks progressed, until it suggested the deeper notion that the murders themselves might have been a misdirected or transferred attempt to kill the devil which inhabited him.

When he came to read the depositions against him, he perceived, as anyone would, that the tone of his answers during police interrogation was cold and even. 'I was unburdening a heavy weight on my conscience for four years,' he said, 'and I was anxious to get everything out as quickly as possible.'[15]

There had been no breaking down, no display of emotion. Whatever tears there were lay deep, and had to be summoned. 'It must be the most wonderful gift to be able to throw your arms around someone and just weep,' he wrote.[16] There is evidence, however, that the tears did rise spontaneously one day in his cell, not from the recall of his own crimes, but as the result of an incident which brought vividly before him the vision of those crimes without the intercession of voluntary memory.

An inmate whose name we must protect (not Martin) had

185

tried to hang himself and failed. He was left looking drugged, with staring eyes, scarcely human. When Nilsen first caught sight of him, the experience was as powerful as a catharsis, stirring pity and fear until they churned and overwhelmed him. 'I hope he has not suffered irreparable brain damage,' he wrote. 'In his pain and condition I see all the effects of my past and of this case. I am the guilty man who has caused this pain in others.' He questioned one of the hospital officers who, according to Nilsen, confirmed that brain damage was a possible outcome. Nilsen in his cell scrawled across the page, 'NO NO NO NO NO NO NO', the words progressively more illegible and unformed, finishing in a desperate scribble as his pen ran away to the right in a jagged line. It is the mark of a man about to burst, and is clearly genuine.[17] In fact, the other prisoner recovered in the course of time.*

The only mitigation Nilsen could find as he searched his soul was the certainty that he had not maliciously planned any of the deaths for which he was responsible. He wrote as much in his letter to D.C.S. Chambers, to which reference has been made, but one might cynically expect a statement of the sort in a letter which would go to the prosecution, as it touched crucially upon the issue of premeditation. He returned to it again and again in less guarded moments. Pondering the charges of attempted murder, he wrote, 'It is my belief that whatever prompted the initial attacks on these occasions . . . they were not committed with a great deal of resolution and force.' The assaults were sudden, and equally suddenly discontinued. If he had wanted to kill a man who was already unconscious, surely he could have done so? Why did he stop? Why did he spend hours afterwards trying to revive Carl Stottor? These are the thoughts of a man who has seen the demon in himself, and recoiled; he must find the

---

* It should be pointed out, however, that a graphologist who has examined this page draws a quite different conclusion, according to which the scrawled sequence of NOs demonstrates deep-seated frustration arising from the vision of the half-throttled man and Nilsen's inability to finish the job. It was the killer, in this view, who rose to the surface and directed his pen.

angel in himself too, to preserve sanity. The future of his self-regard depends on the existence of that angel.

Sometimes, too, Nilsen would turn the blame upon 'society'. Perhaps nothing of the nightmare would have occurred, he implied, if we lived in a social ambience where people cared about their neighbours, where society as a whole did not permit homelessness and despair in the young. There is confusion here. At moments, Nilsen seems to suggest that his victims might not have become victims if there had been people to take notice of them. The newspapers, he told Mr Chambers, would have a field day after the trial, but the 'Des Nilsens, Stephen Sinclairs, Billy Sutherlands and Martyn Duffeys will still stagger along their blind worried way, unnoticed and alone. Society is more interested in a death than in a life.'[18] By placing himself among the victims, Nilsen wants to express solidarity with them against an unfeeling world. Perhaps, he thought, he made the mistake of trying to take on his shoulders alone all the care that the selfish world refused (just as he had tried to represent all the workers at his branch and been largely despised for it); the emotional pressure was too fierce. 'Part of their destruction [the victims] may have been my frustration in not being able to solve their problems.'[19] It sounds absurd, but Nilsen may partly have murdered in anguished assault against social injustice; he was not killing individuals, but society itself. And what had society done? Apart from neglecting its duty to care for the individual, it had neglected Nilsen himself. So the confusion is circular. General anger against social crimes is honed down to specific anger against neglect of Des Nilsen. If people had cared, they would have seen the plight of Stephen Sinclair, his arms cut to pieces in self-laceration; they might also have seen the obscure and distant Mr Nilsen. 'My signals were going out right from the start but nobody seems to have bothered to notice them.'[20]

Such a displaced view of responsibility could not be sustained for long. Ultimately, Nilsen could not bring himself to shirk the truth or shift the blame. Self-analysis must be pursued:

Killing is wrong, and I have reduced my own principles to ashes. The extent of this calamity is immeasurable and the responsibility for it lies with me alone. It would be a just result if I were taken from the courtroom and hanged so that I might be free from guilt. It would also appease public opinion whose mob enthusiasm is more appreciative of sixteen corpses than fifteen. I have strangled to death these men and youths. I have stolen from them their rights to life . . . my murders were for no useful end as murders never are.[21]

I believe my offences are motivated by emotional disorders under unique conditions of extreme mental pressure which release areas in the subconscious when I have lost control . . . I cannot conceive myself breaking the law and injuring people for material or financial gain, jealousy, sexual lust, hate or sadistic pleasure in inflicting pain. Mine is a disease peculiar to me which I should have sought to cure or control. There is no excuse for taking the lives of fifteen innocent people and trying to kill eight others. The buck stops here.[22]

It would not do for me to escape just punishment. I am an irresponsible selfish bastard who deserves everything that is coming to him . . . Society has a right to call me a cold mad killer. No other category fits my results.[23]

These passages reflect the mood of Nilsen's most acute depression during the weekend of 29 April to 2 May, when he was sending out letters declaring that he was unfit to be with humans and should be considered as already in the tomb. That crisis, it will be remembered, followed directly upon his alleged rejection by church-going prisoners. As the mood subsided, it left in its wake a revelation: as soon as he saw himself in the tomb, Dennis Nilsen also saw the last memory of his grandfather, lying silent in a box in the front room at 47 Academy Road, Fraserburgh. In a flash, all paths met in that box — his near-drowning in the sea, his attachment to the earth in Shetland, his narcissistic fantasies with the mirror image, his presentation of himself as a corpse to be adored, the feeling of love (or anger?) as he killed, the ritual washing and caring for dead men at his feet. Coolly, Nilsen surveyed his situation in the light of this new insight. It had come as an intuition and was pursued with labour. Might it also contain the key to his emotional disorder?

> I could only relate to a dead image of the person I could love. The image of my dead grandfather would be the model of him at his most striking in my mind. It seems to have been necessary for them to have been dead in order that I could express those feelings which were the feelings I held sacred for my grandfather. It was a pseudo-sexual infantile love which had not developed and matured. It has taken me until now to identify it and grow out of it practically overnight . . . great relief. Self-knowledge arrived too late to save the dead or myself . . . misplaced love out of its time and out of its mind.
>
> In the post-death awakening these men were as I last remembered Andrew Whyte, the sight of them brought me a bitter sweetness and a temporary peace and fulfilment. I could not see this at the time, it is all clear to me now.[24]

Nilsen advanced this hypothesis tentatively. He knew it was imperfect, and held spurious logic. He looked forward to the more professional views of the psychiatrists, Dr Bowden and Dr MacKeith. Moreover, the explanation, if such it was, did not promise the end of the road. Far from it. Several dams were unblocked by this neat conclusion to his ruminations, the long-delayed responses to his crimes suddenly released. He now thought he could see with clarity, and what he saw was hideous. The first reaction was to open, at last, the way to remorse.

On 10 February 1983 Nilsen had been taken by the police to his former address at 195 Melrose Avenue, and had pointed out exactly where they should dig in order to find forensic evidence of human remains. At that stage, his purpose was practical, his method speedy and accurate. With the passage of time and the temporary relief at having adumbrated a possible solution to the mystery of these events, Nilsen now felt quite differently towards those who had died at Melrose Avenue. Released from the shackles of incomprehension, he had the freedom to test and explore his regret:

> I look back with shame that the small space on that living-room floor could have witnessed twelve deaths, and that small back lot, twelve incinerations . . . I made the garden, I looked after its growing things. The high cost of fertiliser has ruined me . . . That ground will always have their dust in it.[25]
>
> How can I *ever* make amends or respond to the suffering and loss caused to the next of kin of those whom I have killed? . . . Will they forever hate me, or will they forgive me in the fullness of time?[26]

At times he thought it might have been better to leave them in peace at Melrose Avenue and not tell the police they were there. At other times, he forced himself to bring them back, to people his cell with their images, by drawing the dead bodies as he remembered them. This portfolio, entitled 'Sad Sketches' (some of which are reproduced between pages 305 and 316), would be ghoulish in the extreme were it done for amusement. Nilsen says he was filled with self-loathing as he put pen to paper, and wrote in the margin around the pictures what he was feeling. 'They are as I remember them – worse when you can recall the detail of real flesh, hair, and skin.'[27]

He reserved a special degree of remorse for Ken Ockendon and his parents, for many reasons. In the first place, Ockendon obviously had family ties, and came from a home with love in it; had he lived, he would have had somewhere to return to. Secondly, Nilsen and Ockendon had been happy together for a whole day, much longer than had been the case with any of the other victims, who generally died after an acquaintance of three or four hours. The death of Ockendon seemed even more inexplicable to Nilsen than the others. It was not only arbitrary, not only impulsive, but a cruel and horrid parody of what might have been. The two men could have continued as friends. His attitude towards Ockendon's parents underwent several metamorphoses. He felt protective, and did not wish them to know that he had met their son at a pub frequented by homosexuals; this is why he withheld the name of the pub from the police. (To this day he has no idea whether Ockendon was homosexual or not — their conversation never touched upon the subject.) Then he longed for a romantic redemption which he expressed in high-flown language:

> To Mr and Mrs Ockendon, what can I say? Apologise? I would be sorrier than they at his loss by my hands . . . I feel forgiven by him. All he asks is that I spend a lifetime in his chains and make him real to those he never knew. I must pay for their [Mr and Mrs Ockendon's] pain.[28]

Forgetting for a moment the offensive presumption that he could 'outdo' the Ockendons in their grief, the passage throws additional light on Nilsen's complex personality. Suffering in the abstract (the sort of suffering inflicted by a faceless state authority, for instance) he cannot endure. Personalised suffering, as a penance *for* someone, carrying *his* chains, he can understand, even welcome. He positively enjoys the responsibility of 'standing in' for Ken Ockendon, or of representing him in some way, of speaking for him. To do so would be a form of giving, a form of love. One move further, and Nilsen almost *becomes* Ockendon the better to represent him. However distasteful the idea that he could somehow replace the murdered man, the notion is important to an understanding of the murderer. He aspires to nothing less than absolution through love:

> The Ockendons must be made fully aware of the guilt of my hands, but also of the guiltless heart . . . If I had remained silent, his fate might never have been known. I must behave as they would expect their son to behave, for the rest of my life. I am the only living material of their son Ken. It is almost unbearable to think that they should ever accept *me* as a son. It may be that they would prefer another corpse. I am at their disposal.[29]

Allied to this desire to be identified with the victim is Nilsen's oft-repeated contention that he has absorbed the essence of the dead into himself. 'I have always believed they are, in a sense, living on within me,' he writes.[30] It is perhaps necessary at this point to make clear that the meaning of this and similar statements is not to be construed literally; there is no evidence that any of the murders were followed by cannibalism. Nilsen's claim to have assimilated the dead is intended to be taken in a spiritual sense, as was the case when he watched the bonfire at Melrose Avenue (see p. 151) and declared that the vanished life of the burning corpses had entered into himself. To his mind, this was a mark of the deepest benevolence, and it thoroughly confused his newly-discovered feelings of remorse. If he felt contrite for having killed, he could not always feel a suitable remorse for having taken upon himself the sufferings of his victims without denying what he saw as the 'angel' within him. The result was a sorry ethical jumble. Here he is reflecting upon the death of Stephen Sinclair:

> Here in this cell he is still with me. In fact I believe he is me, or part of me. How can you feel remorse for taking his pains into yourself? I loved him much more than anyone else he had ever met in his twenty years. The image of the sleeping Stephen is and will be with me for all of my life. No court or prison can ever take that from me, or this almost holy feeling.[31]

Quite apart from the odd presumption that no one else had ever cared for Sinclair (how could he know? they were only acquainted for about four hours), there is a very clear impression that Nilsen's deepest yearning is to assume another identity, any identity other than his own. Thinking about Sinclair, his self-image melts into the contemplation, so that one is not quite sure if he sees two people or two aspects of the same person:

> Stephen had to die to get attention for his plight. I would give anything for him to walk into my cell now alive and warm, and shoot me dead. But then only to return to the

junked-up slow twilight of his misery. He might just pause long enough to feel the sticky warmth of my blood before blowing himself away. The moment we met we were both long ruined. All the pious aftercare comes now it is too late. A fatal trio, two men and a dog sitting through the mad moments . . . Stephen got temporary release from the needles and I from the bottle, but it couldn't last. The spartan reality of a cold new day would almost certainly have led to him stealing for dope and me killing for company . . . Stephen may depart up the chimney at Golders Green. They must bring me in chains, naked to Piccadilly Circus, and pour his ashes on my head in the healing sun.[32]

The confusion is even more pronounced in the commentaries he wrote to the drawings — 'Sad Sketches'. One sketch shows a body slumped in the wardrobe, another depicts two bodies under the floor, a third the body of a blond youth ritually stripped after the killing:

After twelve hours his body had become cold and rigid with rigor mortis and his arms became fixed as they had been left. I would have to force his limbs loose after another twelve hours had passed. I put a clean undergarment on him and left him on the spare bed. *I wept for us both.* [Author's italics]

A fourth drawing shows a body lying on a table and another man, evidently Nilsen himself, standing by it and looking down upon it:

I stood in great grief and a wave of utter sadness as if someone very dear to me had just died . . . amazed at such a tragedy . . . ritual washing . . . waited for arrest. I sometimes wondered if anyone cared for me or them. That could easily be me lying there. *In fact a lot of the time it was.*[33] [Author's italics]

The conclusion is obvious, and Nilsen had to face it. 'It may be that when I was killing these men I was killing myself.'[34]

The progression from a static admiration of his own body in the mirror, to feigning death, and finally, to the actual contemplation of a real corpse which represented himself, was complete. The victims had died to satisfy Nilsen's search for an identity, and the only identity he yearned for was a dead one. It followed that a punishment ending in death would be a consummation.

It seemed to Nilsen that the capital sentence, fallen into desuetude since 1967, would have been the fitting solution to his life. He admitted that it would be a relief to walk into the prison yard one day and be hanged, and he meant not only relief from oppressive guilt but from uncertainty and doubt. It would at last make sense. 'I was destroying myself and the destruction of others could have been instruments in a binge of guilty self-punishment.'[35] If this was really so, then the self-punishment must finally be self-directed; there would, he knew, be no more victims to take his place. While he would welcome hanging, he could not countenance suicide which would assuage guilt rather than embrace it:

> I would step up there [on the scaffold] safe in the knowledge that the books were now to be balanced for the good of all. I've thought of hanging myself but I can't bear the prospect of it being interpreted as an act of cowardice on my part and running away from my responsibilities and punishment. It would also have a ruinous effect on my mother, relatives and friends . . . I'd like posterity to know that I can take anything that they choose to throw at me. Suicide is an escape from justice, and I have handed myself over so that justice may be seen to be done.[36]

Rejection of suicide did not amount to a stubborn attachment to life. On the contrary, Nilsen's death-wish grew steadily more persistent throughout his remand, invading his dreams and distorting his judgment. He would imagine himself in a room, possibly at Melrose Avenue, with all fifteen victims lying dead around him, except that he was dead too. He was one of them, with a noose around his neck. The only sound of life was Bleep whining and howling in the garden. The interesting aspect of such a vision is not so much that Nilsen should receive attention in death (the dog's lamentations offering proof that he mattered), as that he should be where he *belonged*, where he felt at home. The corollary of this attitude is that he is a foreigner, an alien in the living world, a permanent and helpless outsider. Perhaps, after all, the church was right to ban his attendance at services; perhaps he really was not fit to be with humans, as he was not essentially part of the human race himself. Perhaps he was the incarnation of evil, the instrument of diabolical designs.

'I wish I was "consciously" evil, so that I could at least have a god to worship,' wrote Nilsen. 'I do not feel like an evil person. I doubt if I could kill someone now, even under *orders* and *with* lawful authority. I am about the least likely killer that I know.'[37]

This is potentially one of the most revealing passages in all Nilsen's writings, for it is obviously a genuine cry of bewilderment, and if we turn later to consider the religious view of his crimes, and the possibility of possession, we shall see that according to this view the devilish influence works insidiously and subtly to convince the person selected to act on its behalf of his essential innocence. Nilsen once wrote to me that he must not lose sight of this innocence. He did not, of course, mean to deny that he had killed, but to give voice to the feeling that he had in some way been used by a power to which he had surrendered control. It was not a thought which occurred to him often. Most of the time he accepted total responsibility for his acts. But it was there, latent and subdued, the last glimmer of self-esteem.

'We are born with a skull wherein a great harvest can be sown . . . they cut away the goodness and leave the field barren, to spray their deadly chemicals within and bring forth a poisoned yield.'[38] Who, exactly, are 'they'? Supporters of a Manichaean vision of the world and of man's predicament would identify them as messengers of Lucifer. Psychiatrists might call them pressures of a personality disorder brought on by morbid imagination. Medical men could say that they are chemical imbalances in the body, or an inherited tendency towards madness. Environmentalists would blame amorphous 'society'. Do they all amount to the same thing dressed in different words? And where, in all this, does human will fit? 'The fashion of treating human behaviour as conditioned by events in infancy or by impersonal forces in history has been conveniently used to exempt individuals from moral responsibility,' Noel Annan has written.[39] It might equally be said that intimations of possession by evil forces postulate a similar exemption. The whole question of free will ultimately comes into play.

One of the letters which Nilsen sent me was written as he emerged from this long period of introspection. It touched upon the themes of alienation and evil, of guilt and punishment, and reverted once more to his grandfather. It might serve to illustrate how the prisoner saw himself five and a half months before his trial:

My case has produced a series of delayed emotional and moral shocks as the mind slowly accumulates the enormity of events. My range of emotions recently have all arrived at the same destination — self-punishment. I am now in a void of uncertainty. I remember the past and I remember some of it with vivid clarity. I recollect these images from the past and I sometimes wonder if anything that transpired was somehow meant to be. I think I am two stark contrasting poles of man's character. I have played the angel's role, unimpeachably, balanced disastrously by momentary and uncontrollable outbursts of primitive evil. In my life at its most important junctions there was no middle of the road. At these critical moments there were no grey areas. I had seen through my union principles to a conclusion of absolute defeat or absolute victory. Moderation became alien to me. When my feelings directed its love on another living being I would overpower that person with overwhelming emotion. In a moderate conventional world this is considered bizarre and alien. I had always held within me a fear of emotional rejection and failure. I seemed always to travel at 100 m.p.h. in a stream of traffic with an upward limit of 30 m.p.h. Nobody ever really got close to me. I was a child of deep romanticism in a harsh plastic functioning materialism . . . I am an odd personality for today. There never was a place for me in the scheme of things . . . My inner emotions could not be expressed, and this led me to the alternative of a retrograde and deepening imagination. I turned to self-love and found myself competing against the advances of others to win my affection. I think (now) that I was jealous of giving myself to anyone completely. I led a dual life — one life was constantly pulling against the other. I had become a living fantasy on a theme in dark endless dirges. I think that I must have subconsciously wished to be in the tomb with my grandfather. My emotional development had become arrested at that traumatic moment long ago.[40]

Explanation, however, was no exoneration. As he searched deeper, he became more contrite and more intent upon atonement. Of the victims, he wrote, 'I must keep their memory alive. I must be reminded constantly and never be allowed to forget.' Expiation for such vicious deeds was impossible, the offence was too great, too far beyond the reach of punishment. Nilsen sought wildly for some dramatic sign he might give. Should he change his name to Stephen Sinclair, thus forcing himself to face reality every day? It was an absurd notion, scribbled down one afternoon, but it conveyed the same impulse as his vain hope that he might be a son to Mr and Mrs Ockendon — namely that he must strive to escape the devil of Dennis Nilsen, to become someone else. In similar vein, he asked me to find out how he might change his name by deep poll and assume his real name of Moksheim. If a way could only be found, 'Nilsen' must somehow be left behind.

Set against these advances in self-knowledge, the forthcoming trial began to look less significant to him. Justice would be done, but he was at a loss to see how that would assist him in finding a way to live with himself. Naturally, that was not the purpose of justice; it was for him to come to terms with his soul during whatever sentence might follow. 'What advice can all the legal men in the world now give me that will resurrect the dead?' he wrote. 'I shower much longer than other prisoners because there is so much blood on *me*.'[41]

Meanwhile, he would make a start with whatever tiny opportunities might be afforded him. He would 'try to improve by the small daily acts of communion with my fellow beings. My effort must be greater as my sins are many and of enormous proportions.'[42] A month later he wrote:

> I believe that there is much in my past which I need to morally redress and I will spend the years remaining to me in acquiring knowledge in order to give all my talents to my fellows. I am a grain of sand who just has to face the oncoming tide and I will expect no miracle.[43]

This mood was severely tested in August, when Nilsen was given fifty-six days' punishment at Brixton Prison for 'assaulting' prison officers, a sentence which he thought vindictive. He grew more combative and difficult. He dismissed Ronald Moss as his solicitor not for any personal reason (he always maintained that he held Moss in the highest regard), but because Moss had been unable to alleviate the conditions of his punishment despite letters and representations. He would discharge legal aid altogether as a protest. Then he met Ralph Haeems. After many years' experience representing notorious criminals, Haeems cheerfully welcomed any challenge to authority, a characteristic which appealed to Nilsen immediately. Besides, the same solicitor had recently taken on David Martin's case. On Mr Haeems's advice, having studied all the evidence, it was decided that there was a case for 'diminished responsibility' due to a mental abnormality in Nilsen. This would mean that the victims of attack, like Paul Nobbs and Carl Stottor, would have to be called to the witness-box; this he had previously intended to avoid, to spare them the anguish of reliving experiences in open court. He had hoped that the prosecution could accept their written statements without question, but this would no longer be possible if his state of mind was to receive full consideration.

Now, at last, Nilsen saw the photograph of human remains found at 23 Cranley Gardens. The experience acted like an exorcism. 'My mind is depressingly active', he wrote, 'as I am now deep into the horrific details of the case. The weight of the mountainous burden of my past presses heavily upon me . . . the details of this case are horrible, dark and alien . . . I *must* relive the past.' He says he felt nauseous and disturbed. When he saw what was left of John Howlett, he wrote, 'I must be a really terrible, horrific man . . . I am damned and damned and damned. How in heaven's name could I have done any of it?'[44] That night he had a dream in his cell, in which he was dragging a part of a body, putrefying, across the floor of the office at Kentish Town trying desperately to conceal it. The office floods, and someone* calls the fire brigade.

In the final week before his trial, Nilsen's attitude swung evenly between recognition of guilt for his acts, and protestation that they were committed involuntarily. The conflict between 'angel' and 'devil' continued, and who could tell when, if ever, it would be resolved? The court would reach a decision in the light of the law and the evidence. Nilsen's own decision might be many years ahead. He clung to the efforts of Dr MacKeith, for whom he secretly wrote a quotation from Spinoza: 'I have striven not to laugh at human actions, not to weep at them, nor to hate them, but to understand them.'

Two sentences serve to illustrate his frame of mind before his trial: 'I have judged myself more harshly than any court ever could';[45] 'We are not dealing with murder here, although I have killed.'[46]

*The author.

9

TRIAL

The remark at the close of the previous chapter was written
by Dennis Nilsen not on the eve of the trial, but months
before. Rephrased in unfamiliar legal or psychiatric jargon, it
was in effect to be the one central issue which dominated
proceedings over the next two weeks. No one disputed that
Nilsen had killed.* The prosecution counsel, Mr Alan Green,
maintained that he did so with full awareness and deliberation,
and should therefore be found guilty of murder. Defence
counsel, Mr Ivan Lawrence, would suggest that at the time of
each killing the defendant was suffering from such abnormality of mind as to substantially reduce his responsibility for the
act, and should therefore be guilty of the lesser charge of
manslaughter. Prosecution would rely entirely upon Nilsen's
own account given at Hornsey Police Station, while defence
would bring expert psychiatric evidence to establish the
degree of abnormality involved.

One difficulty arose even before the trial began. On the six
charges of murder the burden fell upon the defence to prove

---

* The *actus reus* (state of affairs caused by the conduct of the defendant)
was agreed. Dispute centred upon the *mens rea* (state of mind of the
defendant at the time).

'diminished responsibility'. On the two charges of attempted murder, however, the law did not permit a defence of diminished responsibility, and the burden of proof reverted to the prosecution. Mr Lawrence submitted to the judge, Mr Justice Croom-Johnson, that this conflict might confuse the jury, whose task could be simplified if the charges of attempted murder were removed from the indictment, or tried separately. The point was valid, for if the jury were to find Nilsen guilty of attempted murder, but guilty only of manslaughter on the murder charges, they would in essence be saying that his responsibility was diminished when he succeeded in killing but not at all reduced when he failed. In order to avoid this logical nonsense, their decision on the murder charges might be influenced by their virtually inevitable verdict on the charges of attempted murder; denied the opportunity of considering his mental state at the time of the attempts, even if they wanted to, they were bound to find him guilty on the evidence of surviving witnesses. Mr Lawrence's submission was unsuccessful, the judge ruling that the matter was not so intolerably complicated as to confuse the jury. For at least two members of the jury the final verdict was to prove him wrong, and there are indications that a further four jurors struggled to resolve the non sequiturs which the law had forced upon them.

On the morning of Monday, 24 October 1983, the chief administrator of the Central Criminal Court, Mr Michael MacKenzie, read out the charges, that Dennis Andrew Nilsen murdered Kenneth Ockendon, Malcolm Barlow, Martyn Duffey, John Howlett, Billy Sutherland and Stephen Sinclair, and attempted to murder Douglas Stewart and Paul Nobbs, at the end of each charge asking, 'How say you, Nilsen, are you guilty or not guilty?' To each the defendant replied, 'Not guilty,' and those were to be the only two words the court would hear from him. The jury was then sworn in with the oath: 'I swear by Almighty God that I will faithfully try the several issues joined between Our Sovereign Lady the Queen and the Prisoner at the Bar and give a true verdict according to the evidence.' There were eight men and four women, dressed unspectacularly in jeans and shirt-sleeves, crumpled suits, or skirts and jumpers, collectively an eloquent demonstration that the ultimate decision rests in law with twelve ordinary men and women of the world. They might have walked off the street, their very incongruity in the awesome surroundings of Court Number 1 acting as a kind of reassurance.

Alan Green, for the prosecution, opened his case by relating in detail the events of early February 1983 which led to the arrest, including a description of the human remains found in the drain at 23 Cranley Gardens and subsequently hurled over the back garden fence. He promised the jury that the photographs they would be shown were only of the house and garden; and they would not be asked to look upon photographs of an unpleasant nature, by which he meant those pictures of the contents of plastic bags found at the flat. Mercifully, these were never produced in court.

Counsel went on to say that seven victims had been identified, although only six were listed on the indictment. The seventh, Archibald Graham Allen, aged twenty-eight, from Glasgow, was the fourteenth person to die (the 'omelette' death), but he was only identified by dental records after the indictment had been drawn up. Similarly, the jury would hear evidence from three victims of attempted murder, whereas there were only two on the indictment; Carl Stottor had been traced, with information given by the defendant, too late for inclusion in the indictment. Mr Green claimed that all the murders fitted into a pattern:

(a) Every victim was a man;
(b) Each one met the defendant in a public house;
(c) They were all unknown to him until that meeting;
(d) They were all (with one exception) without permanent address;
(e) They were all strangled;
(f) Some were homosexual, and a few were male prostitutes.

On the last point, counsel implicitly conceded in advance the defence contention that none of them had died because they had rejected sexual advances from the defendant; homo-sexuality was a coincidence arising from the nature of the pubs where they had been picked up, and was not put forward as an indication of motive.

Selecting relevant passages from the lengthy confession at Hornsey, Mr Green took the jury through all fifteen killings, with particular emphasis on how Nilsen had described them. The death of the emaciated young man whose legs rose in a cycling motion as he died, that of Malcolm Barlow, killed as he lay unconscious because it would have been a nuisance to call an ambulance for the second time, and that of John the Guardsman, three times strangled and finally drowned, brought the court to an incredulous hush. Counsel's strong, theatrical voice needed no exaggeration or embellishment of manner to have effect. He called the account of John the Guardsman's death 'chilling' (the judge would nine days later call it 'appalling'), and the evident shock on the faces of several jurors showed that the adjective was well chosen. The public gallery, high near the ceiling of the courtroom, looked down upon the silent defendant with a concerted, fascinated gaze.

Counsel also made the telling point that Nilsen had acquired certain butchering skills in the Army Catering Corps, and confirmed that a search of the garden at Melrose Avenue yielded evidence that 'at least eight bodies' had been disposed of in bonfires there. Rather less relevant, but even more effective, were the quotations Mr Green chose to bring before the jury, taken from Nilsen's confession. Of killing the emaciated young man he had said 'it was as easy as taking candy from a baby'. Of another he remarked, 'end of a day, end of the drinking, end of a person'. Asked about his ties, Nilsen had said he started out with fifteen and only had a clip-on tie left, and questioned as to how many bodies lay beneath the floor at any one time, he had replied, 'I am not sure. I did not do a stock-check.' It has to be remembered that the interviews at Hornsey were conducted in an extremely relaxed manner. Messrs Jay and Chambers needed to keep the accused 'sweet' in order to coax as much information from him as they could (he was, after all, their only source at that stage), and Nilsen did not want to make matters any worse for himself by being difficult. The result was much laughter and casual rapport as they addressed each other in a friendly manner to alleviate the intolerable tension created by the revelations themselves. Jokes in the circumstances may well have been tasteless, but they are not important. They assumed importance as presented to the jury. So also did Nilsen's remark that he had taken on a 'quasi-God role'. Given undue emphasis this suggests the delusions of a missionary, which would be misleading. 'At the time of the killings I don't remember saying any such things,' wrote Nilsen that evening in his cell. 'The interviews with police were given with hindsight.' To me he wrote:

Now that the court has accepted the 'evidence' that I am God I've begun to get looney letters from religious freaks . . . all this because I casually threw the police a psychiatrist's cliché. I wonder if the press would print it if I said 'At that moment I really believed I was the Emperor of China'?[1]

The 'quasi-God role' was to be mentioned in court half a dozen times and would make headlines in one newspaper.

Jurors' attention was specifically drawn to two points in Mr Green's address, both concerned with quotations from the confession. Describing the problem of disposal after the death of John the Guardsman, Nilsen had said to Messrs Chambers and Jay, 'I decided to dissect the body in the bath and flush the pieces of flesh and organs down the lavatory. This proved a slow process so I decided to boil some of it, including the head. I put all the large bones out with the rubbish.' One could almost feel the shivers of fear and repulsion emanating from the jury benches, as the vision of dustmen carrying away bits of people loomed before them. A lady juror stared at Nilsen as if she did not believe he was real.

The second point Mr Green made concerned Nilsen's state of mind. Very cleverly, he planted the seed of the defence's case for them, as if in a spirit of generosity and understanding, but leaving them with precious little to add. Police officers had asked Nilsen whether he needed to kill, said Green, and Nilsen had replied, 'In some cases I am aware that at the precise moment of the act I believe I am right in doing the act. If there was a bomb blast at the time, nothing would stop me.' One could hardly imagine a more vivid portrait of a man apparently 'out of his mind', and some jurors nodded slightly in recognition of this possibility. Mr Green seemed to acknowledge the shakiness of his own case, but then he added, 'The Crown says that even if there was mental abnormality, that was not sufficient to diminish substantially his mental responsibility for these killings.' In other words, Nilsen could be sick, but still guilty of murder; the jury's entire task would pivot on the weight they must give to the one adverb — 'substantially'.

The first witness for the prosecution was Douglas Stewart, aged twenty-nine, from Thurso, Caithness, whom Nilsen had attacked on 10 November 1980. Dressed in an ill-fitting three-piece green suit, he gave an impression of extreme self-possession, even cockiness. He spoke with a pronounced Scottish accent which the jury found difficult to follow (and they were not alone), and at such speed that the judge had frequently to ask him to slow down. One of the charms of the English legal system is that evidence should be given at such a pace as to allow a judge to copy it down in longhand with a quill pen. It was established immediately that Mr Stewart had married in July 1981 and was not homosexual.

Mr Stewart told how he had met Nilsen in the Golden Lion pub in Dean Street, with a number of other people whom he had assumed were Nilsen's friends. The defendant had introduced himself as 'Dennis' and had suggested, after closing time, that they go back to his flat to continue drinking. It was very late, and they were the last to leave the pub. Mr Stewart thought the invitation was extended to all present, and was somewhat surprised to discover he was the only guest. They drank two more pints of lager, after Stewart had refused the vodka which was offered, and Nilsen eventually went to bed on the raised platform at Melrose Avenue. He invited Stewart to join him and Stewart declined, on the grounds that he 'did not do that sort of thing'. Stewart fell asleep in the chair.

When he woke up, his ankles were secured with a tie, and his own tie had been removed and replaced around his neck under the collar. Nilsen had his knee pressed against Stewart's chest. Stewart fought him off, scratching him wildly beneath the eye and drawing blood, and finally pinned him to the ground, whereupon Nilsen shouted several times, 'Take my money, take my money!' This would later be represented by the Crown as evidence of cool presence of mind, in that Nilsen hoped his voice would be heard throughout the house and blame might then be shifted on to Stewart. Nilsen also said, in a calm voice, 'I could kill you,' when he was in no position, beneath Stewart, to harm anyone. This, said the defence, showed that his state of mind was abnormal.

They got up, and Nilsen then went to the kitchen whence he emerged carrying a large knife. He did not seem to be brandishing it, but was calm and 'normal' throughout. Stewart decided to humour him, apologised for hurting him, and went with him to the kitchen to wipe the blood from his face. He stayed another ten minutes, had a drink, and left. Going to the nearest telephone box in the street he called the police, who sent an officer to 195 Melrose Avenue, where he heard conflicting reports from Nilsen and Stewart and concluded that there had been a lovers' quarrel. It is not uncommon for the police to be called to intervene in a domestic squabble, and most of them are settled without further action. In this case, Stewart was informed that the C.I.D. would take a further statement from him, but they could not trace him the next day, and he did not renew contact with them. The matter was forgotten until after Nilsen's arrest more than two years later.

Throughout Stewart's evidence, Nilsen had been leaning over the dock and passing hasty notes to his solicitor, Ralph Haeems, who handed them to counsel behind him. Ivan Lawrence requested a short adjournment to take fresh defence instructions arising from these notes, and the court reassembled half an hour later.

Ivan Lawrence's cross-examination of Douglas Stewart

sought to undermine his credibility as a witness, at least on matters of detail. He suggested that Stewart had drunk more than two pints of lager during the two and a half hours he spent in the pub, was therefore more drunk than he admitted and his memory less clear than he claimed. Stewart had made three trivial mistakes which lent weight to Lawrence's contention. He said that Nilsen had introduced himself as 'Dennis', a name he never used; that he had offered vodka, a drink he never kept in the flat (it was always rum); that the house bore a number-plate '195', which it did not. Why had Stewart not pointed out to the police the scratch he had inflicted upon Nilsen, which would have supported his story of the attack and scuffle? There was not time, said the witness, 'and I am not used to people half-killing me'. Why did he not run for his life, instead of staying for another drink? There was no adequate response to this question. Lawrence finished by asking the witness if he had sold his story to a newspaper. Yes, he had. Mr Justice Croom-Johnson asked which newspaper, and made a note of the reply, 'The *Sunday Mirror*.' 'And of course, newspapers want details, don't they, not hazy recollections,' commented Mr Lawrence as he sat down.

The next witness was the police constable summoned by Stewart on the night of the attack. From notes he made at the time, it was clear that no injury to Nilsen's face had been pointed out, or been noticed by the constable. On the other hand, his notes did indicate that Stewart's tie was missing when he called to investigate, the strong inference being that Nilsen had secreted it.

On the next day, Tuesday, 25 October, the court heard frightening evidence from two young men who almost died at Dennis Nilsen's hands. Baffling evidence, too, for they were both reprieved by their assailant, who could easily have dispatched them but chose not to — in the one case, before he finished the act and had a 'change of heart', in the other case after he thought his victim was already dead. This 'change of heart' was for the prosecution damning evidence that the defendant was constantly in control of himself, had free will and exercised it by playing with life and death as if they were in his gift. For the defence, the same curious behaviour indicated extreme instability of mind and a temporary state of what psychiatrists call 'dissociation'. But for the court, the evidence heard that day was a painfully intense personal drama which few of us have ever had to experience.

Paul Nobbs, aged twenty-one, was the first in the witness box. With dark, straight hair, clean-cut and good-looking, Nobbs was clearly nervous at the prospect of being questioned. He stood way back in the box and could scarcely be heard. Although he was a prosecution witness, the junior prosecution counsel who questioned him appeared to intimidate him, telling him to speak up a dozen times. The judge also intervened with the stern admonishment, 'Keep your voice up.' Nobbs looked as if he could not wait to be released.

Mr Nobbs told the court how he had met Nilsen in the Golden Lion at lunchtime in November 1981, while he was a student at London University. He used Nilsen as an excuse to escape the attentions of a man who had been trying to pick him up, and went off with him, first to Foyles to buy some books, then home to Cranley Gardens. He telephoned his mother twice during the evening. After some drinking, Mr Nobbs told the court that he got into bed and Nilsen followed him. They kissed, cuddled, and fondled each other, but were both too drunk for anal sex, although Nobbs did make a move to penetrate Nilsen, who asked him not to because he was still 'a virgin'. Nobbs then went to sleep.

He woke up about two in the morning with a stinking headache, went to get a glass of water, sat down for a while and went back to bed. A few hours later he woke again, still feeling ill. 'I went to splash some water on my face and in the mirror over the sink I saw my face. It was very red and there were no whites in my eyes; they were all bloodshot. I had a sore throat and I felt very sick.'

Nilsen had told him, 'God, you look bloody awful,' to which he had replied something like, 'Oh, thanks very much.' There was nothing odd in Nilsen's behaviour, rather the contrary. He was concerned and sympathetic, suggesting that Nobbs was perhaps the worse for wear after too much rum. It was only later, after his tutor had sent him to hospital, that Nobbs was forced to acknowledge he had been strangled, and assumed that his attacker had been Nilsen. He had not wanted to report the attack to the police because they would be unlikely to pay much attention to him when they realised he was homosexual.

When Ivan Lawrence rose to cross-examine the witness, he was smiling, avuncular, and polite. 'I do not wish to challenge anything you have said,' he began, 'but want to ask some questions which may help us.' The point of his first questions was to remind the jury of certain aspects of Douglas Stewart's testimony while it was still fresh in their minds, without actually mentioning Stewart's name. Nobbs confirmed:

(a) That the defendant was called 'Des' rather than 'Dennis';
(b) That the Golden Lion pub was a recognised place for homosexuals to pick up partners. Nobbs did not think that anyone who used that particular pub could be ignorant of its reputation.

The remainder of Mr Lawrence's cross-examination was designed to alert the jury to the lack of any motive for the attack, and by implication to prepare them for the possibility that the defendant was mentally unstable.

'There was no question of his forcing himself upon you, of his stalking you?'

'No. He was doing me a favour by pretending to be with me, by rescuing me.'

'Did he seem to be offering genuine friendship and companionship?'

'Yes.'

'He wasn't saying to you, "Come on, drink up, drink faster, drink more"?'

'No.'

'He didn't stop you calling your mother, or stop you saying anything you liked to her, or stop you from giving the address where you were?'

'No.'

'There were never any sadistic, masochistic, violent or bondage acts which you were asked to perform?'

'No.'

'He didn't try to force you to continue with sex?'

'No.'

Having established that Nobbs first felt the headache at 2 a.m., and then again when he awoke at 6 a.m., Mr Lawrence suggested that the attack must have occurred before 2 a.m. 'He must have let you sleep unmolested from about two to six, with no attempt to murder you while you were utterly at his mercy.' Nobbs could not be sure when the attack had occurred. Lawrence went on:

'Assuming as we must that he attacked you and tried to strangle you, did you give him the slightest justification for doing so, any provocation, any words of anger?'

'No.'

'Nothing you said, nothing you did caused him to behave in that extraordinary way? You didn't reject him, tease him, frustrate him in any way?'

'No.'

'And the next morning he behaved as if nothing unusual had happened in the night?'

'Yes.'

'Did he seemed concerned about your condition?'

'Yes.'

'Was there any sign from him that he thought he must have done something awful in the night?'

'No.'

Paul Nobbs's monosyllabic answers were potentially of crucial significance. In view of later suggestions that Nilsen had stalked his victims, here was one who said that he did not. It would be proposed that Nilsen had been enraged at people not listening to his conversation, and killed them in anger, but here was a living witness who testified to the contrary, maintaining that Nilsen's behaviour both before and after the attempt at murder was unremarkable. The next witness, Carl Stottor, would leave the same impression. Even more importantly, Nobbs's evidence was at odds with the idea that Nilsen purposefully chose victims who were rootless drifters, unlikely to be missed. He had twice stood by while Nobbs had called his mother, but the knowledge that there *was* a mother had not prevented him from trying to kill Nobbs. There was no doubt that Nobbs's disappearance would have been noticed, nor even that there were people who had seen him talking to Nilsen at the pub that day. Was this why Nilsen stopped half-way through, suddenly realising his prey had an identity? If so, why did he not realise it *before* the attempt, and leave Nobbs alone? Or was it that Nilsen was literally 'in two minds', one of which was the mind of a murderer, and that his rational self could not always influence the actions of his murderous self?

If Paul Nobbs was nervous, Carl Stottor was positively terrified by the ordeal of giving evidence. There was the slightest pause in his step as he entered the court and saw for the first time the awesome theatre of his performance. His hands were thrust into the pockets of a loose jacket and held close to his stomach. He wore an open-necked shirt beneath which a neck-chain was occasionally visible, and there was a hint of make-up on his otherwise pale face. Twenty-one years old, effeminate and shy, he would be referred to rather unnecessarily by prosecuting counsel as 'a rather pathetic young man'. Certainly there could be no one in court who did not feel sorry for him as he related the most horrifying story in a quiet, soft, barely audible voice. He, too, had to be told to speak up, but the drama of his narrative was intensified by its mouse-like delivery, and the court was so silent one might almost have heard a feather sway to the ground.

Mr Stottor told how he met Dennis Nilsen in the Black Cap in Camden High Street in May 1982. Stottor was deeply depressed over a love affair in Blackpool which had gone wrong, and Nilsen comforted him, encouraged him to talk, tried to instil an optimistic spirit. 'He said how pretty I was. He seemed a very nice person, very kind, talking to me when I was depressed.' Nilsen paid for all the drinks, and eventually suggested they go back to his flat, promising that he would not touch him. They took a taxi to Cranley Gardens, holding hands for the length of the journey. At the flat, Stottor had said that he wished he were dead, and Nilsen had told him not to be so silly, that he should not throw his life away for one man, that he had a whole future to look forward to. When Stottor felt ill from the alcohol, they both went to bed. Stottor was invited to tell the court what he could remember of the events of that night. In a voice made even quieter by the pain of recollection, he relived a nightmare.

I woke up feeling something round my neck. My head was hurting and I couldn't breathe properly and I wondered what it was. I felt his hand pulling at the zip at the back of my neck. He was saying in a sort of whispered shouting voice, 'Stay still, stay still.' I thought perhaps he was trying to help me out of the sleeping bag because I thought I had got caught up in the zip which he had warned me about. Then I passed out.

Stottor's voice broke with emotion before he could continue; it seemed he might sob, but did not. He had been, he said, semi-conscious:

The pressure was increasing. My head was hurting and I couldn't breathe. I remember vaguely hearing water running. I remember vaguely being carried and then I felt very cold. I knew I was in the water and he was trying to drown me. He kept pushing me into the water. The third time I came up I said, 'No more, please, no more,' and he pushed me under again. I just thought I was dying. I thought this man was killing me and I was dying. I thought, 'You are drowning. This is what it feels like to die.' I felt very relaxed and I passed out. I couldn't fight any more.

To his own amazement, Mr Stottor woke up to find himself on the couch with the dog, Bleep, licking his face. Later he saw a red line round his neck and broken blood vessels all over his face. Nilsen told him he had had a nightmare and that he, Nilsen, had had to splash his face with water to get him out of the state of shock, Later still, he was in bed, gradually getting warm as Nilsen cuddled him.

Counsel for the prosecution established two important facts which pointed to premeditation. First, Nilsen had asked Carl Stottor in the Black Cap whether he had any family, a question which supported the thesis that Nilsen was consciously looking for victims with no decor to their lives. Second, he had warned Stottor about the loose zip on the sleeping bag before he went to bed, which could only mean that he intended to use it as an excuse if need be, since no one can sensibly become entangled in the zip of a sleeping-bag which is lying on top of the bed. (Stottor was not *inside* the sleeping-bag.) The implication was that if Nilsen warned him about the zip, the intention to use it for strangulation was already in his mind before Stottor went to bed.

Cross-examining, Mr Lawrence was concerned to establish the apparent normality of Nilsen's behaviour before and after the attack. Stottor agreed that the defendant was a good listener, patient and genuinely interested. 'I got the impression he didn't want to leave me on my own in the state I was in,' said the witness. He also agreed that he had not been forced to stay, that there had been no word about sex, no sexual proposal, no violent argument, no frustration. Three points emerged from Lawrence's questioning:

(a) The police had traced Mr Stottor only from information given them by the defendant;
(b) As Stottor had been too weak to save himself, the defendant 'must have' let him up out of the water at a time when he could have killed him with ease;
(c) After the event, Nilsen had accompanied Stottor to the underground station.

Was the defendant both calm and concerned before and after the incident, 'as though he was unaware that he had done anything to harm you?' 'Yes.' 'How odd that was,' mused Mr Lawrence as he resumed his seat.

The court would later hear from a page which Nilsen wrote for the police exactly how odd it was, for Nilsen had frantically heated the room and the body of a man he had thought was dead, to save him from the effects of an attack he had himself perpetrated: 'I was desperate that he should live.'

All eyes in Court Number 1 followed Carl Stottor as he walked softly past the jury, the press benches, and back into ordinary life. He looked as if he might remain scared for many years.

Reflecting that evening in his cell, Nilsen wrote that he could not recall Stottor's being in the bath. He remembered wanting him to appreciate the good feelings that music and drink produce: 'I wanted him to share in it so that he would feel happy.' Of course he knew he had tried to kill him, that is why he had told the police about it in the first place, but he did not feel *personally* responsible for the attack (Nilsen's italics). With, apparently, no hint of irony, he further wrote, 'I hoped that these uncontrollable events would not affect our relationship.' Certainly his behaviour after the attack, as confirmed by Stottor, shows that was precisely what he hoped. 'These incidents were not *ends* but bloody disasters which blighted my sexual and social desires. They in no way *enhanced* them.' Of Stottor he wrote, 'I hope he can forgive me (although he will never forget). He must have a prospect of future happiness.'[2]

Mr Green next invited Mr Lawrence to admit certain facts which were not in dispute. Lawrence having made the formal admission, the next witness was called, Detective Chief Inspector Peter Jay. He recounted the circumstances of Nilsen's arrest on 9 February, then read out to the court three statements volunteered by Nilsen after his arrest (including the document entitled 'Unscrambling Behaviour') and the letter he sent to the police from Brixton Prison on 25 May. Mr Jay read slowly and clearly, and once again the courtroom was plunged into attentive silence as everyone strained to absorb the import of these extraordinary passages of self-appraisal.

I guess I may be a creative psychopath who, when in a loss of rationality situation, lapses temporarily into a destructive psychopath, a condition induced by rapid and heavy ingestion of alcohol. At the subconscious root lies a sense of total social isolation and a desperate search for a sexual identity. I have experienced transitory sexual relationships with both males and females before my first killing. After this event I was incapable of any intercourse. I felt repelled by myself and as stated have had no experience of sexual penetration for some years . . . God only knows what thoughts go through my mind when it's captive within a destructive binge. Maybe the cunning, stalking killer instinct is the only single concentration released from a mind which in that state knows no morality. It may be the perverted overkill of my need to help people — victims who I decide to release quickly from the slings and arrows of their outrageous fortune, pain and suffering. There is no disputing the fact that I am a violent killer under certain circumstances. The victim is the dirty platter after the feast and the washing-up is a clinically ordinary task. It would be better if my reason for killing could be clinically defined, i.e. robbery, jealousy, hate, revenge, sex, blood-lust, or sadism. But it's none of these. Or it could be the subconscious outpouring of all the primitive instinct of primeval man. Could it be the case of individual exaltation at beating the system and the need to beat and confound it time and time again? It amazes me I have no tears for the victims. I have no tears for myself or for those bereaved by my actions. Am I a wicked person, constantly under pressure, who just cannot cope with it, who escapes to reap revenge against society through the haze of a bottle of spirits? Maybe it's because I was just born an evil man. Living with so much violence and death, I've not been haunted by the souls and ghosts of the dead, leading me to believe that no such fictional phenomena has, does, or ever will exist.

That ('Unscrambling Behaviour') was written on 15 February. Two days later, he described the ecstatic emotional experience of listening to music and drinking, which released him from the prison of his life. 'I bring back to my prison (flat) people who are not always allowed to leave. Maybe I want them to share my high experience of spirits and music. I still do not know the engine of my performance.'

On 19 February, Nilsen offered the police information on attempted murders, including the passage describing his feverish efforts to revive Carl Stottor, and the bungled attempt to strangle Toshimitsu Ozawa on New Year's Eve 1982.

The final document was the letter of 25 May thanking the police for their professional skill in trying to unravel the case. It asked Mr Jay to believe that he did not maliciously plan any of the attacks, and for the first time touched upon the possibility of remorse.

> My remorse is of a deep and personal kind which will eat away inside me for the rest of my life. I am a tragically private person, not given to public tears. The enormity of these acts has left me in permanent shock . . . The evil was short-lived and it cannot live or breathe for long inside the conscience. I have slain my own dragon as surely as the press and the letter of the law will slay me.

Nilsen finished this letter with a stanza from Oscar Wilde's *Ballad of Reading Gaol* which I had sent him a few weeks before.

Some aspects of these documents deserve consideration. In February, Nilsen said he had no tears for the victims, while in May he was talking of a deep and personal grief. What had happened in the meantime was the discovery of a remorse he had initially striven to suppress, released by his interviews with the psychiatrist Dr Bowden, by his visits from myself, and especially by his 'Sad Sketches', the drawings he made in April of bodies as he remembered them. These images brought at last into his cell the ghosts of the dead which in February had not yet troubled him. It is also clear that he had helped police trace living witnesses to his iniquity, whose existence might otherwise not have been suspected. No one was sure why he should want to 'slay his own dragon' so totally. Nilsen not only provided most of the evidence against himself, but encouraged the discovery of evidence which might easily run counter to his own version of events. Finally, Nilsen it was who first mentioned the possibility of innate evil. Neither prosecution nor defence used the word 'evil', which belongs to the vocabulary of moral philosophy and has no place in legal definitions, but Mr Justice Croom-Johnson in his summing up would give the word a questionable emphasis.

As for the multiplicity of motives suggested by the defendant for his actions, and all rejected by him, there were some who thought he was so clever as to try to confuse judge and jury alike by widening the scope of their deliberations, and others who were convinced that Nilsen was genuinely bewildered. We hoped (vainly, as it turned out) that the psychiatrists would sift the relevant from the muddled.

'Have you ever been involved in a case where the accused seemed to be so willing to co-operate?' asked Ivan Lawrence on opening his cross-examination of Mr Jay. The Chief Inspector agreed that he had never known a defendant be so immediately co-operative, and revealed that even up to the week before the trial, Nilsen had been helping to identify further victims from photographs. On the matter of Carl Stottor's reprieve, Mr Jay admitted that Nilsen had made no mention of having tried to drown him before the dog drew his attention to the body, and Lawrence drew the inference that he had suffered a complete block of that part of the incident, an inference which would assume its importance when Nilsen's state of mind came to be considered. Jay said that the defendant had given his long confession in a calm, unmoved, matter-of-fact manner while he, Jay, had found the substance of that confession 'horrific'. 'Did you find it almost impossible to associate the man you were interviewing with this catalogue of horror?' asked Lawrence. 'Very difficult indeed,' came the reply, and Mr Jay completed his evidence with the formal acknowledgment that Dennis Nilsen was of previous good character, with no criminal record.

Detective Chief Superintendent Geoffrey Chambers spent the whole of the Tuesday afternoon, 25 October, and Wednesday morning, 26 October, reading verbatim the long interviews at Hornsey. Chambers, a 'wise old owl', in Alan Green's phrase, betrayed no emotion as he read this astonishing confession, nor did the defendant, leafing through the

pages and following Chambers's recital word by word, as if
ready to correct any errors of syntax which might occur. The
public gallery, however, was mesmerised by the detailed
revelations of death, scarcely taking their eyes from Nilsen
throughout the four hours that it took to read the interviews.
Some appeared shocked, incredulous, others were near to
tears. A young blonde woman with heavily painted red lips
looked distraught, another stared down at Nilsen with hatred
pouring from her face. The jury showed signs of nervous-
ness, one man repeatedly running his hands through his hair
as he winced at some details. Many of them smiled nervously
when Chambers came to Nilsen's remark that he did not do a
stock-check of bodies under the floor. One juror looked pale
and kept blowing out his breath. The dark-haired lady
occasionally glanced at the prisoner in the dock, quizzically,
searchingly, looking for an answer. At the point when Nilsen
had described unpacking bundles of human remains, the
stench and the colonies of maggots, even the judge looked
repelled by what he heard. Towards the end of Mr Chambers's evidence, several exhibits were produced in court,
including the large cooking-pot in which three heads had
been boiled, the cutting board used to dissect pieces of John
the Guardsman, and Martyn Duffey's knives. The judge's
face then screwed up in unmovable disgust, and two jurors
were so shaken they seemed close to being sick. For the first
time in the trial, there was much nervous coughing in court.
There could hardly have been a more eloquent demonstration
of the gulf which divided ordinary men and women from the
impassive prisoner in the dock. At this point, it was difficult
to believe he was human at all. He himself wondered, he
wrote, if the jury could see him decomposing slowly in the
dock.

A photograph of Martyn Duffey was produced as an exhibit. It had been shown to the accused and positively
identified by him. In his private journal, Nilsen had written
of this moment at Hornsey: 'D.C.S. Chambers passed me a
colour photo of a young man. I recognised it as Martyn
Duffey taken when he was younger. The memory flooded
back. I stopped myself reacting. I wanted to weep but there

were now too many witnesses.'[3] There were now even more witnesses in court. Nilsen kept still, and none of them knew what, if anything, he felt.

Under cross-examination, Mr Chambers agreed that the police had managed to trace fourteen men who had visited Dennis Nilsen in one or other of his flats and had come to no harm. There were probably many more. He further agreed that Nilsen appeared to be unburdening himself, giving precise details on some murders and being unable to recall specifics on others. (Nilsen later told me that he knew from his months as a policeman that too many replies of 'I don't remember' tended to make them impatient, and he was anxious not to be obstructive. He was thinking as a policeman, investigating himself. Sometimes the details of one killing would merge with those of another, until he was unsure which was relevant, but he edited these recollections to make the task easier for the police who were questioning him. The killing of John the Guardsman, for instance, was a montage of flashes from several incidents. He thought of the Hitchcock film *Torn Curtain* as he was telling it.) Chambers said that the defendant showed no remorse, no feeling of horror or disgust, as he told of dissecting rotting bodies and boiling heads on the cooker to make the flesh come away. On this note, Ivan Lawrence sat down. Alan Green had no further questions to put, and the case for the prosecution was completed.

On Wednesday afternoon, Ivan Lawrence rose again to open the case for the defence. He said that he would not attempt to prove that Dennis Nilsen was insane in either the medical or the legal sense, but that he was suffering from an abnormality of mind at the time of each killing, and was therefore incapable of forming the specific intention of murder. The defence has only to prove that he *may* have been suffering from such abnormality, said Mr Lawrence, not that he *must* have been so suffering, at which point the judge intervened to chastise counsel; *he* would direct the jury on points of law, not Mr Lawrence! He concluded his opening remarks by exhorting the jury not to give way to the temptation of thinking that the killings were so horrible, the killer so vile, that they need not waste their time on subtleties

219

which would affect the sentence. 'Society, whom you repre-
sent, requires that you give the matter proper consideration.'
With that, Lawrence called his first witness, Dr James
MacKeith of the Bethlem Royal Hospital.

Dr MacKeith began with the stark contention that on each
of the six occasions of homicide, Dennis Nilsen had been
suffering from a severe personality disorder which substantially reduced his responsibility. There were, he said,
maladaptive patterns of behaviour which continued from
youth into adulthood. He then summarised Nilsen's early
life, with which the reader is familiar, and made three
interesting points very early in his evidence:

(a) Nilsen had always experienced difficulty about express-
     ing any feelings apart from anger.
(b) He had a tendency to attribute to others certain attitudes
     and feelings without checking if they were true.
(c) He always fled from situations where personal relation-
     ships had gone wrong.

Dr MacKeith said that Nilsen's trouble was an unspecified
type of personality disorder, which did not fit any particular
category. He showed signs of disorder in all categories, but
insufficient to diagnose when taken alone; it was the combination of these signs which convinced Dr MacKeith that
Nilsen was a severe, but hidden, case.

Two stories were presented before the jury as being related
to the concepts of nakedness and unconsciousness in a sexual
context. The first was Nilsen's recollection of walking into
the sea at Fraserburgh when he was ten, and being rescued
by an older boy who masturbated over him. The second was
the story of the Arab he killed in self-defence in Aden. They
were both bizarre stories, said the psychiatrist, like fantasies.
'I do not say these two stories are important if accurate, but
important because he has consistently told both stories to
at least one other person, and they demonstrate an extraordinary interest in the concept of unconsciousness.' The one
other person to whom Nilsen had told these stories was
myself, and he had admitted to me that there were elements

of fantasy in them, though they were based upon true events. Dr MacKeith told the court that it did not matter whether the stories were true or false; what mattered was that they were in his mind.

Having told the court of Nilsen's interest in mirrors and his habit of masturbating by a corpse before dissecting it (without, it must be said, revealing the significance of these unusual symptoms), Dr MacKeith went on to consider his occasional amnesia brought on by excessive drinking ('You mean he passed out because he was drunk,' said the judge), and his aggressive manner. He had the ability to separate his mental functions and his behaviour to an extraordinary degree, as was indicated by his behaviour towards the victims of attempted murder, when two parts of him appeared to operate a few minutes apart in total discrepancy.

Nilsen was unduly suspicious, with a paranoid reaction to immediate circumstances, and a craving for attention which amounted to 'grandiosity'. He had an unlimited need for interest in himself and his viewpoint. Dr MacKeith suggested that this might provide a clue to one reason why people died, namely that they did not pay attention to what he was saying and undervalued his opinion. 'It was the ultimate to pay for apathy.'

Finally, Dr MacKeith touched upon the defendant's impaired sense of identity and his habit of 'depersonalisation'. He was capable of apparently purposeful activity without its being under his full conscious control, perceiving himself at a distance in a manner not unlike that of a sleepwalker. Psychiatrists had a name for this neurosis; it was called 'dissociation'.

The cross-examination of Dr MacKeith began on Wednesday, and continued for most of Thursday, 27 October. It was not difficult for Alan Green to throw doubt upon the reliability of psychiatric jargon, which to a lay person seems nebulous and elusive. What, in the end, was the basis of Dr MacKeith's diagnosis? Nothing more than what the defendant had told him, and the way in which he had told him. Was there any evidence of 'deeply ingrained maladaptive behaviour' before the first killing occurred in 1978? The witness could not say. Was there any evidence of 'retarded or arrested development of mind'? Quite the contrary; the defendant's intelligence was above average, but Dr MacKeith insisted that this legal form of words was, for a psychiatrist, too narrow. It ought to cover retarded or arrested development of *personality*, which would certainly apply to Nilsen. After consultation with counsel and the judge, it was agreed that 'personality' should be included in the definition, but this did not advance precision much further, as the judge intervened to ask what was meant by 'personality'. When the witness said 'character', Mr Justice Croom-Johnson replied tartly, 'That's what I thought you would say.'

Referring to the two stories which Dr MacKeith had related to the court, Mr Green asked, 'Did you believe a single word of those stories was fact?' The witness would not be forced into a short answer, in spite of being asked the same question three times, until the judge intervened again. 'Was it *true*?' he said. 'What's your answer?' Dr MacKeith replied, 'Highly unlikely.'

Mr Green continued to build a catalogue of lies which Nilsen had told, to try to establish the point that he was a consistently untruthful person. Nilsen had, for example, told Paul Nobbs that his scar had been inflicted in Northern Ireland, when it was the result of a gall-bladder operation, and he had told the Japanese man that he was married.*

Quoting from Nilsen's own words, counsel said that he had managed to suppress all thoughts of morality from his mind, and invited Dr MacKeith to agree that whereas 'repression' was subjectively not deliberate, 'suppression' certainly was. The witness conceded this was correct. Green also said that Nilsen displayed resourcefulness, cunning and presence of mind, to which the witness replied that he would not use such words, but would prefer to be more illuminating. Mr Green then proposed that the separation of mental functioning to which Dr MacKeith had referred meant nothing more than that Nilsen was 'a jolly good actor'. It was becoming clear to

*Nilsen denies ever having said he was married.

the court that antagonism between lawyers and psychiatrists was endemic; at one point Mr Green leant forward and said to the witness, 'You know you really must *make up your mind* about your diagnosis.'

Mr Green presented several examples of Nilsen's plausibility and cunning. He had never, for example, faced the fact that he *invited* people back to his flat, using neutral terms instead, yet the initiative must have come from him. This was because he did not want to show the police that the purpose of their visits was to die at Nilsen's hands. He had hoodwinked Nobbs and Stottor into believing that nothing untoward had happened to them. He had allowed Martyn Duffey's knives to rust before throwing them out, and had collected Duffey's belongings from the left luggage at Euston Station. He had been able to stop midway in the course of strangulation, demonstrating that the root of this case was the extent to which the defendant was able to wield power over life and death. He was able to exercise self-control and desist when he wanted to, the implication being that he could also kill when he wanted to. Dr MacKeith disagreed, pointing out that it was striking how Nilsen recalled some physical aspects of his victims, but scarcely anything about them as people. They were objects who filled his assumptions, indicating a strange depersonalised state.

Mr Green took the witness through Nilsen's own account of four killings, in order to show awareness and deliberation. The most significant of these were the long and painfully vivid murder of John the Guardsman, and the almost casual killing of Malcolm Barlow. Nilsen, faced with an unconscious epileptic in his flat, had said that he had a problem and dealt with it. He had thought for twenty minutes wondering what to do. Dr MacKeith agreed that in this case there was no evidence of dissociation or depersonalisation. 'And yet you say his responsibility was diminished at the time?' asked Green. 'Oh come, doctor,' he shouted. 'Face up to my question!'

The cross-examination terminated in confusion. Mr Green asked if the witness still maintained that the defendant's responsibility was diminished in all six counts of murder. MacKeith was reluctant to use such words, so the judge requested counsel to put the question again. MacKeith said that the defendant was suffering from a mental disorder which profoundly affected his judgment. Mr Green put the question a third time. 'I hope it's simple,' he said. 'Do you yourself think he was of diminished responsibility?' 'I cannot answer that as an expert witness,' replied Dr MacKeith. 'That is for the court to answer.' 'I am pressing you, doctor,' pursued Mr Green, supported by the judge, who said to the witness, 'You are an expert. Why don't you say?' Dr Mac-Keith said that he could not say whether the defendant's responsibility was diminished, as that was a legal form of words which was for the court to determine on the basis of psychiatric evidence as to his abnormality of mind. 'Would your answer be the same on all six counts of murder?' asked Mr Justice Croom-Johnson. 'Yes.' 'In other words, you will not say?' 'No.'

Having begun his evidence by claiming diminished responsibility for the defendant, Dr MacKeith was forced to retract and in effect say that he was unable to judge as it was not a matter for him to determine. The lawyers and the psychiatrists did not speak the same language.

Dr Patrick Gallwey was the second psychiatric witness for the defence. He, too, began with the statement that the defendant suffered from an arrested development of personality (though not of intelligence) which substantially impaired his responsibility for his actions.

At the root of Nilsen's trouble was a condition of which Dr Gallwey had made a special study. It carried the impossible name 'Borderline False Self As If Pseudo-Normal Narcissistic Personality Disorder', but Dr Gallwey, no doubt mindful of the impatience such a mouthful might kindle in judge and jury alike, settled for the 'False Self' syndrome. Its essential feature was a combination of paranoid and schizoid elements and an apparent normal functioning of the personality. Because Nilsen can behave normally, without pretence (maintained Gallwey), he is able most of the time to keep at bay those schizoid disturbances which cause him to behave differently, but the strain involved in this conflict causes periodic breakdowns when the schizoid features predominate.

224

These outbreaks would display the same characteristics — sudden, episodic, motiveless, violent, psycho-sexual — not understood as normal extensions of personality. The emotional experience of oneself and of others is at these times drastically altered.*

On Friday, 28 October, Dr Gallwey returned to the witness-box to elaborate on his False Self analysis. There was evidence, he said, in the accounts of survivors to indicate the kind of breakdown he would expect to see. The murders followed the same pattern of breakdown, with one exception. Dr Gallwey was not happy with the reasons Nilsen gave for killing Malcolm Barlow, which made the attack differ in a significant way from the others. He did not say why.

False Self personalities, Gallwey continued, are kept in proper order when surrounded by affectionate relationships, but are more likely to disintegrate when socially isolated. They positively need good relationships to hold them together. In Nilsen's case, his liability to breakdown became severe when the relationship with David Gallichan collapsed. Anyway, 'Gallichan did not provide sufficient contact with human goodness.' He then clung to his office work obsessively, like a 'man drowning in his own nightmares', desperate to keep them under check. The killings (again with the one exception of Barlow) were 'motiveless from any point of view that a normal person could understand'.

After the first killing, Gallwey said, Nilsen tried to pull himself together. He thought it must have been the drink which caused it (he was wrong in this), so he laid off drinking for six months, and when he started again he was relieved to discover that he was all right. He was trying to explain his behaviour to himself.

The defendant's lack of feeling when he was killing was a crucial part of Dr Gallwey's analysis. 'The victims had no meaning to him as real individuals,' he said.

* The idea of the False Self was put forward by R.D. Laing, adapting some theories of Jean-Paul Sartre. The false self was an artificially created self-image designed to concur with expectations, while the true self remained hidden and protected.

He was muddled as to their identity, and frequently felt they threatened his private world. Divorced from normal awareness that his victims were real people enlivened with human properties, they became objects to him. Sometimes they seemed to be himself. This is very relevant to depersonalisation. The motiveless murder of John the Guardsman shows horrifically the effect of treating another person as if he were just an object. A normal person enriches experience and life with imagination. A schizoid personality indulges imagination for its own sake. This can produce artists, but in schizoids it can be dangerous, causing a split in personality. Nilsen's imagination eventually took him over, causing recurrent breakdowns.

Mr Justice Croom-Johnson interrupted to ask on what Dr Gallwey's conclusions were based, with reference to the defendant. The witness said Nilsen's fantasies provided evidence. What fantasies, asked the judge, tell us what they are! The witness said that Nilsen did not have the ability to separate his perception from his imagination, but this answer did not satisfy the judge, who was obviously angry when Dr Gallwey had to admit that he could not specify any one 'fantasy' which supported his thesis. He simply had not investigated them at all.

Returning to the absence of an emotional content to Nilsen's actions, Dr Gallwey said, 'I cannot see how he can be guilty of malice aforethought if he is entirely without feeling, since feeling is an integral part of a person's intent and motivation,' whereupon the judge told him that he was trespassing on the law, and should confine himself to medical opinion. The evidence of Carl Stottor's 'reprieve' indicated that Nilsen had emerged from an episode of dissociation and was 'reassembling' his personality; he was guided by some feeling, which had been absent during the attack.

When the court adjourned for lunch, Douglas Bence, a journalist, rushed up to the witness in front of the jury to ask a question about the disposal of human remains. Dr Gallwey refused to answer and reported the matter to the court administrator, as a result of which Mr Bence was reprimanded

by the judge at the beginning of the afternoon session. He
had been guilty of a gross contempt of court (which everyone
present realised) and could be imprisoned forthwith (which
many would have welcomed). But Croom-Johnson accepted
the man's apology and Gallwey took the stand once more for
cross-examination by Alan Green.

Mr Green suggested that the witness accepted some things
the defendant had told him, and flatly rejected others. This
was normal practice in psychiatry, said Dr Gallwey.

'Do you believe the account he gave to the police of the
killing of Malcolm Barlow, John the Guardsman, and the
emaciated young man?' asked Green.

'No.'

'Why not?'

'He is giving an account of actions when he must have been
in a very abnormal state of mind.'

'If the defendant's account to the police is indeed substantially true,' continued Green, 'then there's an end of your
diagnosis as far as those three killings are concerned?'

'I could be wrong.'

'Aren't you putting the cart before the horse, doctor?
You've come along here with a theory . . . '

'No,' interrupted Dr Gallwey.

' . . . a diagnosis . . . '

'That's not a theory.'

'Let's not split hairs.'

'It's not splitting hairs.'

Dr Gallwey explained his position with an analogy. If a
man complained of an ingrowing toenail and claimed it had
given him gonorrhoea, he would discount the evidence of the
toenail and look elsewhere. Counsel pounced upon this as a
trivial example, causing Dr Gallwey to explode in a rare show
of anger. 'I treat this case extremely seriously,' he said. 'It has
caused a great deal of distress and tragedy to a number of
people, and I strongly object to the way counsel has taken my
answers.' Wisely, Mr Green let the matter drop.

Green then concentrated on the degree of awareness shown
by the defendant and his ability to make choices and decisions.
He *chose* to invite men to his flat when he was perfectly aware

what might happen to them. He *decided* to kill Malcolm Barlow rather than do anything else. With John the Guardsman, he had offered to ring for a taxi, then decided to kill him instead. Giving emphasis to each word, Green said, '*He knew exactly what he was doing*. It is impossible to imagine a clearer picture of that event.'

'Leaving aside emotion, yes,' said Gallwey, 'but his emotional condition is *vital*.'

'You in no way dispute that he was intellectually aware of what was going on?'

'No.'

'He knew what he was doing?'

'I don't agree with that. The distinction between intellectual and emotional awareness is not a trivial matter. If his emotions were removed, then he would behave like a machine.'

'Did he know the nature and quality of his acts?'

'No. He knew the nature of the acts only, he did not know the quality of them.'

Mr Justice Croom-Johnson then made an intervention which was important in giving the jury everyday words with which to wrestle rather than abstruse medical concepts. 'By reason of his emotions not being involved, he is acting in cold blood. Is a cold-blooded killer not responsible for his acts?' Dr Gallwey replied that such words were not within his discipline.

The re-examination of Dr Gallwey by Ivan Lawrence on Monday, 31 October, was designed to clarify certain concepts which had arisen in evidence the previous week, namely:

(a) The acts of murder prevented Nilsen from going insane, by pointing destruction outwards instead of inwards. Without them, his mind would have collapsed into psychosis.

(b) A person cannot know what he is doing unless he has *emotional* awareness of what he is doing. With the emotional factor drained from him, he would be like an automaton.

(c) 'Cold-blooded' does not mean the same as 'without emotion'. A crocodile is cold-blooded. Applied to human behaviour, it is merely a metaphor and can be misleading. It departs from scientific precision.

(d) There is nothing abnormal in fantasising as such; the abnormality lies in what the fantasy *serves*. The schizoid trait can push it over the edge.

Mr Lawrence experienced some difficulty in framing questions which could extract these answers without 'leading' the witness, a cardinal sin for a barrister to commit. After putting one question three times without either the witness or anyone else in court understanding what he meant, the judge with a hearty chuckle said, 'Put it in a *leading* form, Mr Lawrence, come on.' Mr Lawrence did not look abashed, but rather grateful.

He also introduced a significant ruling in the case of Regina *v*. Rose, to the effect that 'a man may know what he is doing and intend to do it and yet be suffering from such abnormality of mind as to substantially impair his judgment.' If the jury could be reminded of this precedent frequently enough, Mr Lawrence might yet be able to show that Dennis Nilsen was such a man. In addition, he invited the court to consider the Appeal Court judgment of Lord Chief Justice Parker in the Byrne case. Parker had said that abnormality of mind was, 'wide enough to cover the mind's activities in all its aspects and meant a state of mind so different from that of ordinary human beings that the reasonable man would term it abnormal.'

For the moment the case for the defence rested, and there remained only the 'rebuttal' psychiatrist for the prosecution to hear, Dr Paul Bowden, the man whom Nilsen called a 'cold fish' but who had seen the defendant on no less than sixteen occasions covering fourteen hours spread over eight months. There could be no disputing that he had been more thorough than the other doctors, nor, as he stood in the witness box, that he was indeed icy.

Questioned by Alan Green, Dr Bowden examined the precise wording of the Homicide Act 1957, Section II, Subsection 1, and declared that he could find no abnormality in

Nilsen which fitted the definition of the Act.* There was no arrested or retarded development of mind (whether in intellect or personality), no mental disease, no injury, no inherent cause. There was no genetically inherited or constitutional component which would predispose the defendant towards a depressive condition. (Dr Bowden plainly had not inquired after the history of fishing villages in Aberdeenshire, and knew nothing of the chronic incidence of clinical depression among Nilsen's immediate antecedents — the Stephens and the Duthies.)

Bowden gave the impression that the defendant had been busy trying to manipulate him and that he had resisted. He painted a picture of a gregarious boy, intelligent, artistic, in a close family atmosphere, with a mild feeling of being an 'outsider'. 'Latterly the defendant has been more emphatic in presenting his boyhood as lonely and withdrawn,' he added. He also challenged Nilsen's account of the relationship with David Gallichan, which he had said was based only on sex. Gallichan denied this in interview with Dr Bowden.

The witness dismissed various motives for murder which Nilsen had postulated, offering his own version, to the effect that Nilsen had transferred his feeling of guilt about his homosexuality into guilt at being a murderer. (In other words, I feel guilty already, so why not do something *really* bad?)† 'I found the case extremely harrowing, at least initially,' said Dr Bowden. 'Latterly, putting aside the horrendous nature of the crimes, I felt strong sympathy for the defendant and believed I understood him, however imperfectly.'

There was no evidence, in his view, of dissociation, such as occurs during an epileptic fit, a diabetic coma or an incident of sleepwalking. Dissociation invariably involved amnesia,

---

*'Such abnormality of mind (whether arising from a condition of arrested or retarded development of mind or any inherent causes or induced by disease or injury) as substantially impaired his mental responsibility for his acts and omissions in doing or being a party to the killing.' (Homicide Act 1957)

† The reader is invited to read again Nilson's poem on p. 145, which deals with the transference of guilt in a graphic manner.

whereas Nilsen could remember some of the murders in great detail. Those that he found painful to recall he had suppressed from his memory.

There was no evidence, either, of especial loneliness or withdrawal apart from the usual sense of distance felt by homosexuals. As for the masturbation beside the corpse, which occurred only once (Sinclair),* this was not sexual in nature (*sic*), and the powdering of corpses was merely by way of disinfectant to smother the smell. There were no paranoid tendencies and no difficulties in forming personal relationships. There was no impaired sense of identity, and the grandiosity referred to in court was too recently acquired to be considered a long-standing personality defect; it showed in his relaxed interviews with the police as 'a transparent defence against the hopelessness of his position'.

Dr Bowden revealed to the court one incident which, he said, demonstrated Nilsen's capacity to feel very deeply and to conceal his feelings in order to preserve appearances. Only once had he walked out of an interview with the psychiatrist, when he was asked to recall the death of John the Guardsman. He did not want to allow his feelings about that killing to come forward, having until then put the episode at the back of his mind. He would not talk about it, his eyes filled with tears, and he left the room rather than be vanquished by emotion. Remorse was evident, said the doctor.

(The interview to which Dr Bowden referred took place on 13 April 1983. Immediately afterwards, Nilsen confided his own reflections on his distress in his prison journal. 'He presses me, yet again, for all the details of a "killing",' he wrote. 'I have run these images over and over in my mind and they are unbearable. It was bad enough when I had to keep control during the police statement sessions at Hornsey Police Station. I cannot bring myself to keep remembering these incidents over and over again. These are ugly images totally alien to me. I seem to have not participated in them, merely

---

*It occurred more often, but Nilsen had not told Dr Bowden this. See Chapter 6.

stood by and watched them happen — enacted by two other players — like a central camera.'[4] This sounds not unlike the phenomenon of 'depersonalisation'. The prison journals were available to but not requested by any of the psychiatrists.)

Dr Bowden could find no evidence of maladaptive patterns of behaviour ameliorating (as they generally do) in middle age. On the contrary, Nilsen's admittedly abnormal behaviour only emerged in adult life. Asked to give his view of Dr Gallwey's 'False Self' syndrome, Bowden said it was no more than a theory and therefore impossible to refute. One either has to believe such theories or not believe them, and Dr Bowden did not believe this one. It conflicted with what evidence there existed, which was of a man displaying purposeful integrated behaviour as he wilfully encouraged his victims to relax or fall asleep. There was no disintegration of the personality either before or after the killings, no high degree of anxiety, but rather a rational and goal-directed mind. Dr Gallwey's theory was an attractive medical explanation, but no more.

A page of doodles prepared by the prisoner for Dr Bowden in March 1983.

Mr Lawrence's cross-examination attempted to show, in essence, that Dr Bowden was a rather poor psychiatrist. The last sentence of the doctor's report dated 20 September stated, 'I am unable to show that Dennis Nilsen had an abnormality of mind.' Little more than one month later, Dr Bowden was stating the opposite, that he did have an abnormality of mind but not a mental disorder. Why had he changed his conclusion? And why should we place more reliance upon what he says now than on what he said on 20 September? Dr Bowden explained that he had previously thought the two expressions (abnormality of mind and mental disorder) were synonymous. For the first time in his career he had to admit they were not. Nilsen was a unique case. Though abnormal, he was not mentally defective.

Mr Lawrence asked why so many cardinal events in Nilsen's life were ignored by Dr Bowden. The death of his grandfather, for instance? 'I do not believe it was psychologically damaging to him at that time,' said Bowden. His increased social isolation after 1978? That was due to the fact there were bodies all over the place.

There were some giggles in court when Mr Lawrence insisted on the abnormality of Nilsen's conduct and drew from the witness the blandest of replies tinged with weary impatience.

'Of course strangling people is not normal behaviour,' conceded Dr Bowden.

'How then do you interpret his attitude towards the victim?'

'I suspect he wanted to kill him.'

As for the defendant's stark lack of emotion, Bowden at first maintained that, on the contrary, his ability to share feelings with another person was extensive, then added another common-sense remark. 'In my experience,' he said, 'the vast majority of people who kill *have* to regard their victims as objects otherwise they cannot kill them.'

When the cross-examination of Dr Bowden resumed on Tuesday, 1 November, there was a further altercation over the definition of terms. Counsel wanted to dwell upon 'diminished responsibility' but witness refused to comment, because 'diminished responsibility is not an illness like the 'flu but a subsection of the Homicide Act.' All right. Mr Lawrence tried again. Was not Nilsen's obsessive guilt about homosexuality indicative of a mental disorder? 'No,' said Bowden, 'it is preposterous to suggest that if a person is homosexual he suffers from a mental disorder.' So it would be, but that was not what Lawrence had suggested. Dr Bowden's remorselessly colourless response to questions was frustrating counsel, who seemed unable to prise from him the smallest admission that there was anything at all wrong with Nilsen (except his by now obvious enjoyment in killing people), until they touched upon the period of Nilsen's remand at Brixton Prison. Bowden agreed that Nilsen had shown an unusual degree of complaint, and further agreed that this might point towards paranoid tendencies. When he said that there were no such tendencies in Nilsen, he carried little conviction, especially since the court had heard examples of Nilsen's conduct in prison. It transpired that Bowden had been responsible for consigning Nilsen to the hospital wing in prison because he thought he was a suicide risk. Is it not true that a man who is liable to commit suicide is suffering from some disorder of the mind, asked Mr Lawrence? Not in Nilsen's case, answered Dr Bowden, though he was subsequently pressed into admitting that the majority of remand prisoners who commit suicide are indeed suffering from mental disorder, and Nilsen was initially thought to be one such person. But Dr Bowden had since changed his mind.

It was then the witness's turn to win a point. You cannot infer mental abnormality from the killings and then explain the killings in terms of mental abnormality, he said. This was a circular argument, tantamount to saying the man was mad because he killed and killed because he was mad. The next point he made was considerably less persuasive. Surely the fact that the defendant gave Carl Stottor his name and address after he had almost killed him, and allowed Paul Nobbs to telephone his mother and say where he was before attempting to kill him, indicating extraordinary irrationality, asked Mr Lawrence. Not at all, said Bowden, 'it points to the pleasure he derived in being so powerful.' There were not many in court who could imagine such coolness in full clarity of mind.

Dr Bowden's long ordeal in the witness-box finished with another clash over the definition of terms, in which he for the first time betrayed his irritation. 'People with prodigious memories have an abnormality of mind,' he said, 'in that their behaviour is not normal, not usual, but that does not amount to a mental disorder.'

'But on 20 September you said that Nilsen's abnormality did amount to such a thing. You've got your terminology wrong, haven't you, doctor? How many times before have you got your terminology wrong?'

'Several.'

'And on those occasions did the courts act upon your report?'

'No.'

'I should hope not,' said Lawrence, pausing to fix the floor with a long look of disbelief before sitting down.

With that, the evidence in the case of Regina v. Nilsen was complete. Both Mr Green and Mr Lawrence went to some trouble in their closing speeches to remove from the jury's mind the clutter of psychiatric classification with which they had been bombarded for four days and to reduce the case to its basic recognisable elements. For Mr Green, they were dealing with a defendant who liked killing people and derived satisfaction from the act itself. For Mr Lawrence, they had before them a man who was simply out of his mind. 'The defence says he couldn't really help it,' opened Mr Green. 'The Crown says, oh yes he could.'

Mr Green depicted Nilsen as a man who was able to exercise self-control over his actions, able to choose whom to leave alone, whom to kill and whom to reprieve. He was resourceful and cunning, coherent and articulate, 'a plausible fellow, able to bluff his way out of many a tricky situation'. Taking the jury through the many points counted against Nilsen (his warning to Stottor about the zip on the sleeping-bag, the trouble he took to construct a ligature of tie and string with which to kill Sinclair, his rusting of Duffey's knives before throwing them out), he ended each one with the air of a man stating the obvious — 'So there it is!'

'There were no nightmares for Mr Nilsen, whatever the

psychiatrists may tell you,' said Green. 'The motives he has offered are not motives at all, but pretexts latched on to by Nilsen to explain his actions after the event.' Quoting from the police interviews the sentence, 'I could see what had happened before would happen again,' Green maintained that this showed conclusively that Nilsen was not a man of moral blindness, that he knew right from wrong, and went on inviting young men to his premises in the full knowledge that they might end their lives there. Alcohol he dismissed as forming no part of diminution of responsibility. 'A drunken intent is still an intent,' he said.*

Green's oration, which continued into Wednesday, 2 November, was a powerful piece of plotting, free from invective or drama, clear and disarmingly polite (it was noticeable that he often referred to the defendant as 'Mr Nilsen', whereas his own counsel invariably called him 'Nilsen'). When he terminated with the quiet invitation to the jury to find the man guilty of murder, there was a moving sense of awe in the court.

Ivan Lawrence picked up this sense of awe as he began his closing speech for the defence. He was going to state, he said, what was blindingly obvious. 'Does not common speech oblige one to say of the perpetrator of those killings, he must be out of his mind? Even if the law were an ass, members of the jury, you are here to apply your common sense.' Echoing Mr Green's 'So there it is,' Lawrence went through a catalogue of horror, pausing after each item to ask the rhetorical question, 'Is there nothing substantially wrong with the mind of a man like that?' It was a Ciceronian performance which concealed the fact that there was little legal substance in what Lawrence was saying. He was appealing to naked innocence, inviting the jury to regard the law as inadequate to deal with such a freak as Nilsen and suggesting that they might know better. The only evidence he considered at length was that

*In this he is supported by Wolfgang and Strohm, 'Relationship between Alcohol and Criminal Homocide' in *Quarterly Journal of Studies on Alcohol*, vol. 17, no. 3 (1956), wherein it is stated that intoxication does not preclude deliberation and premeditation.

offered by Dr Bowden, whom he called the 'Dr No of Central Criminal Court Number 1' because he had consistently refused to see any sign of mental disorder in the defendant, whereas men and women of the world could see it without looking very far. *'Res Ipsa Loquitur,'* he intoned, 'The thing speaks for itself.' It did not need psychiatrists, it did not need lawyers, it just needed a sensible jury [or Lord Chief Justice Parker's 'reasonable man'] to see that the defendant was, in effect, crazy.

For nearly four hours, Mr Justice Croom-Johnson summed up the issues raised in the case and clarified the subtleties of the task which faced the jury. To the public at large, it might have appeared easy, even absurdly so; the man had not denied his crimes, why should so much time and effort be wasted in deciding what label to pin upon him — the sentence would be the same whatever happened. As Nilsen himself wrote in the cell, they had to decide 'Am I outrageously bad or just very bad?' There were indications in the press that such questions were being raised. Here in the courtroom, however, the jury had to cope with a problem set for them by incautious legislators. The concept of 'diminished responsibility' had been introduced into the 1957 Homicide Act to save the Home Secretary from having to send to the gallows a man who was patently so dim-witted as to be not answerable for his actions. Now the gallows had gone, but the 'diminished' clause remained. It was archaic, it had outlived its purpose, and it placed an intolerable burden upon juries, who had to decide whether the mental abnormality of the defendant was substantial enough to impair his judgment.* 'What is meant by "substantial"?' asked Croom-Johnson. 'It doesn't mean total. Nor does it mean slight or trivial. Parliament has left it to you to decide, I'm afraid. You may legitimately differ from the doctors and use your common sense. If you found there

---

*In 1975 the Butler Committee (of which Croom-Johnson had been vice-chairman) recommended a new verdict – 'Not Guilty on evidence of mental disorder'. The Criminal Law Revision Committee has completed its report on Butler's recommendations, but they have yet to be debated in Parliament.

was some impairment, but not enough, you would be allowed to find him guilty of murder.'

The jury would have first to determine if on the six counts of murder Nilsen killed the men, then to decide if he intended to kill them. Should the answer to both questions be 'Yes', then they had a case of murder. Only afterwards should they consider whether or not to reduce the offence to one of manslaughter. (This procedure was followed scrupulously by the members of the jury, with the result that they gave a note to the judge the following day to say they were all agreed on murder, having completed the first two stages of their deliberations, and would like to delay the question of responsibility. The judge had then to correct his earlier instruction and tell them they must decide upon responsibility *before* concluding that the case was one of murder. They were apparently divided six to six on the matter of responsibility.)

The judge's summing up was delivered in a quiet, tired, frail voice, which belied the close attention he had clearly given to every aspect of the evidence. One was left with the impression that Croom-Johnson was the only person in court capable of absorbing and unravelling the complexities of all the evidence. As he proceeded, however, it became apparent which verdict he personally thought the jury ought to return. On one count of attempted murder, there were few who would dispute that the law left no alternative to a verdict of guilty. The fact that Nilsen had spared Paul Nobbs was irrelevant. 'Up until the time that change of heart took place, what was it that Nilsen was trying to do?' mused the judge. The evidence offered by Douglas Stewart was less conclusive. It was by no means clear that Nilsen had even started to kill him, only that he had intended to start. The disparity between the two cases was reflected in the eventual verdict, when all twelve jurors found the defendant guilty of attempting to murder Nobbs, and ten of them (with two dissenting) found him guilty in the case of Stewart.

On the six counts of murder, Croom-Johnson's bias was pronounced. 'There are evil people who do evil things,' he said. 'Committing murder is one of them.' Again, 'A mind can be evil without being abnormal.' (The question as to whether evil represents a departure from the norm or is inherent in the human condition is a metaphysical one, which has been debated by philosophers for centuries and will continue to be debated without any hope of resolution. It cannot be resolved because it is incapable of proof one way or the other, but depends upon the ideas men develop as they contemplate intractable human nature, and the language they use to express them. Ultimately, it boils down to the religious concept of Original Sin. Psychiatrists do not tamper with such concepts. Nor, in the normal way, do lawyers.)

If Dennis Nilsen suffered from a retarded development of personality, that, alas, was not something which could be measured like an intelligence quotient. It was very difficult even to describe it, as the psychiatrists had demonstrated. If it only meant 'character', then the jury should not, warned Croom-Johnson, give it undue weight. 'There must be no excuses for Nilsen if he has moral defects . . . a nasty nature is not arrested or retarded development of mind.' (Lord Denning is on record as saying that 'any mental disorder which has manifested itself in violence and is prone to recur, is a disease of the mind.' This ruling was not mentioned by anyone in court.)

The jury retired late on the morning of Thursday, 3 November. A verdict was confidently expected during the afternoon, but the hours passed and it was not forthcoming. At 4.30 p.m. the judge asked the foreman of the jury whether they might reach a verdict if the court sat until the early evening. 'No, my lord,' he replied without hesitation. They were then sent to a hotel for the night and ordered to resume their deliberations the following morning at 10 a.m. Meanwhile, the London evening newspaper, the *Standard*, had misread the ease with which the jurors would make up their minds, taken a gamble, and published a great deal of background material on Nilsen and his bloody career in clear contempt of court. Frantic efforts were made to gather up copies from the streets of London, but it was too late. The next day, five national newspapers followed suit.*

*The Attorney General's office took no action.

239

Thursday evening, in his cell, Nilsen wrote:

At the end of this day I am tired. I am tired. I face tomorrow and tomorrow is the future. I will be putting on that stuffy civil service garb for the last time in many many years. I do not know what will happen tomorrow . . . I tend to see myself as in jail for keeps. I must make the best of whatever future now remains for me (thirty years or so). I'll survive.[5]

On Friday, 4 November, at 11.25 a.m., Mr Justice Croom-Johnson told the jury he would accept a majority verdict. This came through at 4.25 p.m., with two dissenters on every count except the attack upon Paul Nobbs, when all twelve jury members agreed. Dennis Andrew Nilsen was found guilty of murder six times and of attempted murder twice. The judge sentenced him to life imprisonment with a recommendation that he serve a minimum of twenty-five years. He went down to the cells and was removed to Her Majesty's Prison Wormwood Scrubs. To the last, Nilsen remained strangely impervious to the ghastliness of his crimes. The agony of remorse which had overcome him at least three times during his remand, and had lasted for some days, was not apparent immediately after conviction. Writing of himself in the third person, he says, 'He has committed fifteen homicides and it is other people who think him important.'[6]

10

ANSWERS

'How many more words must I write without arriving at a smooth compact conclusion?'[1] By the time his trial was over, Nilsen had filled nearly fifty prison exercise books with random reminiscences in what looked like a concentrated effort to find himself, to unravel the multiple knots of motive and mind which caused him to become a killer. Like Raskolnikov in Dostoievsky's *Crime and Punishment*, he was a criminal pondering his own crimes and hoping by relentless examination to dispel bewilderment. The need was sometimes so urgent that he would scribble on the back of his depositions; with uncomfortable irony the murderer's self-justifications are found on the reverse of a list of human remains consequent upon his acts. The court had accepted the prosecution's case that Nilsen killed 'in cold blood' to satisfy his own perverted desires. This at least had the merit of simplicity and would obviate the need for any further inquiry:

I probably did enjoy those acts of killing. It was intense and all-consuming. Poor Doctor Bowden won't be satisfied until he has a *reason*. Well, enjoying it (killing) is as good a reason as any. I hope he will be contented with that. How the hell do I know what motivated me to kill someone I had

241

nothing against at that particular time! I needed to do what I did at that time. I had no control over it then. It was a powder keg waiting for the match. I was the match. The more I write, the less I know. I have probably already written the reason somewhere back there amongst all these words . . . everything must be in small neat boxes for these people . . . the real answer might lie in the fact that I could be just a bad bastard.[2]

Colin Wilson, who has made a long study of murder, insists that we must acknowledge the urge to destroy as an inherent characteristic of mankind. He writes:

For whatever reason, man *is* capable of experiencing a morbid involvement in the act of destruction, as if some deep erotic nerve had been touched by a craving for violence. And, like the sexual impulse, this destructive impulse has the power to blind him to everything but its own satisfaction.[3]

As if in corroboration, Nilsen's final statement, written in Wormwood Scrubs Prison a few days after his life sentence began, shows that he had decided to 'come clean' and make a frank admission that the Crown case against him had been essentially correct all along. Here are some extracts from that statement:

The loner has to achieve fulfilment alone within himself. All he has are his own extreme acts. People are merely supplementary to the achievement of these acts. He is abnormal and he knows it.

I had always wished to kill but the opportunity never really presented itself in safe conditions . . . therefore substituted by fantasies which had *me* killed in the mirrored images. I had been killing this way for years, killing my own image.

The kill was only part of the whole. The whole experience which thrilled me intensely was the drink, the chase, the social seduction, the getting the 'friend' back, the decision to kill, the body and its disposal.

The pressure needed release. I took release through spirits and music. On that high I had a loss of morality and danger feeling . . . If the conditions were right, I would completely follow through to the death.

He failed to kill Stewart and Ozawa, he says, because excessive alcohol clouded his judgment. As for Nobbs and Stottor, those attempts were interrupted 'for reasons of survival and had nothing to do with sympathy for the victim'. With Nobbs, he suddenly realised as he was throttling the man that he (Nobbs) had twice telephoned his mother that evening, and would be missed by her. As for Stottor, it was a practical decision not to complete the murder; he simply had no room for the body! Besides, they may have been seen together in the Black Cap. Kevin Sylvester, whom Nilsen rescued one evening (afterwards, the reader will recall, Nilsen felt 'elated' because the man had come to no harm), was spared because he had been found unconscious in the street and therefore fell outside the necessary formula of the 'chase'. The formula had to be right. (Why, then, did he kill Barlow, who also was not hunted, but presented himself twice to Nilsen?) Nilsen names two other men whom he 'really wanted' to kill, but did not because the conditions were not right or the risk of discovery was too great. An untold number of others owed their lives to the fact that there were already too many bodies under the floor at Melrose Avenue and Nilsen could not be seen to have bonfires with uncommon regularity without arousing suspicion. Two more sentences in this 'final' confession, slipped in almost in parentheses, alert one to see a different emphasis. 'The decision to kill was never taken until a few moments before it was attempted or transacted,' he writes; and 'I wished I could stop but I could not. I had no other thrill or happiness.'[4]

Quite obviously, there are some inconsistencies in the statement which make it difficult to accept in every detail. Nilsen had, for example, known that Paul Nobbs was a university student, with a firm identity and a home, since lunchtime on the day that they met. It is inconceivable that he should only remember this when he had all but killed him some nine hours later. The problem of what to do with Stottor's body in the attic flat at Cranley Gardens had not prevented him from killing one man only a month earlier (in March 1982), and would not prevent him from killing two more before he was caught. And the risk of discovery in the case of Kenneth Ockendon was very high (it being likely that a good number of people had seen them together during the day, especially at the pub where they drank for two hours or at the shop where they bought food that evening). Yet Ockendon died in a sudden moment of unreflective impulse. The risk was also high with Barlow, with the possibility that Nilsen might be traced through hospital records. Nilsen says he relished the excitement of risk. With his trial out of the way, Nilsen may well have been prone to attach exaggerated importance to his power of decision, almost as a sop to his pride and a childish desire to demonstrate that he had been capable of superlative deception. Added to which, I believe, he was weary of looking for answers.

This is not to say that the central truth of Nilsen's confession, namely that he killed for pleasure, should be discarded. But it would be wholly wrong to regard that as the end of the matter. The degree of control Nilsen was able to exercise over his acts requires further attention, and it is all but certain that he is the last person to measure that degree in any adequate manner. Moreover, to say that a killer enjoys killing is tautological. It offers no answer, but merely restates the question, and to accept it as it stands would be a facile surrender.

Even as one reads these documents, and half-welcomes the summation they represent, one is struck by involuntary revelations which suddenly and temporarily lift Nilsen from the unfathomable depths of monstrosity and bring him back into the air where we can recognise him more readily. 'I have unburdened myself and held nothing back,' he writes. 'I have been candid to the point that the reader may be horrified at times.'[5] And again, 'I do not feel like a very acceptable human being when I write these notes directly pertinent to my offences. I feel unclean.'[6]

How can it be that a murderer of so black a hue can first express fear that his revelations might offend, then look upon himself with contempt as if *he* were the one who is offended by them? These are not the remarks of a man without conscience. The moral sense, suffocated almost beyond recall, does still retain a timid voice. A true psychopath, insensible to any understanding of morality, does not make this kind of apology to the susceptibilities of his listeners. Nilsen's last chapter makes him more, not less, enigmatic.

We have already had cause to be reminded of Dostoievsky's great study of motiveless murder in *Crime and Punishment*, in which Raskolnikov in the most profound solitude is driven to endless contemplation of his crime in a desperate effort to repress the guilt which continually surges up by finding an explanation which will at least make him human. His worst punishment is a constant, relentless pondering on his brutal killing of an old woman, a perpetual self-analysis which he cannot escape. One critic has interpreted Raskolnikov's need in these words: 'To sustain himself in the terrible isolation of his guilt he must be in complete possession of a single incontrovertible motive representing his deepest self, his own rock-bottom truth.'[7] It is not too extravagant to recognise in this summary the same preoccupation which has beset Nilsen; any motive is better than none, and the worst fate is insubstantiality. The same critic points out the several personalities which Raskolnikov displays in the course of the novel, and once more they reflect some of the confusing disparities in Nilsen's character as they emerged at his trial and in this book. There was an altruistic Raskolnikov and an egotistic Raskolnikov, 'a despot by nature'; a radical Raskolnikov with ideas of revolution, and a grandiose Raskolnikov who demanded the right to self-assertion, to exercise his own power in his own way; 'and there is the neurotic who acts out his illness through a murder intellectually rationalised but inexplicable except in terms of an unconscious drive.'[8]

There is no need, however, to resort to literary echoes. A number of experienced criminal psychiatrists have studied the phenomenon of the multiple murderer and have attempted to draw a picture of the kind of man whose character and life history mark him out as a potential murderer of this kind. The point of such studies is to enable psychiatrists to spot the clues before a personality finally disintegrates and fulfils itself in destruction. (This is not to say, of course, that *everyone* who fits such a description is a potential killer, only that potential killers will often fit it.) One particular study, by Dr Robert Brittain, builds a portrait of the mass murderer-to-be that is so like Dennis Nilsen in almost every respect that it takes one's breath away. The study was published in a medical journal in 1970, and represented the fruit of twenty years' close study of murderers who killed for no apparent motive other than enjoyment.

The sadistic murderer, says Dr Brittain, is commonly an introspective and rather withdrawn man. He has few associates, and usually no close friends. His pursuits are solitary, such as listening to music. He is studious and pedantic, retiring, essentially shy, and he feels inadequate. Sometimes he presents himself as pseudo-intellectual. He is uncommunicative, and rarely if ever shows his temper. He does not retaliate to violence, and never did, even at school. He is very clean, and meticulous in appearance. He feels different from other people, and is thereby isolated and insecure. He tends not to drink very much. He feels inferior to everyone, except in relation to his offences, when he feels superior to other men. He is at his most dangerous when he has suffered a loss of self-esteem, such as might happen if he were demoted at work.

Nilsen is already recognisable, apart from in the reference to abstention from drink. The reader does not need to be reminded of his loneliness and introspection. At school he did not join in playground fights, and we know also that he felt inadequate in every way when compared to those around him. His pretensions to intellectuality are evident in his writings, where he will occasionally use something picked up from a dictionary of quotations and reveal his source. His first crime was committed after the breakdown of personal relationships and the failure of his superiors at work to recommend him for promotion when he had completed the requisite number of years' service and acquitted himself well.

Dr Brittain goes on to describe his composite man as a

> vain, narcissistic, egocentric individual who, through his
> vanity, may be convinced that he can commit murder and
> escape detection by being more clever than the police. He
> would rather be notorious than ignored and . . . he may
> have ideas of himself going down in history as a major
> criminal and, before detection, read and comment on
> details of his crime reported in the newspapers. He some-
> times expresses very strong and punitive views on what
> should be done with the murderer when he is caught.
> There can be a peculiar arrogance about him.

Other characteristics are tendencies to hypochondria and
homosexuality. He is sometimes regarded as a 'loner'. Beneath
his retiring façade there is a deep aggression which he cannot
normally express.

We should pause here only to remark that Nilsen, ever
protective of his health, was anxious to ensure a regular daily
intake of Vitamin C, and that during his trial he asked that he
should be supplied with the principal newspapers so that he
could read the reports on his case, and correct inaccuracies.
On the other hand, no one would say that he had a 'retiring
façade', and his aggression was frequently expressed in fluent
harangues on political and moral issues.

The murderer has a rich and active fantasy life.

> Even as a child he is likely to have been withdrawn, living
> in part in his own dream world. His fantasy life is in many
> ways more important to him than is his ordinary life, and
> in a sense more real, so diminishing the value he puts on
> external life and on other people. It is almost as if he were
> forced by practical realities to emerge unwillingly from
> fantasy at times, but returns to it as soon as he can.

> He is generally under thirty-five (Nilsen was thirty-three
> at the time of his first murder) and of high intelligence, which
> would be necessary to indulge and develop his complicated
> fantasy life. He is emotionally flattened, shows little or no

remorse and is without pity for his victims. He is indifferent to the moral implications of his acts.

Dr Brittain continues:

> He will frequently express regret if asked, but he does not feel it, or, if he does, his feeling is only transiently sincere, is shallow, and is quite insufficient to prevent him from killing again. Such expressions of regret are commonly to create what he hopes is the right impression and one designed to achieve some advantage for himself. He can detach himself from his killing, being aware of it but not emotionally involved. He knows he is responsible for his offence but regrets only its legal consequences.[9]

After his arrest, Nilsen displayed no hint of remorse under questioning by the police. Subsequently, waves of contrition have possessed him (the first being at the end of March 1983), but they are of short duration and separated by intervals of weeks or months; they are also on occasions disguises for self-pity. Sometimes Nilsen's remorse shows evidence of deep feeling, but he is himself alive to the possibility that it is spurious, and wonders why. He has written, 'Words like "sorry" hold little comfort for the bereaved. I mistrust my own inner sincerity to bear even to utter them.'[10]

There is more to say on the question of feeling. After his crime, the sadistic murderer behaves normally and calmly. 'Intellectually, he *knows* that it is wrong to kill but emotionally he does not *feel* this to apply in his case. He is indifferent to the feelings of others but shows much concern in matters relating to himself and in particular to his welfare or his safety.' This passage recalls Dr Gallwey's evidence in court about acts which are devoid of emotional content. We are also reminded of Nilsen's note, left on his desk on the day he was arrested, pointing out that his death would not be the result of suicide, and also of his many complaints on remand about the way he was treated in Brixton Prison.

Murderers of this kind have little experience of normal sexual intercourse. Nilsen claims to have had coitus with women twice in his life, once with a prostitute in Berlin and once with a Swiss *au pair* girl in London. But the word 'normal' in this context may be taken to include complete homosexual love-making, which Nilsen did not experience until his late twenties. Thereafter, he passed a few years in random promiscuous sexual contact, which probably did include complete love-making on occasions. A letter found among his papers at Cranley Gardens from a man in Birmingham says 'our love-making was so beautiful'. However, a few people who are known to have had sexual relations with Nilsen report that very little activity took place, and there is one passage among his notes which reveals more than it intended. Talking of the death of his first victim, Nilsen says that he examined the body with his hands, and was particularly fascinated to see that part of it which is normally never seen, between the scrotum and the anus. Lovers who are relaxed and are used to exploring each other's body would find this statement odd, and may deduce that Nilsen could only have had limited sexual experience if he was a stranger to the perineum.

The multiple murderer 'may describe opposing forces warring within him, referring to them as good and evil, or God and the Devil.' As we have seen, Nilsen calls himself the 'monochrome man' — black and white — and makes frequent reference to the contrasting poles of man's nature which possess him equally. This is an aspect which we shall have to look at more closely later, untrammelled by the disciplines of psychiatric method. For the moment, one of Nilsen's letters to the author finishes with the sentence, 'I am probably both devil and angel — the darkness and the light. I have had too much darkness — I have dispelled it and I am reaching out to the light.'[11]

There may be evidence of some minor sexual offence before the murders began, or of some fire-raising. In Nilsen's case there is the episode with David Painter in 1975, which arose from a sexual advance, and instances of nearly starting fires at his flat on at least three occasions – with Martin Hunter-Craig, with Trevor Simpson, and with three young men who stayed with him one night in 1978. Nilsen maintains that these embryonic fires had the purpose of asphyxiating the men, and failed, but he may well not be right in thus identifying the source of his own actions.

There is usually no history of mental illness (there is none with Nilsen). The murderer considers himself sane, behaves and talks normally even to psychiatrists, but is afraid that psychiatry may emasculate him.

If the kind of murderer Dr Brittain is describing attempts to resist his murderous drives, anxiety and deep depression result. He is very keen on using mirrors, often has photography as a hobby, and writes poetry (Nilsen concurs on all three points). Also, a surprising number of such people have been professional butchers.

They plan the murders well and cunningly. The victims are always strangers to them. They make plausible liars. At the time of the murder the killer's reason is dulled, all but obliterated by sexual and power drives. Excitement and ecstasy are greatest during the process of killing, leaving the death itself as an anti-climax. ('I am joyful just climbing the mountain,' wrote Nilsen, then speaking of sex rather than murder. 'I never really want to reach the summit because the joy is over.)' The usual method is strangulation, because death is thereby slower and pleasure can be prolonged, and also because the murderer can retain the power to increase or decrease pressure, to take the victim's life or to give it back. It is not unlike a cat playing with a mouse.

'The desire of having power over others is an essential part of this abnormality.' The subjection of the victim to the killer's power is more important than the infliction of pain, which is why these murderers do not feel cruel. Cruelty is not their primary objective, but the unavoidable means by which they achieve their end. (Nilsen has frequently said that he cannot tolerate the idea of cruelty, and that he dispatched his victims in a manner which was short, swift and decisive. He seems unable to understand that cruelty is not thereby erased, nor to reconcile his contention with the slow agony of John the Guardsman and Carl Stottor.)

'Although these are essentially sexually motivated crimes', writes Dr Brittain, 'sexual intercourse or even orgasm does not always occur. Sometimes the murderer masturbates beside his victim.' This passage accords entirely with Nilsen's own account of his behaviour towards the corpses.

Multiple murderers may often talk quite freely about their crimes in great detail. They are blandly unperturbed when so doing, and show no embarrassment. Sometimes they take pleasure in writing a detailed account of what they have done, and are commonly annoyed if any part of their story is doubted. They can be disproportionately irritated if a tiny point is misunderstood. They are 'indignant if they think some injustice is being done to them, seeing no incongruity in this when, at about the same time, they are relating some particularly monstrous actions of their own. They can even then appear self-righteous.'

Dr Brittain concludes his composite picture with the alarming remark, 'this condition is not rare.' Fortunately, it is still rare for the condition to become full-blown and homicidal, though the incidence of multiple murders over the last ten years indicates that complacency would be foolish. Especially in America, there has been a rash of cases which post-date the so-called Boston Strangler of the early sixties (Albert De Salvo), then thought to be a killer without parallel, and surpass him in the horror and magnitude of their crimes. Norman Collins in 1969 killed seven girls in Michigan. In 1973 Edmund Kemper killed eight and dismembered them, in one case burying the head in his garden facing the house, so that he could imagine the victim looking at him. The same year saw the nauseating case of Dean Corll in Houston, Texas, killer of thirty-one teenage boys, and Juan Corona, who murdered twenty-five vagrants at various times in California. In 1980, John Wayne Gacy was arrested in Des Plaines, Illinois, having murdered thirty-two young men and boys. In England, Peter Sutcliffe, known as the Yorkshire Ripper, killed thirteen women between 1975 and 1980. There is every reason to conclude that murderers like Dennis Nilsen are becoming progressively less rare and may well come to represent a type of 'motiveless' criminal who belongs predominantly to the twentieth century. Unless, that is, professional men can recognise his symptoms before they explode. The difficulty is, of course, that the symptoms

251

are either concealed or apparently innocuous; none of Nilsen's acquaintances was aware of his intensely secret fantasy life, nor did his overt personality ever give cause for alarm. One can only deplore that he did not himself feel the need, before 1978, to seek the advice of a psychiatrist. He would almost certainly have been diagnosed as potentially dangerous.

Brittain is not alone in drawing attention to the insidious danger of personality disorder in a tense society. Blackman, Weiss and Lamberti in *The Sudden Murderer*, and Satten, Menninger, Rosen and Mayman in *Murder without Apparent Motive* (both American studies), have identified similar characteristics to those pinpointed by Dr Brittain, including the severe isolation, the confusion of sexual identity and the highly-developed fantasy life, more often than not violent and primitive. Furthermore, they all agree that the subjects they studied showed blunted and shallow emotional responses, and first began to kill when the boundaries between their private fantasy life and reality broke down.[12]

Denied the help of psychiatry, is there any other way in which Nilsen's disorder might have been spotted before he committed murder? I have shown a page of his writing to an experienced graphologist who, with no knowledge of the identity of her subject (or of me), drew a picture which bore a striking resemblance to the personality described by Brittain, and evidently worried her; she asked how well I knew the man before she would give her report, and was relieved to discover that I was in no danger. The writer, she said, had a good brain but had not disciplined himself to educate his mind or direct it. Consequently, instead of turning creative (as he could have done), he turned destructive. He was very cunning and egoistic, wanting to satisfy his needs at all costs and without moral scruple. He was by nature extremely aggressive. He was also very suspicious, and an adept dissembler. He was touchy, unbalanced, and resentful of all authority.

For some reason which she could not define, the subject suffered from a feeling of inadequacy or impotence (*impuissance*, not necessarily sexual). He needed to talk about himself a great deal by way of compensation for this feeling, in search of reassurance. He had a mind open to illusion, to myths, which he increasingly believed in at the expense of his connection with reality. He was stubborn and capable of self-pity, though not of pity for others; or at least, his pity for others would be formed from intellectual recognition of the facts, while his pity for himself was emotionally based. He was as defensive as a cat, but with tremendous physical power which could be released in an irrepressible surge of aggression if he felt himself slighted by some chance remark. He was homosexual, yet virile and masculine. The graphologist concluded by admitting that she found the handwriting very frightening.

Presumably, a handwriting expert who saw evidence of Nilsen's script before 1978 might have recommended a course of psycho-analytic treatment. But none did. We are therefore, tragically, limited to a *post facto* examination of how and why the mind of this particular man grew so distorted as to require nourishment in death. The tragedy is final for his victims; he, at least, may recover. We are aided in the search not only by psychiatry, but by the history of sexual perversions, by philosophy, and by religion. They may all, separately or collectively, throw some light upon why Dennis Nilsen crossed the abyss between thought and deed, why his impulses triumphed over his restraints.

Nilsen's own rationalisations may serve by way of illustration, but must not be allowed to dictate the route. It is well enough known that we are bound to rationalise when one part of our personality seeks to justify to another part acts for which it anticipates disapprobation; that is what repression is about. If the disapproval is likely to be intolerable, then we invent 'causes', 'motives', 'reasons', which may be more acceptable and which will disguise the truth from ourselves. The huge amount that Nilson has written indicates that the rationalisation process is constant, the expected disapproval harsh. The conflict rumbles on within the same paragraph or upon the same page. At one point he knows that the aims of repression should not succeed ('I cannot justify any of these deaths, ever'), but is then sharply reminded by the self-protective side of his personality that 'murder is a sign of alarm'; the two remarks cancel each other out.[13]

The Psychiatric View

1. Schizoid personality

'Homicide can be "caused" by practically any type of major psychiatric illness.'[14] So says Marvin Wolfgang, an acknowledged American expert on murder. At the trial of Dennis Nilsen, it was contested by two psychiatrists that the defendant suffered from several kinds of personality disorder which, when put together, made an impressive heap of problems which he could not possibly hope to solve. Paramount among these was a schizoid tendency.

Schizoid people have such a deep mistrust of others that they regard any really intimate relationship with another person as dangerous. They are inwardly weak and vulnerable (as is the child, whose vulnerability attracts the love of the parent), but because they are afraid of being at the mercy of anyone on whom they are emotionally dependent, they never allow their vulnerability to show. This might arise because the vulnerability was not rewarded in infancy, and they will not risk any such disappointment again. They therefore compensate with a disproportionate desire for power and superiority, and if they cannot attain this in reality, they invent it in fantasy. Their greatest fear is humiliation, which they equate with the position of being loved, as the love might at any moment be withdrawn. Hence, by a sad inversion of cart and horse, they are convinced that they are unlovable, and extreme hostility festers within them as a result. This hostility can be of such intensity that it frightens even themselves, but remains for the most part hidden. It might show in the most bitter resentment of any kind of criticism, however slight. The anger which rages within will reveal itself indirectly in a stream of sarcastic remarks, which defeat of any kind may let loose. As Anthony Storr has written:

> The disposal of aggression is particularly difficult for schizoid people; for, in them, the normal positive aspects of aggression in defining identity and asserting independ-

ence are so intermingled with hatred for past disregard that it is almost impossible for them to be aggressive without being destructive. When rebuff or criticism, however mild, are interpreted as insult, withdrawal or murder may seem the only possible alternatives.[15]

Storr, in his book *Human Aggression*, goes on to point out that schizoid people may be safe if they can attain high power or accomplishment. They may be visionaries or messianic political leaders (Joan of Arc is a fine example), or they may sublimate their aggression in stern, demanding artistic endeavour. One such, according to Dr Storr, was Beethoven, who did not hesitate to call himself a genius:

He was generally morose and suspicious, and never succeeded in making any permanent relationship with a woman. His deafness increased his isolation and mistrust of human beings; but this disability merely accentuated characteristics which were already present. He displayed, in marked degree, the conviction of superiority so typical of schizoid characters . . . in personal relations he was so touchy that even his closest friends were liable to find themselves excluded on account of some supposed slight.[16]

It is when the aggression cannot be channelled into some creative activity, or is not kept dormant in secure social bonds, that it may be detonated by accumulated stress and the schizoid person becomes a danger to himself and to others. The Dutch murderer, Hans von Zon, who killed six people for no clear motive between 1964 and 1967, was a schizoid type. So was Raymond Morris, the Cannock Chase child-killer whose alleged victims died also between 1965 and 1967. He was an adept photographer, had written poetry, and constructed a rich fantasy life. People thought him cold and emotionless, but he was capable of violent rages. His intelligence was above average. Dean Corll, the Houston mass murderer of the seventies, was hypersensitive, morose, unsociable — all possible indicators of a schizoid personality. If we go back to one of the famous cases of the nineteenth century, we find that Pierre Lacenaire was a lone wolf, bereft of emotion, incapable of satisfactory human contact, who murdered out of rage against 'society'. (He is also one of the rare murderers before Dennis Nilsen who wrote his own memoirs; Dostoievsky published them in a journal he edited.)

The reader already knows enough of Nilsen's arid emotional life to judge how far the schizoid diagnosis may apply to him. Nilsen does not regard himself as a violent man, yet these explosions of violence afforded him, in the aftermath, a temporary peace. 'Each one seemed to be its own last time,' he writes.

> In any domestic situation where I had constant contact with people or a person, these things could never have occurred. They were the products of the lonely empty life and the mind therein. I made another world, and real men would enter it and they would never really get hurt at all in the vivid unreal laws of the dream. I caused dreams which caused death. This is my crime.[17]

We recall Dr Gallwey's testimony in court that the schizoid elements in Nilsen's personality lay relatively undisturbed while he maintained human contact with David Gallichan as a flat-mate. After Gallichan there were Martin and Pett, both briefly, followed by collapse towards the end of 1978. Nilsen's isolation was by then complete. Feeling defeated and humiliated on all sides, and unwilling to blame himself for his misfortunes, resentment grew like a cancer and others had to pay the price.

Another manifestation of the schizoid type is a dangerous ability to place false meanings on what people say. Dr Mac-Keith said Nilsen had 'an unusual capacity to invest others with attitudes and feelings reflecting his own feelings'.[18] There are manifold examples of this in Nilsen's life. While on remand in Brixton Prison, he asked a cleaner to get him a cigarette, and was told it would come later. In the interim, he constructed a whole convincing (to himself) portrait of the man as a hypocrite, toady and liar, reflecting on to him the qualities of his own frustration and anger. He did not express his anger verbally, but scrawled it alone across the page: 'A man can't fucking look you in the eyes when he is lying.' The cleaner had only uttered two words to Nilsen, 'Yes, later.' In fact, a roll-up cigarette was pushed under his cell door in time, and Nilsen recognised his own disability. 'I have a knack of misjudging some people — if not all people,' he wrote, adding that he felt ashamed.[19] It is more than likely that he also misjudged the characters of some of his victims, and decided that they were using or humiliating him on no evidence at all.

2. Egocentricity

Allied to the schizoid capacity to misinterpret the feelings and thoughts of others is a desperate, obsessive need that everyone should bend his energies to noticing and understanding the miscreant himself. 'Report me and my cause aright,' said Hamlet; this might be Nilsen's *leitmotiv*, expressing his desire that at last some attention might be afforded him. Of course, it is a truism to say that the need for attention is part of the universal need for love, but it is important to see that this represents the converse of the schizoid's abject failure to recognise love for what it is and to accept it when offered. While he is frightened of loving attention and sees it as a danger, a door to dependency and humiliation, he none the less still craves it, and is reduced to expressing this craving in a comparatively 'safe' way, by noticing every event or gesture in so far as it affects *himself*. The Old Bailey heard of Nilsen's need for attention and his 'grandiosity', and there have been many examples in these pages of his tendency to regard himself as a victim along with those whom he killed. He talks of Duffey, Sinclair, Barlow and Nilsen as all lonely outcasts, thus turning the face of compassion upon himself. Two more quotations from his prison notes may serve to emphasise the point. 'I want crowds around me to listen to my solitude,' he writes. 'I want others to know that I am feeling pain. I want others to see that I suffer. I do not like suffering, but it seems now to be expected of me.'[20] Nothing could better illuminate his condition than that last sentence, with its implication that any stratagem might be countenanced if it would gain the necessary attention; the infant who resorts to tears is doing much the same thing — he will play a role to achieve the desired end. What Nilsen does not fully realise is that the attention, when given, will be misunderstood by him if it contains any element of affection.

A poem that he wrote in September 1983, as his trial approached, underlines both this egocentric characteristic and the schizoid fear of closeness. It was penned with David Martin in mind, but equally can apply to himself:

> Never a man so sore afraid
> To let his feelings shine;
> Never a man so helpless
> To stop and notice mine.[21]

3. Fantasy

All are agreed that a central element in the psychology of the schizoid type is the development of a fantasy life. Time and again it is found in the psychic history of multiple murderers, from Kürten to Christie to Kemper. It does not arise spontaneously, from a void, but is a link in a chain of circumstances which may ultimately lead to murder or suicide unless the chain is broken. Fantasy begins as a solace to the lonely child (and is then very common and quite harmless); it takes hold if the loneliness is not relieved in adolescence; and it grows more complex and sophisticated with the adult. It answers the search for immediate satisfaction. Danger looms when fantasy becomes more cherished than reality, and when people from the real world impinge upon it, innocent of the terrible intensity they are jostling.

I have tried to show in these pages how Nilsen's fantasies gradually developed alongside his overtly normal life. At about the age of ten he was aware of sexual attraction towards other boys, and at the same time knew that he must therefore be wicked. The thoughts had to be suppressed.

I assumed that there was something abnormally wrong with me when contrasted with other boys. I felt apart, alien and inferior (and more than a bit soiled). I had no person to confide in, and it is there that my road to isolation began to lengthen and be really ingrained in my personality.[22]

So a fantasy, originally quite safe, took the place of bleak reality. The boy imagined himself happy with a friend, such as the boy in the playground, but did not dare to try translating the happiness into real life, for fear of rejection and scorn. Next, the fantasy attached to a drawing, in a French grammar, of a boy who could not possibly respond. The fantasy was fed, also, by the cinema, where everyone was beautiful, popular and famous. When the memory of the one love of his life, his grandfather, entered the fantasy and became co-mingled with it, then it took a new and morbid turn. The loved object became himself as a corpse, viewed in the mirror (this development dating from Nilsen's early manhood, immediately post-adolescence). At the same time, the cinematic fantasy was gratified by his own movie camera and projector, which he used in particular to film the young soldier with whom he fell in love in the Shetlands (and to whom, significantly, he never declared himself). Together they would enact dramas in which the young soldier had to 'play dead' while Nilsen filmed his prostrate and apparently lifeless body. Afterwards, he would sometimes masturbate when watching these films alone. Until his mid-twenties, his sexual experience in the real world was nil, as the fantasy life was already a far more enticing alternative. When he entered his promiscuous period, after the age of twenty-seven, we have the word of at least one man who spent the night with him that Nilsen would pretend to be asleep or lifeless and wait for the lover to entertain his motionless body. 'He went dead on me.' Meanwhile, the solitary experiments with the mirror continued, with ever more complicated stratagems to make himself appear dead, that is, by covering his body with powder, making his eyes bloodshot, his lips blue, and so on. The fantasy, it should be noted, is not the source of the problem, but the instrument by which the problem is tamed — until, that is, its greed makes it impossible to contain any longer and it spills over into the real world. We recall that when Nilsen began to kill, he would frequently hold the body up in front of the mirror and 'love' the mirror image. The two worlds had collided.

Here now are some extracts from Nilsen's own understanding of his fantasy life:

> I wandered aimlessly through a life and found only the shadows of my own imagination weeping in front of those spent lives.[23]
>
> The need to return to my beautifully warm unreal world was such that I was addicted to it even to the extent of knowing of the risks to human life. That was my irresponsibility, that is my crime. It is just as bad as any premeditated act in my view. I had the power to say *no* to my trips but I only thought of the sublime pleasure these feelings gave me. It was a great and necessary diversion and escape from the troubled reality of life outside . . . The pure primitive man of the dream world killed these men . . . [24]
>
> I have been my own secret scriptwriter, actor, director and cameraman . . . I took this world of make-believe, where no one really gets hurt, into the real world, and people can get hurt in the real world . . . These people strayed into my innermost secret world and they died there. I'm sure of this.[25] [Kenneth Ockendon went too close to the fantasy world by listening to Nilsen's 'magical' music through headphones.]

Nilsen also touches upon the dreadful irony that his crimes have made him 'someone' for whom there is no longer any need to take refuge in fantasy. 'I have *become* the *real* character in the movie. The notoriety of arrest and imprisonment in Brixton became *more* real than anything I could have created in the movie world.'[26] Cynics will suspect that this is what he intended all along, and his bearing since conviction would give them support. But that would be to misconstrue the purpose of the fantasy, which is not merely to imagine fame, but to caress death. He will never kill again. Either the fantasy has been melted away by exposure, or exorcised by examination. Or, if it remains, it can only be consummated by his own death, the most pleasurable 'trip' of all. Peter Kürten, the Düsseldorf sadist, said that he looked forward to hearing the sound of his own blood rush out as his head was severed on the block. Nilsen has said he would welcome the hangman's noose.

4. Control

If Nilsen's fantasies were kept in check for years, what finally broke down the barrier and made them trespass into the real world? 'Often a criminal is a man who does what other people merely think,' writes Frederic Wertham in his study of murder, *Dark Legend*.[27] People normally restrict their fantasies to 'thinking' because they have an inherited ability to control their impulses which is sometimes given the word 'morality'. But this ability to control is fragile in all of us, and when it is under strain it can lead to neurosis — anything from a headache to a mental breakdown. Nilsen lost control over his secret amoral world.

Aggression is a natural and beneficial aspect of the human condition. It enables the child to grow independent and the adult to master his environment. It is a necessary part of any endeavour which strives to improve upon given premises or to open up new avenues of knowledge. It is not confined to violence between individuals or warfare between nations, as the word normally implies in daily conversation. If the aggressive drive is totally blocked then illness must result. The Ute Indians are neurotic almost to a man, because their rigid ethical laws prevent any discharge of aggression.[28] On the other hand, aggression has to be controlled if it is not to run amok, and nature has evolved a subtle method of control which is termed an 'appeasement gesture'. You can observe how these gestures work in animals. Geese swoop and undulate their necks as a way of showing aggression or working it out of their system without actually coming to a fight. Similarly, herring gulls tear up grass. Even the neighbourhood dogs will demonstrate the mechanism by offering their hindquarters to a potential aggressor in order to 'appease' and avert catastrophe. We do virtually the same thing by shaking hands, thus offering proof that we carry no weapons. One cannot fail to have a sense of admiration, writes Konrad Lorenz, 'for those physiological mechanisms which enforce, in animals, selfless behaviour aimed towards the good of the community, and which work in the same way as the moral law in human beings'.[29] The moral law, then, is a fact of evolution passed down through the species, and not an invention of man.*

The point here is that Nilsen's natural control of aggression faltered and gave way to selfish rather than selfless behaviour. Instead of displaying appeasement gestures, he treated people who crossed the threshold into his fantasy world in much the same way as we might treat an ant. According to accepted psychiatric theory, aggression in such a case *has* to be released in order to prevent something worse. (Is this what Nilsen subconsciously meant when he said that he *had* to squeeze somebody's throat to 'stop something terrible from happening'? That 'something terrible' would have been the complete collapse of the personality which Dr Gallwey described in court.)

Let us hear some psychiatric definitions of murder. Murder is 'a defence against impending psychotic ego rupture'.[30] It is 'episodic dyscontrol which functions as a regulatory device to forestall more extensive personality disintegration'.[31] In his study of 'Gino', Wertham writes, 'the act of murder appears to have prevented consequences far more serious for Gino's mental health.'[32] Murders result from 'severe lapses of ego control which make possible the open expression of primitive violence born out of previous, and now unconscious, traumatic experiences'.[33] The eighteen-year-old American killer William Heirens left a note which said, 'For heaven's sake catch me before I kill more. I cannot control myself,' and the psychiatrist Dr Brussell claimed that the Boston Strangler, Albert De Salvo, was 'progressing' through murder towards greater maturity.[34]

All this makes uncomfortable reading, for it seems to suggest that murder is somehow excusable on grounds which

*Erich Fromm comments mockingly on Lorenz's method, claiming that the argument from analogy is specious.

have nothing to do with morality as we understand it. But the point is not that it is excusable, but explicable in terms of the breakdown of control, the smothering of that inhibiting factor which works so well in the animal kingdom. Dr Wertham gives a name to this breakdown of control. It is a 'catathymic crisis'. 'A violent act', he writes, 'is the only solution to a profound emotional conflict whose real nature remains below the threshold of the consciousness of the patient.' The catathymic crisis has five stages, namely:

(a) Initial thinking disorder;
(b) Crystallisation of a plan;
(c) Extreme tension culminating in violent crisis;
(d) Superficial normality;
(e) Insight and recovery.[35]

It is interesting to note that Nilsen's history can be made to fit this pattern, if one accepts that the crisis can be episodic and occur over a period of five years (Wertham was dealing with only one murder).

If this is true, then we have identified the process by which the schizoid's control over fantasy breaks down and allows subdued aggression to explode, but we still do not know the origin of the conflict which artificially kept the aggression in check.

Nilsen has been asked about his lack of control. He says he was enraged by apathy, especially that of his colleagues in the trade union. He would talk incessantly, and wanted people to understand, but they would get bored and fall asleep.

All these frustrations came down to someone sitting in my armchair or on my bed and everything dear to me became nothing but boring trifles to them. My views, me, my emotions, my love and aspirations meant nothing to them. Life itself seemed to mean nothing to them . . . I think I was giving them a last chance to fight for something. It seemed that their own lives were of no importance to them. The only way for them to listen to me and take me seriously was to apply that pressure.

He goes on to imply that he was trying in a way to waken them up, to 'vivify' them. When the killing was over, Nilsen felt 'intense fulfilment and mutual release for us both'.

> They didn't have to listen any more and I didn't have to talk any more . . . I had tried to communicate with them but they had chosen to cease to listen . . . I cared enough about them to kill them . . . I was set off by their silence, by their rejection of everything that I was . . . I was engaged primarily in self-destruction . . . I was killing myself only but it was always the bystander who died.[36]

It would be easy to dismiss this as more rationalisation, self-justification or righteous bombast. It does not mention the hunt or the chase for a victim, nor the sexual attraction of a corpse. Nilsen's case is by any standards a complex one, requiring not one answer but the congruence of several. However, it is interesting to discern clues in his statement which may trigger recognition. The need for release of tension is obvious. Somewhat less clear, at the moment, is Nilsen's insistence upon the illusion of self-destruction.

5. Precedents

The temptation to compare Nilsen with other mass murderers need not be resisted, for analogies can be instructive. His case clearly echoes to some extent that of John Christie, hanged in 1953 for the murder of six women at 10 Rillington Place in London. Christie also brought his victims home and made them drunk, he also strangled them, masturbated over the bodies, and placed them under the floorboards. He said he would have continued to kill had he not been caught. Lacenaire compares with Nilsen in other ways, being a fierce radical who despised the complacent rich and wanted to teach 'society' a lesson. Landru, the Frenchman executed in 1922, shared Nilsen's black sense of humour, offering to surrender his seat in the dock to a lady who could not find room in the public gallery, and he also refused all religious comfort. But until now, the only time an opportunity was afforded to investigate the mind of a multiple killer was in the case of Peter Kürten, at once the most interesting and the most horrifying of all murderers, not excepting Jack the Ripper. Between his arrest and his execution, Kürten formed a relationship of trust with a psychiatrist, Dr Karl Berg, to whom he revealed his most private thoughts and feelings. Berg published the text of their conversations, with his conclusions, in a unique book which appeared in English translation in 1938 (it is now extremely rare). Many of the characteristics which emerge about Kürten are strangely familiar and when Kürten speaks, it is almost as if one were listening to Dennis Nilsen; on occasion the very words are identical.

Kürten dictated to the police stenographer meticulous details of all his crimes in chronological order, including many with which he was not charged and which came as a total surprise to the officers. He had precise recall, even to exact addresses and the day and time of murders which were committed up to thirty years before. There were some imaginary embellishments, but Kürten was always accurate on points of fact. His memory was unreliable only when relating the climactic point of his murderous gratification.

Kürten experienced orgasm as he seized the victim's throat, or as he plunged in the knife. When the urge to kill came upon him, he went out in search of a likely victim. He accepted his guilt, because he thought he ought to have been able to control his urge, but did not. He was ready to shoulder his punishment, and admitted that people were right to call him a beast, although he suspected his execution might be seen as an act of vengeance rather than justice, to placate the public mood. He agreed that he enjoyed talking about his crimes and watching the astonished look on the faces of his listeners. He had amazingly cool presence of mind, and had been able to bluff his way out of awkward situations. Dr Berg found in him an odd mixture of mendacity and frankness, but was convinced that essentially he told the truth and showed genuine interest in Berg's interpretations. In the period leading up to his trial, Kürten grew introspective and tried to come to some self-understanding. He was also preoccupied with the question of his legal responsibility.

He showed no emotion at all in the dock, apart from

irritation at inaccuracies and discrepancies in the evidence. In a speech before sentence, Kürten declared that he would make no excuses for his detestable deeds, but hoped that the relatives of his victims might one day forgive him. His last wish was to write thirteen letters to those relatives, seeking pardon. His exuberant fantasy life entirely disappeared after his arrest.

Here are some of the statements made by Kürten in conversation with Dr Berg:

Believe me, if I tell you the whole truth, you will hear a lot of horrible things from me.

. . . my blood and the blood of my victims . . . I had no pity for my victims.

Yes, if I had had the means I would have killed masses.

It was not my intention to get satisfaction by normal sexual intercourse, but by killing.

. . . throttling in itself was a pleasure to me, even without any intention to kill.

When I myself think about my deeds, then I abhor myself so much that I am impatient for my execution.

I can't feel remorse, but only regret for the innocent victims.[37]

One must not press the similarities too far, however. Kürten had had a deprived childhood and had been in prison in adolescence. He had been a vicious sadist all his life, glorying in the sight, smell and taste of blood. At the age of nine, he had pushed little boys into the Rhine, and by the time he was thirteen he had been amusing himself by stabbing sheep as he sodomised them. He admitted that if he happened to be near a road accident he would ejaculate involuntarily, and when his lust rose he would cut the neck from a swan and drink the blood. None of this is relevant to Nilsen. On the other hand, they were both pedantic, remorseless, and alarmingly normal. Kürten's colleagues at work were quite certain that a mistake had been made when he was arrested, and Dr Berg stated that his patient was not insane.

There is a feeling with both Kürten and Nilsen that they welcomed the opportunity for self-analysis (albeit far too late) in order to identify their monster and gain the freedom that is born of knowledge. 'Introspection is the key,' wrote Nilsen. 'We ignore our inner natures . . . We are attracted only to the darkness of others' lives, never our own. Our own demons are relegated to the subconscious.'[38] If the psychiatrists are right, then these 'demons' can be rooted out by prolonged and sustained psycho-therapy. The first step is to recognise them and accept responsibility for them, even if they seem to possess the strengths of renewal and tenacity. As George Meredith wrote:

> In tragic life, God wot,
> No villain need be! Passions spin the plot;
> We are betrayed by what is false within.[39]

Nilsen may not yet know what has caused (if anything?) the falseness within, but he does know it has made him an irredeemable killer. 'I could not kill now,' he writes, 'because I now know myself and my past. I now have some kind of identity (even though it be one that I would rather not have). There are no longer any mysteries about me to trouble me. Knowing yourself is everything.'

'I regret everything that is past. But we do not control everything.'[40]

Sexual Aberration

If Nilsen's crimes could be explained in terms of distortion of the sexual need, that might provide sufficient answer in itself. There is certainly no lack of precedents, and any experienced prostitute will confirm that the varieties of sexual stimulation are seemingly endless. The Hungarian murderer Sylvestre Matuschka could experience sexual excitement only when he saw trains crashing, and so made a habit of causing dramatic collisions with consequent (and to him

267

irrelevant) loss of life. A Freudian might consider this as symbolic of penetration, one train forcing entry into another. The 'Thames nude murderer' of 1964 removed the teeth of his female victims after death so that he might use their mouths as a vagina. Kürten, we have already seen, was stimulated by the sound of gushing blood. William Heirens, whose interviews with the police are reprinted in *Sex Perversions and Sex Crimes* by J.M. Reinhardt, revealed that he was more disgusted by sex than by murder, and that his distortion became so acute that he would experience orgasm at the point of entering a strange house through the window, whether it be for the purposes of burglary or murder.[41] (That, also, is capable of a fairly obvious Freudian interpretation.)

Somewhat closer to our purpose is the case of John Christie, who murdered *in order that* he might have intercourse with a female corpse, it being impossible for him to have an erection when the body was animate. Similarly, Sergeant Bertrand, who was in the French army, would visit cemeteries at night to dig up freshly-buried corpses of young girls, whom he would then violate. 'All my enjoyment with living women is as nothing compared to it,' he said. The compulsion was so strong with Bertrand that he once swam an icy stream in order to get to a cemetery.

Christie and Sergeant Bertrand both conform to the popular view of a necrophiliac, that is a man who engages in the sexual act with a dead body. Necrophilia is in fact not quite so simple, a fact which has not prevented even psychiatrists from reducing it to a statement of the obvious: 'A motivating factor in necrophilia', writes P. Friedman, 'seems to be the need to eliminate the risk of rejection by choosing an object that can offer no resistance of any kind.'[42] As long ago as 1919, Wulffen divided varieties of necrophilia into three main categories, namely:

(a) Lust murder (in which the act of killing provides excitement);
(b) Stealing of corpses (which are then hoarded);
(c) Necrophagy (or the mutilation and eating of corpses).

Neither the second nor third of these categories can apply to Nilsen. He kept bodies for several months in some cases, but not in the spirit of a collector; he wanted rather to have them out of sight, until such time as he could dispose of them. Also, the dissection of his victims proceeded from the practical need for disposal, not from the desire for any kind of gratification. Moreover, there was no cannibalism in his case. On the other hand, there are grounds for suggesting that he may belong to Wulffen's first type, the lust murderer, for whom the act of causing death itself, rather than the anticipation of possessing dead bodies, is the passionate stimulus.

Very little has been written on the subject of necrophilia, still less on homosexual necrophilia, and one must search hard in the annals of crime for examples which have received more than perfunctory attention. In Australia, the defendant in Regina v. Forbes was a twenty-two-year-old married man who had homosexual fantasies involving a dead male. One day he went out with a gun, found a complete stranger, and shot him. Afterwards, he played with the corpse and finally sodomised it. His defence, like Nilsen's, tried to establish that he was suffering from a disease of the mind, but the court would not accept this view. His sanity was not in question, yet 'if he was overwhelmed by deviant sexual drives then he could not reason with sense and composure whether mentally diseased or not.' Forbes's own remark was a familiar one: 'I do not think anything would have stopped me. I was mad with power. I had him in my power and nothing could stop me.'[43]

The victim in another Australian case, Regina v. Isaacs, was a nine-year-old boy whose anus was widely open and gaping, indicating that penetration had been forced after *rigor mortis* had begun. Again, the outcome of the trial was satisfactory only in the judicial sense, while the attempt to find a label which could apply to the defendant was fruitless. The disorder of necrophilia appears to be beyond the competence of legal opinion to understand, and court records show conclusively that most necrophiliacs have been adjudged 'normal' and dealt with accordingly.

Two mistakes commonly warp our understanding of

necrophilia. One is to regard it as predominantly a *sexual* devi-
ation, whereas it springs more from a distortion of the desire
for *power*; it is the freedom to do exactly what one wants with
the body that excites, as Forbes's own comment amply demonstrates, and any sexual pleasure per se is tangential. Most
lust murderers talk in a similar way of their compulsion to kill,
to satisfy an exigent and exultant itch for power; their resistance to the drive is so helpless as to be crushed at inception.
The other mistake is to equate necrophilia with cruelty and
sadism. Krafft-Ebing himself promulgated this mistake, writing that necrophilia was a horrible manifestation of sadism,
but Moll corrected him on the grounds than no actual pain
was caused by the necrophile.[44] The connections here are
subtle. The sadist, too, is interested in power rather than sex
(the Marquis de Sade's writings are full of the adoration of
power, and sexual perversions are incidental means towards
this end), but the sadist needs to have his power confirmed
by the screams of pain from his victim. The necrophiliac, on
the other hand, is interested in a corpse precisely because it is
passive, because it cannot scream or protest in any way.
Consequently, the sadist may torture and kill slowly, to
prolong the pleasure, while the necrophiliac kills swiftly and
painlessly, the quicker to produce the beloved corpse. Kürten
was a sadist, Nilsen a necrophiliac; both are lust murderers
who gain pleasure from the selfish gratification of their need
for power, but in different ways. It may even be said that a
necrophiliac is a cowardly sadist, or a sadist-with-a-con-
science, in that he cannot bear to be reminded of the violation
he is enacting and *must* have a silent passive victim. Nilsen
has himself written, 'Mine is the weakness of a coward.'[45]*

The Nilsen case spotlights both these errors. He has consistently maintained that he was not interested in sexual
penetration of a dead body. The idea occurred to him with
the first victim, but his erection subsided before he could put
it into effect, and he never tried again, he says. 'I remember

---

*He has also said that his washing of the victim was a demonstration of
absolute power and control, which accentuated the victim's helplessness
and his authority.

being repulsed strongly even thinking about sexual intercourse. That and the pure after-image could not go together.
They were poles apart.' The pathologist's examination of the
remains of Stephen Sinclair indicated that the condition of
the anus was consistent with having been sodomised, but
there was no evidence of the event having taken place after
death. Nilsen was adamant that he had not even broached the
subject of sex with Sinclair, and that if Sinclair had been
buggered, it was not by him. 'Poor Stephen,' he wrote,
'maybe he thought I would give him something (financial).
Instead, I took everything.'[46] With six of the victims, there
was some sexual activity following the murder, which took
the form of masturbation over or near the body; this Nilsen
terms as 'reverence for the body with sexual associations, but
no direct sex'.[47] On one occasion it involved photography of
the corpse. He also insists that he has never been attracted by
the idea of inflicting pain.

Why, then, this 'reverence' for a dead body? Why this
fascination with death? 'It was as if the spirit of the man still
dwelt within and the decay of death was a consummation of
life itself. I compared my own "living" body with the dead
body and thought how strange it was that they were now
beyond pain, problems and sorrow and I was not.'[48] The
mystery of death grew for Nilsen into an unnatural and
morbid obsession, the seeds of which cannot now be traced
further than his conscious memory will take us, and it would
need a long course of psycho-therapy to discover where they
took root in the unconscious. That voluntary memory reverts
time and time again to the death of his grandfather when he
was a six-year-old boy.

A short story by C.M. Eddy entitled *The Loved Dead* bears
a strong resemblance to Nilsen's emotional history. The
narrator tells how he grew into a necrophiliac (though he
does not use that word) whose solitary pleasure was the contemplation of a corpse. He described his infancy thus:

My early childhood was one long, prosaic and monotonous
apathy. Strictly ascetic, wan, pallid, undersized, and subjected to protracted spells of morbid moroseness, I was

ostracised by the normal, healthy youngsters of my own age . . .

Had I lived in some larger town, with greater opportunities for congenial companionship, perhaps I could have overcome this early tendency to be a recluse . . . My life lacked motivation. I seemed in the grip of something that dulled my senses, stunted my development, retarded my activities, and left me unaccountably dissatisfied.

The narrator's sullen attitude towards life changed dramatically when his grandfather died, and his mother took him into a room to see the body in its casket:

For the first time I was face to face with Death. I looked down upon the calm placid face lined with its multitudinous wrinkles, and saw nothing to cause so much of sorrow. Instead, it seemed to me that grandfather was immeasurably content, blandly satisfied. I felt swayed by some strange discordant sense of elation. So slowly, so stealthily had it crept over me, that I could scarcely define its coming. As I mentally review that portentous hour it seems that it must have originated with my first glimpse of that funeral scene, silently strengthening its grip with subtle insidiousness. A baleful malignant influence that seemed to emanate from the corpse itself held me with magnetic fascination. My whole being seemed charged with some ecstatic electrifying force, and I felt my form straighten without conscious volition.

Now in adulthood, the narrator has grown into a killer, steadily narrowing the interim between one murder and another, forever seeking a renewal of that thrill which comes with the proximity of a fresh corpse. The bind is inescapable. 'I knew, too, that through some strange satanic curse my life depended upon the dead for its motive force; that there was a singularity in my make-up which responded only to the awesome presence of some lifeless clod.'⁴⁹

Fiction, and florid fiction at that, but the story simmers

with pertinent echoes from Nilsen's own account of his obsession. We have seen already in this narrative how the child was transfixed in confusion at the sight of his grandfather in a coffin, and how he felt that the image of death was 'good' rather than 'bad'. In subsequent self-appraisal before his trial, Nilsen expatiated on the theme, and came to his own conclusion that he had been 'fixed by the wrong internal image', and that his emotional development had been sent on a wrong course:

I carried and developed that image inside me . . . I took that hybrid image [i.e. of death being both good and bad, tragic and glorious] with me, intact into maturity. The living grown-ups had somehow lied to me about my grandfather. I always wanted to be like him in my earliest recollections. My sexual and emotional aspirations became entrenched in creating and enhancing the 'dead' image. I became dead in my fantasies. In the mirror I became dead. I did not regard the image as me at all but perhaps as a vision of me in a visually perfect state. I fear pain, but in a real sense I do not mind being dead because 'dead' is a desirable image. I think that in some cases I killed these men in order to create the best image of them. It was not really a bad but a perfect and peaceful state for them to be in.[50]

Could this be another attempt to shift blame to some extraneous cause? We should consider how the above corresponds to other aspects and episodes of Nilsen's life as he recalled them at different unconnected moments over a period of eight months. From the ritual washing of the body after death, back through the fascination at the police morgue in 1973, the filming of his army friend in the Shetlands in 1972, the semi-fantasy of finding himself naked and near-dead in the back of an Arab taxi in 1967, the vision of Mr Ironside's drowned body at Strichen in 1957, back to childhood dwelling on death at sea (his own included), Nilsen's understanding of death has always been askance or awry. We have noticed several chapters ago how the notion of death frequently

273

suggests to him the notion of love (and vice versa), whereas the idea of sexual satisfaction does not arise spontaneously from either notion. The spontaneity of his conceits is best judged when he is himself unaware of it, when he is not seeking to make a point or influence the reader of his random notes, but where the point and the influence emerge unwillingly. A poem which Nilsen wrote about his childhood wandering by the sea at Fraserburgh may serve as an illustration. Entitled 'Kinnaird Head' after the lighthouse at the edge of the promontory, it is ostensibly inspired by the legend of the lady who threw herself from the former castle into the sea with the body of her lover in her arms, but it quickly transmutes into a celebration of the power of the sea, then to a vision of himself 'dead in the womb of cradle rock, whose blood was the sea'. It concludes:

> Her voice in shingle tones,
> She threatened and terrorised and loved me
> To a coldness deep in my bones.[51]

Nilsen's verse rarely rises to the level of poetry, but it has an immediate guilelessness which escapes the restraints of studied form in spite of the versifier's own efforts, and it reveals a twisted, narcissistic soul with a morbid ambition.

Nilsen's dreams, too, betray a constant preoccupation with death. Some have been related already. Others begin with scenes of emotional happiness and end in disaster, though it is forever ambivalent — death bearing the face of peace rather than of pain. Yet others have no image of death at all, and invite rampant speculation. He frequently refers (not only in dreams) to the loved object and/or the victim being 'in' him. When challenged, he claims that he means this to be interpreted in a spiritual sense. Of his fellow-prisoner at Brixton, David Martin, for whom he felt a powerful attachment (the most powerful of his life, he says), he writes 'he is in me for all time'. This could be significant if it is held to mean he wishes to be the receptive partner, the consoler, to be in fact a woman. If Nilsen's instincts are feminine, this would help to explain why he never pursued a person for whom he felt love,

and why in his sexual encounters he was active in performance but passive in spirit. The act of murder could then be a
warped act of love, the only way in which he could give his
beloved the warm embrace of his body, as a woman would
and as his confused sexuality would not permit. I do not
suggest that this innate desire was recognised by his conscious self, but there is evidence that he 'mothered' people in
life, and by his own account he physically embraced them
after death. It is at least possible that had he allowed himself
to be a passive partner on every level, the tragedy that befell
fifteen men who had to be killed to satisfy him might have
been averted.

There is also a dream which has occurred more than once
depicting Nilsen at the mercy of a man who has strapped him
to the wall and forcibly sodomised him. In the dream the
experience is pleasant, and he grudgingly admits that it may
have happened in reality on occasions when he was drunk in a
stranger's flat. He acknowledges the possibility that he may
have enjoyed this, and fancies the encounter ending with his
being strangled. Part-dream, part-fantasy, part-reality, this
welcome nightmare can possibly be a disguised celebration of
necrophilia.

Among Nilsen's papers at Cranley Gardens was found a
peculiar short story entitled 'The Monochrome Man' (incidentally proving that his self-designation in these terms was
not a dramatic contrivance conceived after his arrest, but a
long-standing obsession). It harks back to the semi-fantasy of
his being drowned and rescued as a child,* and contains some
significant sentences:

> The boy stood steady and cold against the wind in awe of
> his doomed universe and the devil and all that he could
> imagine a creator and destructor to be. He was cut off and
> engulfed by the sea, carried away into the numbing pres-
> sures of a silent peace without fear, without panic . . . He
> floated down into the womb of death, the painless seat of

* See p. 51.

freedom. His glazed eyes stared, his body suspended, hair streaming, and limp hanging arms conducting a dreamless world. Natural living forces animated the pale white boy dancing, drunk in a timeless sea . . . The man spoke as he washed the boy's lifeless body in soothing quizzical tones. 'There is something so temporarily attractive in the bodies of dead young men. The limpness of the movable parts, the ineffectiveness of a non-personality. The texture of dead cold skin to the touch. The uses which fantasy can make on an unresisting model of life . . . The hands and fingers are not rigid, not limp, but lie as though undecided between the two. It is an unlovable thing but traumatic in its presence.'

The piece is undated, but it bears the signs of experience more than imagination, and must therefore have been written after December 1978. The role of the imagination is in placing Nilsen himself as the dead youth, being conscious of what is said to him by the man who handles him. Nilsen spoke to the bodies of his victims in similar fashion, and one can hardly doubt any longer that his ultimate unrealisable fantasy was to have the roles reversed.

It should not pass unnoticed that the only mass murderer of recent times whom we know to be a necrophiliac, John Halliday Christie, was at the age of six profoundly affected by the sight of his grandfather dead in a coffin. The difference is that Christie hated his grandfather, and Nilsen loved his (that at least is how they recalled their emotions, though it is always possible that there was some suppressed love in Christie's feeling and some suppressed hate in Nilsen's). The point is that the experience scarred Christie to the extent that he remembered it vividly, and it was never fully explored at his trial. It ought now to be perceived as more than coincidence in the light of the Nilsen case.

We must finally return to our earlier categorisation of Nilsen as a 'lust murderer', a necrophiliac not in the manner of Christie (killing in order to commit the sexual act with a corpse), but in the manner of Kürten (killing as an end in itself, making death). He had, he says, a need for more prolonged excitement and for the thrill of nearness to death, even his own. Yes, he was, before the murders began in 1978, sometimes tied up in a man's flat. 'I half-expected to be strangled. I wanted to live and be strangled at the same time. From stalking until my eventual capture it was all part of this need for thrill and fear!'

> I did it all for me. Purely selfishly . . . I worshipped the art and the act of death, over and over. It's as simple as that. Afterwards it was all sexual confusion, symbolism, honouring the 'fallen'. I was honouring myself . . . I hated the decay and the dissection. There was no sadistic pleasure in killing. I killed them as I would like to be killed myself . . . enjoying the extremity of the death act itself. If I did it to myself I could only experience it once. If I did it to others, I could experience the death act over and over again.[52]

Do any other definitions of this mysterious aberration help towards an understanding? In *On the Nightmare*, Ernest Jones divided necrophilia into two types.

(a) Arising from a frantic aversion against accepting the fact of final departure, as with Periander, who had sexual coitus with his wife Melissa after her death, and King Herod, who was said to have slept with his wife for seven years after hers. This kind of activity is celebrated in some of the work of de Sade and Baudelaire. It is clearly not the problem with Nilsen.
(b) Arising from 'the most extreme imaginable perversion of the love instinct'. This, we have already seen, is applicable to Nilsen, who may furthermore have obscurely hoped for union with the dead and, for a time at least, felt that he had achieved this. But he never went so far as to bite or devour dead flesh, which Jones says is the ultimate manifestation of such necrophilia, and which has been detailed in gruesome case studies by J. Paul de River.

Von Hentig cited five examples of necrophiliac behaviour:

(a) Acts of sexual contact with a corpse;
(b) Sexual excitement produced by sight of a corpse;
(c) Attraction to graves;
(d) Acts of dismemberment;
(e) Craving to touch or smell odour of corpses.

Of these, only the second applies to Nilsen, the fourth being in his case irrelevant (despite appearances) because, far from craving to dissect his corpses, he frequently left them for months unmolested, and finally dismembered them only to get rid of them. But when Von Hentig describes the 'necrophilous character', his remarks may bear more relevance to Nilsen's case. Widely interpreted, necrophilia is 'the passion to transform that which is alive into something unalive; to destroy for the sake of destruction'.

Erich Fromm, who quotes Von Hentig, goes much further in his identification of the character-rooted passion of necrophilia. The semi-autistic child, who is cold and emotionless, is likely to develop a necrophilous character, he says. The trouble is, this 'character' (according to Fromm) can betray itself in so many scores of insignificant actions, without ever burgeoning into aberrant behaviour, that it might apply to half the people we know. It can be seen in the habit of breaking matchsticks in half, in pedantic and 'lifeless' conversation, in a pallid visage, and in the fascination with things mechanical. Relevant to Nilsen, perhaps, is the predilection for black and white rather than colour, but this is only one trait among many which are too common to be precise. Fromm does usefully point out that necrophilia is an extreme extension of narcissism. While the sadist is still actually *with* other people, wanting to control not annihilate them, the necrophiliac lacks even this degree of relatedness. Necrophiliacs are more narcissistic, more hostile, than sadists. 'Their aim is to transform all that is alive into dead matter; they want to destroy everything and everybody, often even themselves, their enemy is life itself.'

To sum up, the necrophiliac is not *only* a man who violates a corpse sexually (as popular belief holds) but, a man for whom death is the ultimate beauty. Why Nilsen should glory in the act of death, and develop into a dangerous man, sane but with what must now be inadequately described as a 'personality disorder', while there are millions among us who have seen dead grandfathers and remain in control, is a question which persistently eludes an answer. 'Men fear death as children fear to go in the dark,' wrote Bacon. Nilsen, it seems, feared life.

The Philosophy of Murder

It would be reassuring to believe that murder was a gross abnormality, a dramatic departure from respected ethical standards which restrain civilised man from surrendering to his baser instincts. This used to be the accepted view, and the murderer was regarded as beyond the pale, irreconcilable with the rest of mankind. Advances made in our knowledge of ethology, evolution and human psychology present challenges to such banal assumptions which cannot be ignored. Not least important among them is the crucial recognition that, far from being an aberration which despoils civilised man, murder *belongs* to civilised man more than it does to primitive peoples or to other species which inhabit the planet. As man has become more civilised, intelligent, creative and dominant, so he has become more murderous, thus posing a problem for philosophers to grapple with.

Statistically, murder is still rare in proportion to the population. In the United Kingdom, the victims of murder in any one year may be accommodated in three or four double-decker buses. Of these, well over three-quarters are killed as the result of a sudden surge of emotion — a violent quarrel or a jealous rage in domestic conditions. So the kind of murder which Nilsen committed, purposeful and repeated yet motive-less, is rarer still. Yet the increase in this type of murder demands attention, however baffling it may appear, because if one can identify the 'causes' of such crimes, one may cast a chink of light on the condition of modern man. Dennis Nilsen is not a stranger among us, he is an extreme instance of human possibility. The psychiatrist who appeared for the prosecution at his trial, Dr Bowden, implicitly said as much when he commented that Nilsen was 'a very rare animal indeed' but not mad. If he were merely a monster we could learn nothing by studying his deplorable behaviour; it is because he is also human that we must make the attempt.

It is pretty obvious that the search for self-esteem is the motive force behind much human activity; when successful, it can engender happiness, stability, and achievement; when thwarted, it can lead to bitterness and failure. It is generally assumed that self-esteem flourishes alongside sexual confidence, even that the one is rooted in the other. A man who is certain of his own masculinity, or a woman of her femininity, may be certain of much else besides, and growth in all directions must begin with this certainty. Conversely, the man who does not think highly of himself, cannot be tolerant towards his fellows, because (such is human nature) he is apt to blame others for his lack of self-regard. It is *they* who think little of him, throwing back at him an image to which he is forced to assent, and unless he can crack the image and replace it with one of which he can feel proud, he is likely to nurse resentment all his life. Even those who have self-esteem need to have it constantly reaffirmed in sexual conquest. Otherwise, the sexually inadequate man may revert to his grim dark prison of frustration and anger, lowering at the world outside which denies him his 'right' to self-assertion. Murderers are always locked in this windowless stultifying prison.

This, broadly, is the view of Freudian analysts who regard self-esteem as arising from sexual confidence. Latterly there have been alternative ideas which, alas, were misinterpreted and vulgarised by the soppy generation of the sixties. Paramount among these is the work of the late Abraham Maslow, whose positive theory of human motivations postulated a 'hierarchy of needs' in which the need for sexual love and the need for self-esteem exist separately and sequentially, the latter only arising *after* the former has been satisfied.

According to Maslow,[53] the earliest and most fundamental needs are physiological, i.e. the need for food, drink and exercise. When these are satisfied, man moves on to the second level and requires security, order, protection. This achieved, he then reaches the third stage and needs social bonds: love, friendship, sexual fulfilment. The fourth and critical stage for our purpose is the need for self-esteem, that is praise, achievement, acknowledgment, status amongst one's fellows. The final rung in this hierarchy (and the one which the hippy philosophy exalted) is 'self-actualisation' — the need to realise one's full potential, to be everything one is capable of being. Few of us ever reach this far, but most of us manage to satisfy the first four salient needs, at least up to a point. Though they must be dealt with by each individual in their proper sequence, none ever entirely disappears. The man who has attained the level of 'esteem need' may have his needs for security or love suddenly reawakened by the loss of his job or the desertion of his spouse, and these needs must be hastily re-satisfied before he can build once more towards rewarding his need for self-esteem.*

It may well be that murderers falter at the 'esteem' level, and that this has less to do with sex than with the exercise of the will. When the will is able to press forward in a purposive manner, encountering obstacles and dealing with them successfully, then self-esteem is safe and healthy, and one may even enjoy what Maslow described as the 'peak experience', that feeling of elation when a task has been accomplished to a degree of satisfaction beyond even what one expected. But if the will is frustrated, a violent act may ensue as a desperate measure to thrust it forward. 'The hungry will, like an empty stomach, craves fulfilment.'[54] This vocabulary is startlingly apt when one remembers how often Nilsen has referred to his own 'peak of feeling' which he says arose when listening to music and drinking alcohol, but which was in fact the prelude to a murderous attack.

The violent act becomes necessary as a means of asserting the will and compensating for real or imagined humiliation. Understood in this way, murder is a purposive deed which,

---

* Fromm regards Maslow's hierarchy as unsystematic and arbitrary.

by horrid paradox, enables the murderer to reach the previously blocked 'esteem level'; in other words, the very act
which makes him despicable to the rest of us renders him
healthy and admirable in his own eyes. The psychiatrists,
remember, talk of murder as a safety valve to prevent disintegration of the personality, or an antidote to impending
insanity. Our sanity depends upon our being able to satisfy
this need for self-esteem, and that in turn depends upon our
image of ourselves. Without self-esteem, the will comes up
against a terminal moraine impossible to dislodge. So self-
esteem must be encouraged by a good self-image, and this
derives, whether we like it or not, from others. Other people
are the mirror which reflects back a picture, and as the
reflection constantly changes with the different people that
we face, and even within our familiarity with the same person
who may subtly alter the picture from day to day, so the
image is sharpened, clarified, made real, defined. Stability
can be undermined in two ways: either the image reflected is
stagnant, always the same, or it is diffuse, blurred, virtually
non-existent. The first danger was graphically dramatised by
Sartre in his play *Huis-Clos*, in which four people are doomed
to spend eternity together in a small room, so that each one is
stuck with the image of himself reflected back in perpetuity
by the other three, and the way forward is blocked. Thus the
famous line from the play *'L'Enfer, c'est les autres'* (Hell is
other people), can be understood as representing the stag-
nation of the self-image with consequent impotence and
absolute denial of any action which can change matters. The
other danger, of having a self-image which is out of focus,
comes to those who know few people, and nobody well, so
that they live as though constantly in the dark. With no
self-image they can have no self-esteem, because there is
nothing there to *value*; they look, and they see a void. This
produces habitual tension which must be resolved in some
way or another, lest it dissolve into self-denigration and
despair.

This is where fantasy comes in, as a route to the resolution
of the impasse. If the image is blurred, then why not *invent* a
sharper one, one that may offer satisfaction and produce the

illusion of self-esteem? Since fantasy carries with it such pleasurable results, it can become addictive, and it must progressively be exaggerated and enlarged in order to simulate that 'way forward' which would evolve for the healthy man in real life. A fantasy of power eventually becomes a fantasy of extreme power, one of beauty grows into an image of flawless beauty. A fantasy of death, however, cannot progress towards its ultimate goal without bursting into the real world. Once again, it is easy to see how Nilsen's story fits into this hypothetical scheme. His actual (not metaphorical) use of a mirror to convey a satisfying view of himself, his constant talk of 'images', the low threshold of his self-regard and the evident frustration of his will to action, all demonstrate that he was floundering at the edge of Maslow's level of self-esteem, unable to break through and compensating wildly for his failure.

The outcome of these theories (which I have intersected at several points) is the disconcerting conclusion that murder is a creative act, a means of self-fulfilment. Colin Wilson has written a great deal about the 'outsiders' in society, an uneasy group which includes modern murderers as well as poets and musicians. Outsiders who become killers, he writes,

> share certain characteristics of the artist; they know they are unlike other men, they experience drives and tensions that alienate them from the rest of society, they possess the courage to satisfy these drives in defiance of society. But while the artist releases his tensions in an act of imaginative creation, the Outsider-criminal releases his in an act of violence.[55]

It is worth noting in this regard just how many multiple murderers have sought to express themselves in verse. Lacenaire, Landru, Peter Manuel, all wrote sonnets while waiting for execution. Paul de River, in *The Sexual Criminal*, devotes a whole chapter to 'The Poetic Nature of the Sado-masochist' which includes many pieces written by one of his criminal patients.[56] And the reader does not need to be reminded how often Nilsen has assuaged his energies in verse since he was arrested in February 1983. He has even (see p. 277) spoken unambiguously about the 'art' of murder. There does seem to be some evidence that the creative urge of the artist and the destructive urge of the murderer may spring from the same source.

This being so, it is hardly surprising that the murderer is reluctant to show remorse for his acts. Why should he disparage the one action which afforded him at last a feeling of self-fulfilment, which lifted him on to the plane of self-esteem? That would be to deny the self-image which he has so lovingly constructed. It would be a retrograde step, a kind of psychological suicide. Kürten, Lacenaire, Nilsen — none was *willing* to show remorse (and the verb is important), except when moral reality impinged, and then they did, for a brief period, show terror and remorse at the same time. The process is vividly apparent in Nilsen; remorse for his actions, coupled with terror at the renewed disfigurement or dissolution of his self-image which remorse must bring, followed by rapid patching up of the image and recantation of the remorse. Only one illogical course is then left open to these men — to turn the blame upon the nebulous concept of 'society', thus keeping their self-image intact and reconciling it with some expression of regret at the same time. Lacenaire vented his wrath against society. So did Ian Brady (the Moors murderer), Peter Kürten, and Charles Manson. Nilsen has done it too.

The Religious View

Stuttering advances in psychological understanding appear to some not to negate the old-fashioned concepts of good and evil, but to reinforce them. When forensic psychiatrists talk of a 'personality disorder' they imply that the personality can be, and generally is, 'ordered', and that something has *dis*-ordered it; when it is in order, then goodness (or peace, or equanimity) prevails, and when disordered, it becomes a vehicle for evil (or distress, or 'maladaptive patterns of behaviour'). The agent of the disorder is a harsh emotional experience in childhood which has the effect of disrupting the passions ever after and forcing the schizoid type to take refuge in fantasy. Some religious men, especially those with a Scottish inheritance, are not alarmed by such talk, but they see reflected in it ancient truths cloaked in new language. A personality disorder indicates for them that the devil is at work, and that the man imprisoned in fantasy has forsaken the world of God to pursue his miserable life in the vivid, seductive, intoxicating world of Satan. From this point of view, psychology has not slain religion, it has on the contrary reaffirmed man's spirituality, previously represented to him in the symbolic language of myth, now muddied by the obtuse jargon of doctors. Psychiatry and religion, apparently at loggerheads, are in fact intimately allied in poring over the springs of human conduct, the difference being that psychiatry is rather more difficult to follow than myth. Simplicity is, after all, the purpose of myth, and when Martin Israel writes that 'the forces of evil rule the distraught passions of unredeemed men',[57] he is not essentially arguing with psychiatrists so much as reducing their insights to symbols. Can a man like Nilsen be understood by parrying symbols?

In her novel *The Philosopher's Pupil*, Iris Murdoch writes of her character George McCaffrey in this way:

Every human being is different, more *absolutely* different and peculiar than we can goad ourselves into conceiving; and our persistent desire to depict human lives as dramas leads us to see 'in the same light' events which may have multiple interpretations and causes. Of course a man may be 'cured' (consoled, encouraged, improved, shaken, returned to effective activity, and so forth and so on) by a concocted story of his own life, but that is another matter. (And such stories may be on offer from doctors, priests, teachers, influential friends and relations, or may be self-invented or derived from literature.) We are in fact far more randomly made, more full of rough contingent rubble, than art or vulgar psycho-analysis lead us to imagine. The language of sin may be more appropriate than that of science and as likely to 'cure'. The sin of pride may be a small or a great thing in someone's life, and hurt vanity a passing pinprick or a self-destroying or even murderous obsession. Possibly, more people kill themselves and others out of hurt vanity than out of envy, jealousy, malice or desire for revenge. There was some deep (so deep that one wants to call it 'original', whatever that means) wound in George's soul into which every tiniest slight or setback poured its gall. Pride and vanity and venomous hurt feelings obscured his sun. He saw the world as a conspiracy against him, and himself as a victim of cosmic injustice.[58]

The 'rough contingent rubble' is a striking phrase for the unplumbable mass of contradictions which may surface in every man, and it must be clear to any reader who has come this far that Nilsen was himself one such contradictory jumble. The language of sin may single out the constituent element which made him evil. St Augustine thought that evil was a perverseness of the will, and certainly Nilsen was at his most evil when his will was strongest, enabling him to show appalling indifference to others when in the grip of a semi-conscious fantasy. At other times his will was healthy, his altruism intact. That the evil was episodic points to a struggle between opposing forces with, if you like, the power of satanic influence winning through when the personality was at its weakest; hence the huge upsurge of will and strength when diabolic possession took hold. The 'devil' must act quickly since the power of good will reassert itself within moments and drive out the evil forces which have taken advantage of weakness. When the murderer is in the throes of his act, it is as if he were momentarily inhabited by a power stronger than himself. Nilsen has said he was amazed at his strength at such times, and the evidence of survivors (Carl Stottor, Paul Nobbs) is uncannily in tune with this metaphysical version of events; Nilsen was, they said, gentle, pleasant, concerned, both before and after his murderous attack. That he now says this was all part of the pretence and guile necessary to heighten the thrill that he needed is insufficient answer. The devil is cunning or he is nothing. Had the judge asked the witnesses whether Nilsen seemed *to them* to be momentarily possessed by an alien force, they would have found it difficult to say no. In fact, they did tell defending counsel that he appeared to behave out of character, like someone else.

The principle of dualism, that our moral natures are equally divided, is centuries old, and persists in everyday speech. Manichaeism held that evil was positive, and resided in matter, whereas good, equally positive, resided in spirit. St Augustine refuted the teachings of Manichaeus, but still thought that evil was a separate power which operated without the volition of the individual. 'It is not we ourselves that sin', he wrote, 'but some other nature (what, I know not) sins in us.'[59] More than fifteen hundred years later, Iris Murdoch has one of her characters say, 'How can another person steal one's consciousness, how is it possible? Can good and evil change places?'[60] Dennis Nilsen's prison journal is replete with dualist or Manichaean undertones. 'We either make good angels or very bad devils.'[61] 'Man comes apart when he doesn't listen to his god at the crucial times of his life . . . I ignored my demons for years, they sprung out and destroyed me.'[62] After his arrest, he began for a short period to call himself Moksheim instead of Nilsen as if in hopeful recognition that the devil of 'Nilsen' was exorcised, commenting ruefully that though 'Nilsen' was dead, there was no provision in law for his continued animation.[63] He maintains that the energy with which he threw himself into work at the Jobcentre was not a front, but just as genuine as the 'other' self which killed: 'This total principled moral purity in its extremes balanced up all the sickening evil of my private world.'[64] It is important for the neat antithesis of this dualistic view of the world that Nilsen be an essentially moral man. The devil has no victory if there is no good to conquer and an amoral soul (if such a thing be possible) is arid ground. Nilsen consistently reiterates that he has no moral excuse, that he is still tied to a moral code,[65] which would seem to indicate that he was prime material for satanic forces. According to this reading of events, the moral code, instilled in him by his grandfather Andrew Whyte, needed to be demolished not once, but repeatedly, by 'killing' Andrew Whyte time and time again. Each death was but a transient victory for the 'demons'.

Incidentally, it is interesting to note that the Greek word 'demon' originally meant 'divine being or god', an etymological curiosity which harks back to the primitive conception of supernatural beings. God and devil were originally one, in language if not in Christian theology. For some early peoples, a supernatural being was at the same time both good and evil, and it is only later in cultural development that a distinction is made between the two, ascribing one quality to one force and one to another. The distinction first appears in the Old Testament. (Similarly, the French words 'dieu' and 'diable' have the same root.) When men like Nilsen talk of themselves as both angels and devils united in one, they are reverting to a pre-cultural idea of supernature which lies deeper than linguistic tradition.*

We should remember just how often the lives and utterances of multiple murderers conform to the dualist pattern. The rapist Edward Paisnel terrorised the Isle of Jersey for eleven years until his arrest in 1971, throughout which time he was known as Uncle Ted to dozens of children, for whom he regularly played Santa Claus every Christmas; he was a kind-hearted man who genuinely loved children, and who (he thought) was periodically possessed by a vicious demon. Ed Gein, of Plainfield, Wisconsin, universally popular and a most reliable baby-sitter, killed a number of women, and ate parts of their corpses. Mack Edwards killed children for seventeen years until he gave himself up in Los Angeles in 1970, declaring that the demon had left him. We have already seen, in the article by Dr Brittain, that mass murderers habitually speak of opposing forces battling within them, and another study quotes a murderer as saying, 'It was as if I was watching myself do it. I knew I was doing it, but somehow it didn't seem like me.'[66] Theodore ('Ted') Bundy killed at least twenty young women in the United States of America between

---

*It is fair to explain that this idea was put forward by a philologist, not a theologian, to whom it appears nonsense.

1974 and 1978. He has never admitted the crimes, but in talking to his biographers he agreed to speculate on the possible frame of mind of a hypothetical murderer; he felt comfortable in the third person singular. Bundy claimed that the killer was inhabited by an 'entity' which acted of its own volition: 'this entity inside him was not capable of being controlled any longer'. When Bundy was sentenced to death, he addressed the court with these words: 'I cannot accept the sentence, because it is not a sentence to me . . . it is a sentence to someone else who is not standing here today.'[67] In Dostoievsky's *A Raw Youth*, Versilov says, 'I am split mentally and horribly afraid of it. It is as if you have your own double standing next to you.' Now listen to Dennis Nilsen:

> I always covered up for that 'inner me' that I loved . . . He just acted and I had to solve all his problems in the cool light of day. I could not turn him in without also destroying myself. In the end he lost. He still lies dormant within me. Will time destroy him? Or was he only lost temporarily? When I was on my high, Bleep would become sometimes frightened. She was only a simple dog but even she could see that it was not the real Des Nilsen . . . She would go off to a quiet corner and hide. She would greet me the next morning as though I had been away . . . dogs know when your mind has been changed in a drastic way.[68]

The idea that 'I' should have to cope with the effects of 'his' acts offers a potent image of the personification of evil, which has often been treated in literature. But it is not, I think, a literary device so much as a groping for language which will convey the *feeling* of possession rather than the *idea* of it. For the idea must, in any rational sense, be an absurdity; yet it is none the less powerfully experienced and can only find expression in the concept of an alter ego. Marie Corelli devoted the whole of her best novel to the theme, in *The Sorrows of Satan*, wherein the hero, Tempest, is corrupted by a man called Rimânez, who Corelli lets us know is the devil disguised in mortal form. The twist in her tale is that the devil is heart-broken whenever men succumb to his

289

temptation, for each evil act takes him further away from the love of God; he yearns to return to God but is cursed in having perpetually to tempt men to his bidding in the full knowledge that they must resist him in order to redeem him. It is an uphill struggle, says Corelli, as man is incurably weak. The Manichaean theme which underlies her novel is apparent in a much earlier poem:

> God said: 'I will create
> A world in the air!'
> Satan heard and answered:
> 'I too will be there!'
>
> God said: 'I will make of Man
> A creature supreme!'
> Satan answered: 'I will destroy
> Thy splendid dream!'
>
> God said: 'I will ordain
> That thou shalt no longer be!'
> Satan answered: 'Thou canst not, Lord,
> For I am part of Thee!'[69]

One of the most persuasive depictions of evil in literature is James Hogg's masterpiece, *The Private Memoirs and Confessions of a Justified Sinner*, written in 1824. Appropriately for us, it is a Scottish work set in Scotland, and imbued with the strict doctrines which surrounded Nilsen in infancy. The central character, Robert Wringhim, is educated in Calvinist determinism and rejoices to be among God's elect, until he meets a stranger under whose influence he commits a number of murders. The stranger assures him that the elect can do no wrong. He is, of course, the devil. Does he exist *outside* Wringhim, does he *become* Wringhim, or is he the personification of part of Wringhim's own self? The novel is a perfection of ambiguity, reflecting the impenetrable indecision of every man who contemplates such matters. The first half tells Wringhim's story in the third person; the second allows Wringhim his own account of what happened to him.

On the very first page of this account, we are reminded of

Colin Wilson's 'outsider' and the psychiatrists' portrayal of the habitual murderer as a 'loner', who feels isolated from the rest of mankind. Wringhim tells us, 'I was born an outcast in the world, in which I was destined to play so conspicuous a part.' His moral education established for him clear discernment of right and wrong, but with the added penalty of a sense of unworthiness; whatever sins he repented, there would always be mountains more to overcome. 'I saw with the intensity of juvenile grief, that there was no hope for me.' (There are grounds for suspecting that the Whyte grandparents in their piety had a similar effect upon Nilsen, who despaired of ever living up to their expectations of him.) Wringhim was accused when young of having a disposition tainted with deceit. (Afraid of being found wanting, Nilsen learned to conceal himself in tight privacy.)

When Wringhim first encounters the stranger, he is struck by the fact that he looks exactly like himself, and he is drawn to him by 'the force of enchantment'. The stranger tells him that by looking at a person attentively he can 'by degrees assume his likeness, and by assuming his likeness I attain to the possession of his most secret thoughts.' The two become inseparable, the stranger gradually gaining an ascendancy over Wringhim which he is powerless to resist. 'I generally conceived myself to be two people,' yet friends remarked that 'instead of being deranged in my intellect, they had never heard my conversation manifest so much energy or sublimity of conception.' The conviction that he was two persons grew stronger, and eventually oppressive.

> When I was by myself, I breathed freer, and my step was lighter; but when he approached, a pang went to my heart, and, in his company, I moved and acted as if under a load that I could hardly endure . . . We were identified with one another, as it were, and the power was not in me to separate myself from him.

The murders are committed, and the reader is left in some doubt as to whether the murderer is Wringhim himself (as other people think), or the weird stranger pretending to be

Wringhim, or indeed whether Wringhim has externalised his evil and invented the stranger to exculpate himself. Perhaps he even imagines him. The two have a conversation on the matter. 'Is it true', asks Wringhim, 'that I have two souls, which take possession of my bodily frame by turns, the one being all unconscious of what the other performs?' The stranger answers at first elliptically. 'Your supposition may be true in effect,' he says, and continues, 'We all are subjected to two distinct natures in the same person.' One could hardly imagine a more bald exposition of the case for dualism.[70]

It remains to point out that Wringhim is eventually driven to such despair by the strain of the struggle within him that he yearns for death, 'wishing myself a worm, or a moth, that I might be crushed and at rest'. But Satan has one last triumph to accomplish, one last sin to instil, when his prey admits to 'a certain pride of heart in being supposed the perpetrator of the unnatural crimes laid to my charge'. Pride reaches its apogee when Wringhim exults at the thought that his own confessions will be printed and published. All this is recognisable in Nilsen, who also has looked forward to death, who also has felt some satisfaction in the contemplation of his notoriety, and who also has been anxious that the present book be written and published.

Nilsen departs from the fictional Wringhim in his conscious knowledge of the deeds of his 'double', thereby providing, perhaps, a still more suitable vehicle for satanic power. Just as Satan must have something substantial to corrupt, and therefore needs a moral man to work upon, so must the moral sense be kept alive, in order to exacerbate the corruption. The murderer must retain a knowledge of right and wrong, must know that what he has done is wrong, or the devil will be emasculated. It would be pointless for the murderer to be *unaware* of the evil of his deeds, or they might never have occurred. Remorse and repentance would likewise dissipate the devilish influence — Satan would have wasted his time. What fulfils his design, and finally demolishes the good, is the evil-doer's active desire for *punishment*, for in being punished he accedes to the power of Satan and implicitly celebrates his success. The reader knows how frequently in the course of this narrative Nilsen has declared his need for punishment, even for public vengeance. We have come full circle since the remark listed on page xi, and can better appreciate its import: 'I have now a guilt and punishment complex. I deserve everything that a court can throw at me.'[71] The devil has won.

It was perhaps folly to entitle this chapter 'Answers'. Men like Nilsen elude classification, their unfathomable depravity resists conclusive analysis. They remind us, depressingly, of the essential unknowability of the human mind. They are themselves aware of their uniqueness, and look upon attempts by the rest of us to distil their characters into a shape that we can apprehend with something like amused disdain. Theodore Bundy said that society wanted to believe it could identify evil or bad people, but that there were no stereotypes; Nilsen has written scornfully of the desire to perceive him as a 'type'. There are selfish reasons for this attitude; if Nilsen could be categorised, he would lose some of his ability to excite interest, which depends almost entirely upon his being enigmatic. At the same time, one must reluctantly concede that he and Bundy are right. We may scurry around looking for answers, but we will not find a single one which closes all the questions. The 'rough contingent rubble' is always there to make us stumble.

For these reasons, I have avoided using the word 'psychopath' which seems to me to be a *passe partout* noun dragged in to apply to any criminal whose motives are inaccessible. Its connotation is so wide as to be useless. Doctors admit that it is employed too freely, and furthermore point out that it is virtually undiagnosable. So-called psychopaths can be to the expert as well as to the casual observer perfectly normal people who are so adept at concealing their disturbance that they can live among us undetected for years. A man has to be called a psychopath before the symptoms of his condition stand out in relief or slot into place; the label usually precedes the diagnosis. By this yardstick, we are all potential psychopaths, yet it is only those of us who do something vicious and inexplicable who earn the label. In other words, the term applies to the deed, not to the condition. Before his arrest, no one would have thought of calling Dennis Nilsen a psychopath. And what does one call a psychopath who commits no psychopathic act?*

Fowler quotes a useful analogy to help fix the relevance of the term: 'In the psychotic we suppose that there has been some radical breakdown in the machinery; in the neurotic we suppose that it is working badly, though perhaps only temporarily; in the psychopath we suppose that the machinery was built to an unusual pattern or is faulty.' One might add that the pattern is lost and the fault invisible.

Similarly, to call Nilsen a monster is to avoid the issue. People identified as 'witches' were once burned without further ado, it being simpler to get rid of them than to examine the questions which their alleged conduct, and society's hysterical reactions to it, raised. Nilsen has done monstrous things, and the responsible attitude would be to study his personality probingly in the hope of finding out why. Not for his sake, to give him the chance of redemption, but for ours, to deepen our knowledge and improve the chances of detecting such an aberrant personality before it does harm and causes grief. If the death penalty were still in force, it would now be idiotic to kill Nilsen, for that would be to destroy the only evidence worth exploring.

Until this detailed exploration occurs (if it occurs) we can look only to theory and experience for an explanation. Psychiatry offers one answer, fragmented into a dozen smaller answers; philosophy offers another, the theory of sexuality a third, and diabolism a fourth. None has the translucent clarity of unassailable truth, and we have seen that they contradict one another often on essentials. The untutored intuition of a novelist might do as well as any of them. For my

*Sir David Henderson, Professor of Psychiatry at the University of Edinburgh, first defined the term in his *Psychopathic States* (1957). His views influenced the drafting of the Mental Health Act 1959, wherein the notion of psychopathy is given legal recognition. Further debate on the subject may be found in the Royal Commission on Capital Punishment, and in a section of the Butler Committee's Report.

own part, I think there are certain threads which run through Nilsen's life which are not adequately encompassed by any of the tentative explanations so far postulated. I have hinted at them in previous chapters.

Nilsen's concepts of love and death are inextricably entangled in his mind. This has little to do with psychology, or even with ethics, but is bound up with the perception of ideas. We still know nothing of how ideas, represented by words, are formulated in the mind. Why does the word 'love' persistently strike a chord which releases the word 'death' in Nilsen's sentences? There have been manifold examples of this in the present narrative. 'I searched for love and in my struggles made death,' he writes. Even if this is conscious rationalisation, an artful stab at trying to make tangible the dichotomy which he wishes us to believe is the root of his illness in a neat antithetical sentence, why did those two words rather than any others serve his purpose? Antithesis is stylistically dramatic, enabling the mind to grasp quickly an arresting idea, but one must venture beyond form and semantics to see why Nilsen's mind always thinks in opposites, and always tries to fuse them.

Inevitably, I must return to the grandfather. Andrew Whyte was the one love of Nilsen's infancy. The boy's last view of the loved object was as a body, which he only gradually perceived to be dead. It is a commonplace that the infant wants first to possess the parent, then to be the parent, finally to be like the parent. Whyte was 'parent' to Dennis Nilsen as no other member of the family had been. I believe that he never ceased wanting to be 'like' him, as a demonstration of love, and that when Andrew Whyte was dead, the only way that Nilsen could still 'feel' that love was in simulating his own death, and finally the death of others. The idea of death resurrected the idea of love as nothing else could. When simulation ceased, and reality took over, his behaviour towards the corpses of his victims (in the immediate aftermath) was that of an affectionate parent.

The confusion of ideas must have existed in the infant mind before the vision of grandfather's corpse; he was, after all, already six years old. (There are plenty of grounds for believing that character continues to be shaped after this age, anyway.) Andrew Whyte had been a seafaring man, absent for long periods and frequently. Each departure must have seemed like a death to the child, and each return a renewal of love. Unable to accept that the final departure meant the disappearance, for ever, of love, the boy morbidly clung to its last manifestation in the coffin, the last return.

(There is surely some connection between the powerful influence of the sea in Nilsen's childhood and the fact that several of his victims were drowned after strangulation. The image of water never lost its grip on his imagination.)

We remember, also, that the mentality in fishing villages is deeply fatalistic, and that some of the genes of Nilsen's ancestry contributed to a depressive predisposition. Without these factors, Nilsen might not have fallen into morbidity.

There is a further possibility. Semi-autistic children who cannot feel warm love for the mother none the less *need* to feel it for someone. If the mother is not the object of that love but is replaced by someone else, then the love may well haul guilt along with it. Young Dennis gave his love to Andrew Whyte, all the time feeling that he should not, that he should reserve it for his mother. His inability to show even a little affection for his mother made his guilt inevitable and permanent. In a sense, the murders arise from this guilt, and his real love for his mother lies far deeper than even he suspects. Interestingly, it is not unusual for children like this to dream of suicide in the sea, which is the ultimate mother-symbol.

When Nilsen now talks of the excitement and thrill in tracking down a suitable victim and pursuing his plan as far as the kill, he thinks it is pleasure in the act of murder which motivates him, but he could be wrong. The excitement might derive from his anticipation of the return of that beloved object — the corpse. Generally speaking, lust murderers experience anti-climax when the deed is accomplished. Nilsen appears on the contrary to have devoted unnecessary care and attention to the corpse, washing it, drying it, making it 'comfortable' and helping it to look 'good'. (This of course cannot apply to those anonymous victims, like the 'emaciated young man', whom he placed almost immediately under the floorboards.)

At the same time, the 'real' Nilsen is painfully aware that he is alive and thereby hopelessly distant from that state in which his grandfather lies. Hence his repeated flight from his own identity, his tireless denial of the Nilsen who persists in being of this world. We have seen time and again how he will snatch at any pretence to be someone else, to assume another name, to discard the identity he perceives as insulting to his grandfather simply because it is alive, and if he *truly* loved Andrew Whyte he would be dead like him. The one identity which he has consistently embraced is that of the corpse; he would have liked to be one of his own victims. But he was too weak to kill himself, and I fancy he feels more ashamed of this than he does of having murdered fifteen innocent and defenceless souls.

Twice in his life he has felt love for another man, and on both occasions he kept it to himself. To declare it would have been, once more, to betray Andrew Whyte. There can be few more disturbing instances of 'retarded' or 'arrested' development of personality than this. The third love, engendered in Brixton Prison for David Martin, he did declare, in a letter pushed under the cell door (which was later handed back without comment). This was permitted because he now knew that he would be punished for not having loved Andrew Whyte enough by the living death of prison existence; the debt had been paid. As for Nilsen's sexual exploits, it is more than likely that towards the end they amounted to very little, and that they were always preceded by such abandoned drinking that they could be written off by his subconscious as involuntary. Sex was for him less acceptable than murder, for sex pulled him further away from a stern moralist grandfather while murder, in the shambles of his notions, brought him closer.

The role of alcohol in Nilsen's crimes has been misunderstood. Not only is it the trigger that releases inhibitions (as it is with most murderers — between 60 per cent and 90 per cent, according to which survey you read), but it is the excuse which exculpates the infant Nilsen. This is how I believe

Nilsen's subconscious morality might operate: Andrew Whyte
was a strict teetotaller, so if the infant who persists inside
Nilsen suffers (imagined) disapproval from grandfather for
having murdered, the adult can blame the drink, which
grandfather had warned against, thus proving grandfather
right and at the same time demonstrating that drink, rather
than Dennis, is the source of evil. For a long time Nilsen did
blame the alcohol following the first murder in 1978, and is
still apt to attribute undue significance to its ingestion. He
overestimates the power of alcohol in the commission of his
crimes, but underestimates its symbolic significance.

The way in which Nilsen disposed of dead bodies was
revolting. Given that they had to be disposed of in some way
if he wished to escape detection, then from a practical point
of view he was merely efficient. There have been many
murderers who got rid of the evidence in more unpleasant
ways than he (Druse, Webster, Luetgert, Denke, Fish,
Grossman, Haigh, to name only a few). He derived no
pleasure from the task, and there was no sexual element in
dismemberment. (Only once did he cut the genitals from a
corpse, with the first victim at Cranley Gardens, and he says
he felt it was an act of sacrilege.) But this is not the point. It is
not *why* he dismembered bodies that bewilders, but *how* he
could face himself having done so. The police photographs of
human limbs and torn flesh found at Cranley Gardens would
make any normally 'sane' person stagger and sweat. How is it
possible to wake up in the morning to a man's head in a pot on
the gas-stove? How can one place pieces of people in suitcases
in the garden shed and leave them there for months at a time,
then pick them up, rotting, for incineration? How was he
able to tell me, with quasi-scientific curiosity, that the weight
of a severed head, when you pick it up by the hair, is far
greater than you would imagine? I confess I cannot even
guess at answers to such questions, and as I said at the
beginning, it is Nilsen's inhuman detachment, his invulnerability to the squalor of human remains, that makes him
finally unrecognisable.

In this there is an insoluble paradox. For Nilsen *is* a man
who feels, who can bestow loving care on a sparrow or

surprise a colleague with a thoughtful gift. His response to the natural world is that of a sensual romantic. In May 1983 he wrote to me about his lack of close friendship at school.

> My best friends [he said] were the sea, sky, rivers, trees, air, sun, snow, wind, mountains, rocks, hares, rabbits, birds, and the dear land. I was at one with the natural environment, with my face constantly turned to the light or the bosom of the soil and its living grass and broad sweep over the beautiful world. I now know myself too late. I would have been happier as a shepherd up in the desolate reaches with my dog and my flock in a contented harmony with the natural elements.[72]

With people, on the other hand, he was never 'at one'; he was cold, distant, untouchable — his own mother said she could not cuddle him.

Nilsen always knew well enough that it was difficult for him to demonstrate feelings which other people display naturally, recklessly. He can only intellectualise them on paper. That gulf between the Nilsen who feels and the Nilsen who writes is as wide today as it ever was. In trying to bridge the gap, to turn feelings into deeds rather than words, he became a killer of men. Given that he *can* feel, can he feel *enough*? Is the remorse that he has occasionally expressed genuine or false? We are told that 'psychopaths' are adroit at giving voice to emotions which they cannot feel, talking of 'love' and 'remorse' only because they know they ought to. Stavrogin wanted to be tormented by remorse for his act, and felt instead only tepid regret.

We conclude with two passages in Nilsen's own words, contrasting as starkly as the black and white of his own invention, the 'monochrome man', and so deeply in tone, substance, and manner that they might be the voices of two people. The first is a detailed account written after the trial, of how he killed Stephen Sinclair, answering some of the nagging questions about the degree of premeditation and the state of his mind. The second was written in Brixton Prison three months after his arrest.

299

I am sitting cross-legged on the carpet, drinking and listening to music. It finished with the theme from *Harry's Game*. I drain my glass and take the 'phones off. Behind me sits Stephen Sinclair on the lazy chair. He was crashed out with drink and drugs. I sit and look at him. I stand up and approach him. My heart is pounding. I kneel down in front of him. I touch his leg and say, 'Are you awake?' There is no response. 'Oh Stephen,' I think, 'here I go again.' I get up and go slowly and casually through to the kitchen. I take some thick string from the drawer and put it on the stainless steel draining board. 'Not long enough,' I think, I go to the cupboard in the front room and search inside. On the floor therein I find an old tie. I cut a bit off and throw the rest away. I go back into the kitchen and make up the ligature. I look into the back room and Stephen has not stirred. Bleep comes in and I speak to her and scratch her head. 'Leave me just now, Bleep. Get your head down, everything's all right.' She wags her tail and slinks off into the front room. Her favourite place is on one of the armchairs in there, where she curls up. Looking back I think she knew what was to happen. Even she became resigned to it. If there was a violent struggle, she would always become excited and start barking. I was relaxed. I never contemplated morality. This was something which I had to do. I knotted the string because I heard somewhere that this was what the *thuggi* did in India for a quicker kill.* I walked back into the room. I draped the ligature over one of his knees and poured myself another drink. My heart was pounding very fast. I sat on the edge of the bed and looked at Stephen. I thought to myself, 'All that potential, all that beauty, and all that pain that is his life. I have to stop him. It will soon be over.' He was wearing his white running shoes, very tight drain-pipe black jeans, a thick jersey, leather jacket and blue and

* The earliest mention of the Thugs is in 1356, and they were still operating in India in the nineteenth century. They were professional assassins, killing according to strict religious ritual. Their method was strangulation. The modern word 'thug' is derived from them.

white football scarf. I did not feel bad. I did not feel evil. I walked over to him. I removed the scarf. I picked up one of his wrists and let go. His limp arm flopped back on to his lap. I opened one of his eyes and there was no reflex. He was deeply unconscious. I took the ligature and put it around his neck. I knelt by the side of the chair and faced the wall. I took each loose end of the ligature and pulled it tight. He stopped breathing. His hands slowly reached for his neck as I held my grip. His legs stretched out in front of him. There was a very feeble struggle then his arms fell limp down in front of him. I held him there for a couple of minutes. He was limp and stayed that way. I released my hold and removed the string and tie. He had stopped breathing. I spoke to him. 'Stephen, that didn't hurt at all. Nothing can touch you now.' I ran my fingers through his bleached blond hair. His face looked peaceful. He was dead. The front of his jeans was wet with urine. I wondered if he had defecated as well. I got up and had a drink and a cigarette. He had made no noise; I had to wash his soiled body. I ran a bath. I kept the water in it hand-warm and poured in some lemon washing-up liquid. I returned and began to undress him. I took off his leather jacket, jersey and tee-shirt. Then his running shoes and socks. I had difficulty with his tight wet jeans. He still sat there, now naked, in the armchair. He had only urinated. He obviously had not had a square meal in a couple of days. I had not really known that his hair had been bleached until I had stripped him. I discovered that he had ginger pubic hair. Otherwise his body was pale and hairless. He had crepe bandages on both forearms. I removed these to reveal deep, still open, recent razor cuts. He had very recently tried to commit suicide. His heart was stopped. He was very dead. I picked up his limp body into my arms and carried it into the bathroom. I put it into the half-filled bath. I washed the body. Putting my hands under his arms I turned him over and washed the back of his body. I pulled him out. He was very slippery with all that soap. I sat him on the loo and towelled the body and his hair as best as I could. I threw him over my shoulder and took him into the back room. I sat him on the white and blue dining chair. I sat down, took a cigarette and a drink and looked at him. His head hung back with his mouth slightly open. His eyes were not quite closed. 'Stephen,' I thought, 'you're another problem for me. What am I going to do with you? I've run out of room.' I dismissed the future problems from my mind. I would cross that hurdle when I came to it. I laid him on top of the double bed. It must have been well into the next morning of 27 January. I lay beside him and placed the large mirror at the end of the bed. I stripped my own tie, shirt and grey cords off and lay there staring at both our naked bodies in the mirror. He looked paler than I did. Being ginger haired he would anyway. I put talcum powder on myself and lay down again. We looked similar now. I spoke to him as if he were still alive. I was telling him how lucky he was to be out of it all. I thought how beautiful he looked and how beautiful I looked. He looked sexy but I had no erection. He just looked fabulous. I just stared at us both in the mirror. Soon I felt tired. I got in between the sheets as I was starting to become cold. He still lay there beside me on top of the bedclothes. I knew he would become cold very soon and I did not want to feel his coldness actually in bed with me. The coldness of a corpse has nothing endearing in it. Bleep came into the room and jumped up on the bed beside me. 'Come on, old girl, get your head down. Stephen is all right now. He's O.K.' She settled down at the end of the bed stopping only to sniff once near Stephen's leg. She knew that the warm friendly Stephen was no more and ignored his body completely. I turned his head towards me and kissed him on the forehead. 'Goodnight, Stephen,' I said, switched off the bedside light and went to sleep. I was up a few hours later. It was an ordinary day of work for me ahead. Stephen was cold. I carried him into the front room and laid him on the floor under a blanket. I straightened him, as I knew that rigor mortis would set in soon.

In postscript, Nilsen added, 'People understandably will find the description of me killing Stephen Sinclair very horrifying. Nevertheless, that is the way it was.'[73]

Eight months earlier, he had written in different vein:

> The sun has burst through on this late April day. The music from a radio wafts down through the bare prison corridors. It's Abba — 'Lay All Your Love on Me'. It removes me from this place and back to the sun-drenched garden of Melrose Avenue with Bleep on my lap, a tall glass, and all is well. I look in through the French windows and see the body of Martyn Duffey lying on the floor. Here in my cell I struggle to regain control. I succeed but I have tears in my eyes. I am struck as if by a blow, by a realisation in a new way. The gross moral obscenity of these slayings. Murder under Trust. Under my roof and under my protection — the most horrible thing imaginable. I would, at this moment, think it a proper vindication of natural justice that I be hanged, drawn and quartered for having been the perpetrator of these acts. These killings have been contrary to every rule of humanity. Mitigating circumstances pale into insignificance when they are measured against the enormity of these events. They had put an absolute trust in me and I had betrayed that holy trust by killing them, suddenly, without any reason. Nothing that anyone can do, public, law or relatives, will ever match a heart that will ache until it is finally stilled in death. I have exercised the power of pit and gallows upon my inner mind. I am beyond *any* redemption. I need their vengeance, hate, punishments, curses and screams to make the rest of my life tolerable. I have gone a million miles beyond the pale and in the depths of my space I can't even hear myself scream.[74]

After all that has been said in these pages, it would be absurd now to speculate on which of these voices is the more authentic. They both give expression to the thoughts of a man who has constructed his own hell and dragged others into it, without, in the end, really knowing why. It is because one needs to ask why that this book has been written.

Words like 'sorry' hold little
comfort for the bereaved. I
mistrust my own inner sincerity
to bear even to utter them.

— *D.A. Nilsen*

MONOCHROME MAN

SAD SKETCHES

APRIL 1983

195 MELROSE AVENUE NW2

D. A NILSEN

NILSEN
BOOK NINE (B)

The monochrome man is a dream
It is the black and it is the white of life.
There he stands near himself and distant
He is the cameo who activates, now and then
can't cope with metropolitana
Waking him sometimes to this, numbing chant.
On the waste he laid before him
Peaceful, pale flesh on a bed
Real and beautiful — and dead.   23.4.83

I stood in great grief and
a wave of utter sadness as if
someone very dear to me
had just died. I knew that
I had brought this result
but like life itself that
scene looked right and
at the same time I was
amazed that such a
tragedy could not be
averted in this day and age
like a ritual the body had
to be undressed and
washed after each one
I washed and prepared
myself for my arrest.

I sometimes wondered
if anyone cared for
me or them That could
easily be me lying
there. In fact a lot
of the time it was

on III

WARDROBE
MELROSE AVENUE

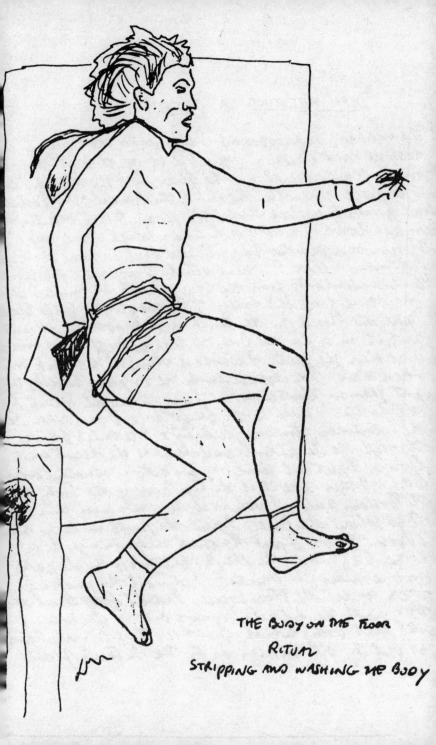

THE BODY ON THE FLOOR

RITUAL

STRIPPING AND WASHING THE BODY

DISMEMBERING A BODY

I prised up the floorboards. I uncovered the body and took it by the ankles. I pulled it up through the gap in the floor and along the floor into the kitchen on to a piece of plastic sheeting. There were other bodies and parts of bodies under the floor. I got ready a small bowl of water a kitchen knife, some paper tissues and plastic bags I had had to have a couple of drinks before I could start. I removed the vest and underpants from the body. With the knife I cut the head from the body. There was very little blood I put the head in the kitchen sink, washed it and put it in a carrier bag I then cut off the hands and then the feet. I washed them in the sink and dried them. I wrapped each one in paper towelling and put them in plastic carrier bags I made a cut from the bodies navel to the breast bone I removed all the intestines, stomach, kidneys. I would break through the diaphram and remove the heart and lungs. I put all these organs into a plastic carrier bag. I then seperated the top half of the body from the bottom half. I removed the arms and then the legs below the knee. I put the parts in large blue carrier bags I put the chest and ribcage in a large bag and the thigh / buttock / private parts (in one piece) in another. I stored the packages back under the floor boards I would leave the bag with the entrails / organs out. I uncovered the next body which had been there longer. I pulled it out by the ankles on to the kitchen floor

There were maggots on the surface of the body. I poured salt on them and brushed them off. The body was but uncoloured. I was violently sick. I drank a few more glasses of spirits and finished the wash as with the other. I got a bit drunk that afternoon. The french windows were open and I had to go out every so often. I was naked = sure soiling my clothes. After I replaced the whatever under the floor I had a bath.

To carry out these directions I only used a kitchen knife — no saws or power cutting tools

Afterwards I would listen to music on the head phones and get really drunk and perhaps take the 'weed' out to Gladstone Park (She was (Bleep) always at it afterwards and stayed in the garden while I carried out these tasks)

While at Melrose Avenue where there were 2 dead bodies involved the only method of disposal I employed there was dismemberment — all after death and burning (2 fires in the back garden and one just behind the garden fence on the waste ground) while drunk I may have taken the carrier bag full of organs on bus me to Gladstone Park (not the dog) and left the bag somewhere. I can't recall how. There were no fires involved in the attempts to fully dispose of the 3 bodies at Cranley Gardens. No part of the last body was disposed of at all — it has been dismembered usually and fully disposed the parts recovered by police. Parts of the other two included large ones and the heads

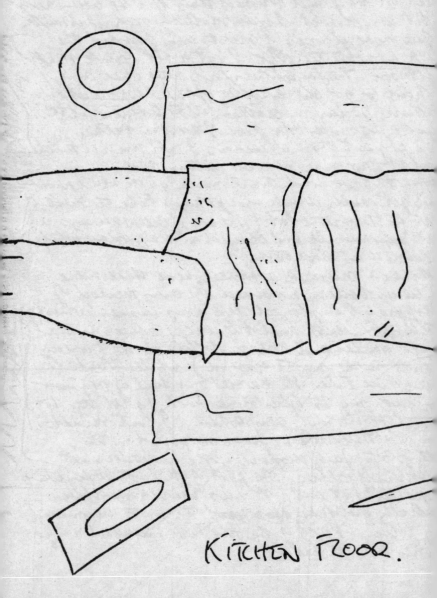

MELROSE AVENUE   NILS

KITCHEN FLOOR.

FAULTILY FAULTLESS, ICILY REGULAR,
SPLENDIDLY NULL,
DEAD PERFECTION, NO MORE

1ST LORD ALFRED TENNYSON

I stripped the body of its clothing. The vest and pants had been soiled with his urine and excrement. I carried him into the bathroom and washed him in the bath. I dried him, put him over my shoulder and laid him on the bed. He was very clean and looked sublimely at peace

I sat smoking looking at him ~~magnetised~~

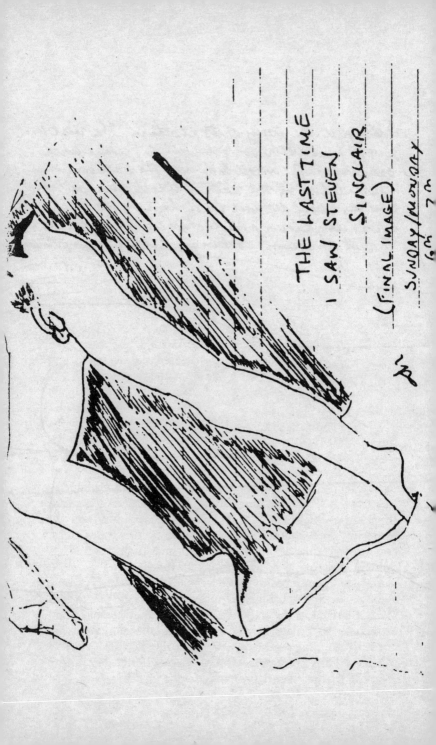

THE LAST TIME
I SAW STEVEN
SINCLAIR.

(FINAL IMAGE)

SUNDAY/MONDAY
6.h 7.h

POSTSCRIPT
by Anthony Storr F.R.C.P., F.R.C.Psych.

I am glad to add a postscript to Brian Masters's study of Dennis Nilsen, although he has performed his task so expertly that he has left me very little to say. Multiple murderers are extremely rare, and Nilsen is unique amongst multiple murderers. Brian Masters has not only read and assimilated virtually all the relevant literature on multiple murderers, but has also become closely acquainted with Nilsen himself, and, so far as is possible, has won the trust of this emotionally isolated, suspicious individual. His portrait of Nilsen is, therefore, the most intimate and the most authentic which we can expect. I do not think that, however many hours a psychiatrist might spend with Nilsen, he would be likely to discover more about him, or be able to provide a more convincing explanation for Nilsen's crimes than Masters has done in this sober, unsensational account.

Only two minor points of criticism occurred to me. First, I think it possible that Masters underestimates the part which alcohol played in the murders. He states that Nilsen 'overestimates the power of alcohol in the commission of his crimes, but underestimates its symbolic significance'. As Masters rightly points out, alcohol releases inhibitions, and is a factor in the majority of murders and other crimes of

violence. Nilsen may indeed be blaming alcohol for murderous aspects of his personality for which it cannot be held
responsible; but I think it probable that he would not have
embarked upon his first murder unless he had been drunk at
the time. Once the inhibition against murder had been overcome, the other murders could follow much more easily.
Alcohol played a considerable part in conditioning the S.S.
guards in Nazi concentration camps to engage in appalling
cruelties and mass executions from which new recruits at first
turned away in horror.

My second criticism is related to the first. One of the
features of Nilsen's conduct which Masters finds incomprehensible is the revolting way in which he disposed of the dead
bodies which he accumulated. Masters writes, 'It is Nilsen's
intense detachment, his invulnerability to the squalor of
human remains, that makes him finally unrecognisable.' Yet
medical students, near the beginning of their studies, rapidly
become accustomed to dissecting preserved human corpses;
and, at a later stage, become inured to post mortems in which
recently dead bodies are slit open and their organs removed
in a way which at first may revolt them. Human beings
become more easily accustomed to, and detached from,
horrors than Brian Masters allows.

It must be extremely rare for murderers to make drawings
of their victims. Nilsen's careful, ritualised washing of the
corpses and the way in which he portrays them shows that he
did indeed regard them as beautiful. The piece which Nilsen
wrote dated 23.4.83 which accompanies the drawing in which
Nilsen is standing contemplating the body is, I think, revealing. Nilsen writes,

> Peaceful, pale flesh on a bed
> Real and beautiful — and dead.

On the other side of the same drawing, Nilsen writes, 'I stood
in great grief and aware of utter sadness as if someone very
dear to me had just died . . . I sometimes wondered if anyone
cared for me or them. That could surely be me lying there. In
fact a lot of the time it was.'

If one has given up all hope of making any permanent, loving relationship with another living human being, as I think Nilsen had, phantasies of a perfect relationship in death may become insistent. Swinburne is expressing something of the same idea in 'The Garden of Proserpine' when he writes, 'And even the weariest river, Winds somewhere safe to sea.' Wagner, in 'Tristan and Isolde', imagines his lovers achieving perfect union in death in a way which had been impossible in life. There is a sense in which Nilsen can be regarded as a terribly distorted romantic, as his drawings demonstrate.

Masters's account of Nilsen's trial highlights the gulf which still exists between legal and psychiatric ways of thinking. During my lifetime, the relationship between lawyers and psychiatrists has greatly improved. This is largely due to the efforts of forensic psychiatrists such as Dr Peter Scott and Professor Trevor Gibbens, both of whom died only recently. Before their day, the psychiatrists who regularly appeared in Court were often the dregs of their profession, and it is not surprising that lawyers took against them. It is also the case that judges who nowadays serve on the Parole Board often come to regard criminals in a new light, as individuals, because they are required to read the detailed reports upon them which are furnished by prison governors, probation officers, prison medical officers and others. This brings home to them that individuals who commit the same crimes are often very different types of person; that the reasons why a man becomes a criminal are both complex and ill-understood; and that legal categories of 'responsibility' and the like are grossly over-simple. In spite of this, there are still some judges who, wilfully or otherwise, close their minds to psychiatric evidence, which they either treat with contempt or dismiss as too imprecise to be useful. It is not surprising that many psychiatrists are wary of appearing in Court. The three who took part in Nilsen's trial were all experienced forensic psychiatrists, who must have given evidence on many previous occasions. Yet all three were made to look foolish, either by Counsel or by the Judge.

One thing which clearly emerges from the Nilsen trial is that both psychiatric classification of mental disorder and legal concepts relating to it are totally inadequate. The defence of 'insanity' requires that the individual be shown to exhibit symptoms and signs of some clearly recognisable mental 'disease' such as schizophrenia. That is, he must be shown to be suffering from delusions of persecution, or hallucinations, or obvious thought disorder. If he believes that his thoughts are not his own, but inserted into his mind by God or the Devil, so much the better. In cases where mental disorder follows upon brain damage, like that caused by severe head injury, or arteriosclerosis, or senility, juries readily accept that such a person cannot be regarded as fully responsible for his actions. In Nilsen's case, no such defence was possible. He was not suffering from schizophrenia or from manic-depressive psychosis, or from organic brain disorder. He was highly articulate, above average intelligence, a fluent speaker and writer, who wrote a full confession of his crimes, and thousands of revealing words about himself. Although the man in the street might say that anyone who did what Nilsen did must be mad, even the defence lawyers decided not to attempt to prove that Nilsen was insane in either the legal or the medical sense. The lawyers therefore tried to get the charge of murder reduced to that of manslaughter on the grounds of diminished responsibility, alleging that, at the time of each killing, Nilsen was suffering from such abnormality of mind that he was incapable of forming the specific intention of murder.

The two psychiatrists appearing for the defence were, I think, faced with a hopeless task. Psychiatric evidence is, from the legal point of view, intrinsically unsatisfactory, because so much of it is based upon what the patient tells the psychiatrist, which may be feigned or false, rather than upon objective observation of behaviour. Persons suffering from brain damage, or mental defect, can be shown to be so suffering by means of objective tests and physical signs in much the same way that persons suffering from heart disease or kidney disease can be demonstrated to have these diseases. Although severe cases of mania and depression generally exhibit disordered behaviour, milder cases may not do so, and the same is true of schizophrenia. In fact, the diagnosis of schizophrenia is bound to depend largely upon what the patient tells the psychiatrist. This is even more obviously so in cases of 'personality disorder', which is the label which the defence psychiatrists decided to attach to Nilsen. The ninth revision of the International Classification of Diseases, Mental Disorders Section, lists some ten or so 'personality disorders' which are defined as 'deeply ingrained maladaptive patterns of behaviour generally recognisable by the time of adolescence or earlier and continuing throughout most of adult life although often becoming less obvious in middle or old age.' The list includes such varieties as 'Schizoid personality disorder', 'Explosive personality disorder', 'Anankastic personality disorder', and so on. Although, from the point of view of the psychiatrist, such classifications of unusual personalities are useful, and convey immediate information about the person concerned to other psychiatric professionals, they in no way match the accuracy of medical diagnosis of disease. Nor, unlike medical diagnoses, does this type of classification provide much opportunity for accurate prognosis. If a patient is suffering from heart disease, or from brain damage, or even from manic-depressive illness or schizophrenia, it is possible to make an informed guess as to whether he will get better, how long he is likely to live, and so on. The diagnosis of 'personality disorder' is one of those classifications which makes one wish that psychiatry was not dogged by the so-called 'medical model'. No wonder Dr Mac-Keith was torn to pieces by the Counsel for the prosecution.

On the other hand, the lawyers are equally constrained by the assumptions and classifications of their profession, and can be made to look equally silly as a result. When Mr Green said that Nilsen showed resourcefulness, cunning, and presence of mind; that he showed initiative in inviting people back to his flat and that he sometimes appeared to be a plausible liar, he was quite rightly trying to show that the defence of diminished responsibility could not be maintained because Nilsen was capable of rational planning and therefore capable of forming the intention of murder. But persons who are obviously mentally ill are also capable of forming such intentions. The man Hadfield who discharged a blunderbuss at George III because he thought it necessary for the salvation of the world was clearly suffering from a mental disorder consequent upon a severe head wound sustained during the Napoleonic wars. He was held to be not guilty on grounds of insanity. But he was perfectly capable of forming the intention of murder and clearly had done so. The *mens rea* beloved by lawyers often fails to distinguish the mentally abnormal from the mentally normal.

Dr Gallwey, the other psychiatrist for the defence, had an equally hard time in the witness box. He laid emphasis upon the 'False Self' syndrome which is characteristic of schizoid personalities. The idea that schizoid personalities present to the world a mask which conceals their real feelings both from others and from themselves is actually valuable to psychiatrists attempting to treat such patients. There is 'another side' to such patients which, as Dr Gallwey said, may manifest itself in sudden outbursts of irrational behaviour. However, the lawyers, not surprisingly, found it difficult to believe that Nilsen was conveniently overwhelmed by uncontrollable feelings on each occasion on which he committed murder, whilst behaving normally at other times. The total failure of the defence psychiatrists and the Counsel for the prosecution to communicate is obvious. Each side is concerned with different problems. The lawyers want a hard-and-fast definition of mental illness which cannot, in cases like this, be given. The psychiatrists are concerned to show that their client is mentally abnormal, but, because psychiatric classification is so inadequate and legal concepts of mental abnormality so primitive, are unable to persuade the lawyers.

Dr Bowden, the psychiatrist called by the prosecution, fared no better than his colleagues appearing for the defence. He had interviewed Nilsen on sixteen occasions, but affirmed that he could find no abnormality of mind in him which fitted the definition demanded by the Homicide Act of 1957 (see p. 230). Counsel for the defence made much of the fact that Dr Bowden had said that he was unable to show that Dennis Nilsen had an abnormality of mind on one occasion, and then said that he had got an abnormality of mind on another. What

322

Dr Bowden had meant to say was that Nilsen was not suffering from a mental disorder of the definable kind to which I have already referred, which is certainly arguable. Is 'mental disorder' the same as 'abnormality of mind'? Dr Bowden had thought so at one time, but then changed his mind. This enabled Counsel to make him look foolish.

All that emerges from these deplorable exchanges between lawyers and psychiatrists is that, if you ask silly questions, you are bound to be given silly answers. Many of the most important things in life are not susceptible to exact definition. A friend of mine was once foolish enough to ask his wife how much she loved him. After a moment's thought she gave the answer 'Eight,' which neatly revealed the stupidity of his question. The degree of mental abnormality or mental illness is no more easily defined than the amount of love in a marriage. It is easier for lawyers to make psychiatrists look foolish than vice versa, because they are in charge of proceedings in Court. Psychiatrists can retaliate by pointing out that legal definitions of 'mental illness' or 'abnormality of mind' are totally inadequate. Indeed, some psychiatrists, of whom Thomas Szasz is the most articulate, argue that mental illness, in the absence of definable brain damage, is a meaningless term which should be dropped altogether.

Is there any way out of this impasse? Yes, there is, if only we can persuade the lawyers and Parliament to adopt it. The defence of insanity should be dropped altogether. What the Court should be asked to decide is whether or not the accused committed the offence or offences with which he has been charged. If the Court finds that he did commit the offences, and there is reason to suppose that he is suffering from some form of mental abnormality or illness, psychiatrists can be called in to help decide upon his disposal. If Drs MacKeith, Gallwey, and Bowden, who are all experienced and competent psychiatrists, had been asked to examine Nilsen after his guilt had been determined by the Court, I venture to think that they would all have agreed about the pragmatic question of whether he was treatable by any known psychiatric method, and also about the question of whether or not he should be confined in prison or in a mental hospital.

Psychiatrists should not be called as adversarial witnesses, but should be employed as independent assessors after the trial is over.

The law is obsessed with the question of responsibility, but responsibility cannot be so easily determined as lawyers would like it to be. Norval Morris, Professor of Law and Criminology in the University of Chicago, has suggested that, if the defence of mental illness is allowed as something which either diminishes criminal responsibility or exculpates an offender altogether, then other defences are equally applicable. In the United States, being brought up in a Negro ghetto is statistically more productive of crime than is insanity. Why not a defence of 'dwelling in a Negro ghetto', or, in the case of the United Kingdom, 'dwelling in a Glasgow slum'? The more we understand about an individual's background and psychopathology, the more we can begin to comprehend his actions, whether good or bad, and the more difficult it becomes to decide which of his actions were inescapably determined by circumstance, and which were decided upon freely. In many cases, if not in all, we are in no position to decide whether a man who has committed a crime should be punished because he is responsible, or freed or 'treated' because he is not. In our present state of knowledge, a pragmatic approach is the only rational one to adopt. Society must be protected from dangerous criminals. Whether they are confined in prisons or in mental hospitals should not be a moral one, but a practical one. Habitually violent offenders should usually be kept in prisons, because prisons are better equipped to cope with them. If they require psychiatric treatment, they can be treated within the prison. Other types of offender may be better dealt with in mental institutions.

Brian Masters's excellent account of Dennis Nilsen's crimes and trial demonstrates that the latter was largely a waste of time and public money. A very brief trial would have established whether or not he had committed the crimes of which he was accused, since he himself had furnished detailed accounts of them, accounts which, in some cases at least, could be confirmed by studying what remained of his victims. Then it would be up to the Court to decide what best to do with such a man, and, at this point, the Court might well feel that psychiatric advice would be helpful. Both lawyers and psychiatrists need to find a common language in order to understand each other and become able rationally to communicate. There is a long journey ahead of us. The sooner we embark upon it the better.

APPENDIX

Even before the trial of Dennis Nilsen had finished, there were suggestions in the national press that he might possibly have been caught earlier, and some of his victims spared, had the police been more efficient. The *Sun* carried a thick banner headline on Thursday, November 3 which announced NILSEN POLICE BLUNDERS, and on November 6 the *Sunday People* suggested in an editorial that 'a cynic might say, on recent form, that the more people a man kills the longer the police will take to catch him.' The basis for these accusations was three reports on police files.

1. Andrew Ho

In October 1979, Mr Ho made a complaint to police that he had been attacked by Nilsen. When invited, he declined to make a written statement or to attend court if required. The complaint therefore remained unsubstantiated, there being no other witnesses to corroborate. No police officer could have accused Nilsen of assault on unsubstantiated evidence, and if such a charge had been made, the National Council for Civil Liberties would have been justified in making an objection.

APPENDIX

2. *Douglas Stewart*

Stewart was eventually a witness for the prosecution against
Nilsen. At the time of his initial complaint, the situation had
been quite different. Stewart said he had been attacked by
Nilsen a year after the incident with Andrew Ho, during
which time over 9,000 other allegations of major crime had
been made at Kilburn Police Station. Stewart called the
police to 195 Melrose Avenue in the early morning of 11
November 1980. A police constable and inspector went immediately, arriving at 4.10 a.m. They noticed that Stewart
had been drinking. It is a matter of course that no police
officer will take a written statement from a potential prosecution witness who has been drinking, so they determined
that the statement should be taken the following day when
Stewart would be sober. That night, they made out a crime
report at Kilburn Police Station. On 12 August they contacted the station at Northwood to make arrangements with
Mr Stewart for an interview. There was no reply from the
address which Stewart had given as his résidence. A second
visit produced the same negative result. A detective sergeant
found the address unoccupied, and inquiries with a neighbour revealed that nobody called 'Douglas' had ever lived
there, only a 'Tommy' and his wife, who had moved two
days before. In fact, that address had belonged to Stewart's
brother, while Douglas Stewart himself had been living in
Holland Park. It was not possible to reach him for interview.
Why Stewart should have given this address, and why he did
not himself contact the police to pursue his complaint, are
questions which remain unanswered.

3. *Robert Wilson*

It was stated in the press that Mr Wilson, a biology student,
had found a bag containing what he knew to be human
remains half a mile from Nilsen's address. The truth is otherwise. Eighteen months before Nilsen's arrest, Mr Wilson did
find such a bag, which he handed to the police and which
was taken to the station. He did not say that he was a biology

327

student, nor did he say that he thought the remains were human. It happened that a similar bag had been found in the same area a few days before. That bag contained animal remains, and had been successfully traced to a local butcher. It had been destroyed as a health hazard. Wilson's bag was likewise destroyed. In any event, there was no clue which could have traced it back to Nilsen, then a quiet civil servant giving no cause for suspicion. Furthermore, the police constable who received the bag had previously been an undertaker's assistant and had had experience of mortuaries; he might have been expected to recognise human remains if that was what they were. And if they were, they might have been stolen from a mortuary, an event which occurs far more frequently than one might think.

There was no evidence to link these three incidents or point them to one source. Nor could police officers have properly behaved differently in each case on the evidence before them. Press allegations of 'blunders' are easy to make, and very tedious to substantiate.

BIBLIOGRAPHY

A Manuscript

The prison journals of Dennis Andrew Nilsen, in fifty volumes (1983), in the possession of the author.
Letters from D.A. Nilsen to the author.
Private correspondence of D.A. Nilsen, in the possession of the author.

B Legal

Regina *v.* D.A. Nilsen, Statements Tendered in Evidence, Statements Not Tendered in Evidence, Further Statements, Exhibits 14–21.
'Unscrambling Behaviour', page prepared by D.A. Nilsen for police.

C Articles

Bartholomew, A., Milte, K. and Galbally, F., 'Homosexual Necrophilia', *Medicine, Science and the Law*, vol. 18, no. 1 (1978).
Blackman, N., Weiss, J.M.A. and Lamberti, J.W., 'The Sudden Murderer: A Comparative Analysis', *Archives of General Psychiatry*, vol. 8 (1963).
Blom-Cooper, L., 'Preventible Homicide', *Howard Journal*, vol. 11.
Bluglass, R., 'The Psychiatric Assessment of Homicide', *British Journal of Hospital Medicine* (October 1979).
Brittain, Robert P., 'The Sadistic Murderer', *Medicine, Science and the Law*, vol. 10, no. 4 (1970).
Friedman, P., 'The Phobias', *American Handbook of Psychiatry*, vol. 1 (1959).
Gibbens, T.C.N., 'Sane and Insane Homicide', *Journal of Criminal Law, Criminology and Police Science*, vol. 49 (1958).
Klaf, and Brown, *Psychoanalytic Quarterly*, vol. 31.
Menninger, K. and Mayman, M., 'Episodic Dyscontrol: A Third

Order of Stress Adaptation', *Bulletin of the Menninger Clinic*, vol. 20 (1956).

Reichard, S. and Tillman, C., 'Murder and Suicide as Defences against Schizophrenic Psychosis', *Journal of Clinical Psychopathology*, vol. 11 (1950).

Satten, J., Menninger, K., Rosen, I. and Mayman, M., 'Murder without Apparent Motive: A Study in Personality Disorganisation', *American Journal of Psychiatry*, vol. 117 (1960).

Wolfgang, M.E. and Strohm, R.B., 'The Relationship between Alcohol and Criminal Homicide', *Quarterly Journal of Studies on Alcohol*, vol. 17 (1956).

D Books

A Psychiatric Glossary (American Psychiatric Association, Washington, 1975).

Berg, Karl, *The Sadist* (Acorn Press, London, 1938).

Eddy, C.M., Jnr, 'The Loved Dead', in *Collected Ghost Stories*, ed. August Derleth (1952).

Fromm, Erich, *Anatomy of Human Destructiveness* (Jonathan Cape, London, 1974).

Hart, H.L.A., *Punishment and Responsibility* (Oxford University Press, 1968), Chs 7 and 8.

Hogg, James, *Private Memoirs and Confessions of a Justified Sinner*, ed. John Carey (Oxford University Press, 1981).

Jones, Ernest, *On the Nightmare* (International Psycho-Analytic Library, London, 1931), Chs 3 and 4.

Maslow, Abraham, *Motivation and Personality* (Harper & Row, New York, 1954).

Michaud, Stephen G. and Aynesworth, Hugh, *The Only Living Witness* (1983).

Morris, Terence and Blom-Cooper, Louis, *A Calendar of Murder* (Michael Joseph, London, 1964).

Pinkerton, M.W., *Murder In All Ages* (1898).

Reinhardt, J.M., *Sex Perversions and Sex Crimes* (Charles Thomas, Springfield, Illinois, 1957).

River, J. Paul de, *The Sexual Criminal* (Charles Thomas, Springfield, Illinois, 1950).

River, J. Paul de, *Crime and the Sexual Psychopath* (Charles Thomas, Springfield, Illinois, 1958).

Wertham, Frederic, *Dark Legend: A Study in Murder* (Victor Gollancz, London, 1947).

BIBLIOGRAPHY

Wertham, Frederic, *The Show of Violence* (Victor Gollancz, London, 1949).

Wilson, Colin, *Order of Assassins: The Psychology of Murder* (Rupert Hart-Davis, London, 1972).

Wilson, Colin and Pitman, Patricia. *Encyclopaedia of Murder* (A. Barber, 1961).

Wilson, Colin and Seaman, Donald, *Encyclopaedia of Murder 1962–1982* (Pan Books, London, 1983).

Wolfgang, M.E. and Ferracuti, Franco, *The Subculture of Violence* (Tavistock Publications, London, 1967).

Other books which have been consulted are listed in the notes.

NOTES

In the notes which follow, the abbreviation NP refers to the Nilsen Papers, notes and prison journals written by Dennis Nilsen between February and December 1983. Letters from Nilsen to the author are represented by DN to BM, with the date. All other references are given without abbreviation.

1 Arrest

1 DN to Hornsey police, 11 February 1983, Exhibit 15.
2 Ibid.
3 Untendered statements, p. 109.
4 DN to Leon Roberts, 8 February 1983.
5 NP, vol. V, pp. 4–5.
6 Ibid.
7 Statements tendered, p. 16.
8 NP, vol. V, pp. 6–7.
9 Ibid.
10 NP, vol. XIX, p. 19.

11 NP, vol. V, p. 11.
12 DN to Hornsey police, 15 February 1983, Exhibit 18.
13 NP, vol. V, p. 10.
14 NP, vol. V, p. 32.
15 DN to Hornsey police, 11 February 1983, Exhibit 15.
16 NP, vol. II, p. 16.
17 NP, vol. XIII, p. 14.
18 NP, vol. II, p. 37.
19 DN to BM, 11 May 1983.
20 DN to BM, 6 June 1983.
21 Ibid.

2 Origins

1 NP, vol. II, p. 27.
2 *The Christian Watt Papers*, ed. David Fraser (P. Harris, 1983), pp. 23, 45.
3 Ibid., p. 27.
4 Ibid., p. 53.
5 Ibid., p. 22.

6 Ibid., p. 108.
7 NP, vol. II.
8 NP, vol. VII, p. 1.
9 NP, vol. XXVII, pp. 1–5.
10 NP, vol. I.
11 NP, vol. XXVII, p. 9.
12 NP, vol. VII, p. 1.

3 Childhood

1 NP, vol. I, pp. 1–7.
2 NP, vol. VII, p. 1.
3 NP, vol. XI, p. 39.
4 NP, vol. I, pp. 8–9.
5 NP, vol. II, p. 35; vol. III, p. 26.
6 NP, vol. XIV, p. 1.
7 NP, vol. XIV, p. 2.

8 NP, vol. II, p. 80.
9 NP, vol. II, p. 43.
10 NP, vol. XII, p. 12.
11 NP, vol. II, pp. 41–7 *passim*.
12 NP, vol. XXIV, pp. 29–33.
13 NP, vol. II, pp. 41–7.
14 Ibid.

4 Army

1 NP, vol. XIII, p. 7.
2 NP, vol. XIII, p. 8.
3 Ibid.
4 NP, vol. II, p. 30.
5 NP, vol. II, p. 26.
6 NP, vol. I, p. 12.
7 NP, vol. II, pp. 55–7.
8 NP, vol. II, p. 62.
9 NP, vol. I, p. 12.
10 NP, vol. II, p. 4.

11 NP, vol. II, p. 5.
12 NP, vol. I, p. 13.
13 NP, vol. III, pp. 1–2.
14 NP, vol. II, p. 17.
15 DN to BM, 25 April 1983.
16 NP, vol. IXB, p. 24.
17 NP, vol. IXB, pp. 25–6.
18 NP, vol. II, pp. 1–3; vol. I, pp. 14–15.

5 Police and Civil Service

1 DN to BM, 3 May 1983.
2 NP, vol. XIV.
3 NP, vol. II, p. 25.
4 NP, vol. II, p. 34.
5 NP, vol. IXB, p. 10.
6 NP, vol. IXB, p. 11.
7 NP, vol. I, p. 17.
8 NP, vol. XXXV.
9 DN to BM, 8 June 1983.
10 NP, vol. IXB, pp. 2–3.
11 NP, vol. I, p. 19; vol. IXB, p. 14; vol. XIV, pp. 11–18.
12 NP, vol. II, p. 18.

13 NP, vol. II, p. 19.
14 NP, vol. VII, p. 10.
15 D.A. Nilsen's file of correspondence with his employers.
16 NP vol. XIV, p. 8.
17 NP, vol. II, p. 78.
18 Untendered statements, p. 122.
19 NP, vol. II, p. 5.
20 NP, vol. II, p. 53.
21 NP, vol. II, p. 13.
22 NP, vol. I, p. 19.

6 Victims

1 NP, vol. II, p. 13.
2 NP, vol. VIII, pp. 1–7. I have removed from this account some words describing the youth which might cause unnecessary anxiety to the families of missing persons. Police found the description insufficient to identify him conclusively from files.
3 DN to Hornsey police, pp. 53–4, Exhibit 17.
4 NP, vol. VIII, pp. 8–10.
5 NP, vol. VIII, pp. 10–11.
6 NP, vol. XII, p. 1.
7 DN to Hornsey police, pp. 108–9, Exhibit 19.
8 NP, vol. II, pp. 31–3.
9 DN to Hornsey police, pp. 120–3, Exhibit 20.
10 DN to Hornsey police, pp. 129–31, Exhibit 20.
11 DN to Hornsey police, p. 17, Exhibit 15.
12 NP, vol. I, pp. 19–20.
13 NP, vol. VIII, p. 8.

7 Disposal

1 NP, vol. XIII, p. 14.
2 DN to Hornsey police, p. 38, Exhibit 16.
3 NP, vol. XIII, p. 4.
4 NP, vol. IXB, p. 18.
5 NP, vol. IXA, p. 5.
6 NP, vol. VI, pp. 28–9.
7 NP, vol. IX, pp. 8–9.
8 DN to Hornsey police, pp. 17–18, Exhibit 15.
9 NP, vol. III, p. 19.
10 NP, vol. V, p. 35.
11 NP, vol. IXB, p. 33.
12 NP, vol. V, pp. 33–5.
13 NP, vol. VII, p. 5.
14 Ibid.
15 NP, vol. IXA, pp. 8–9.
16 NP, vol. XV, p. 12.
17 NP, vol. VII, p. 3.
18 NP, vol. II, p. 72.
19 NP, vol. II, p. 81.
20 NP, vol. VI, p. 27.
21 NP, vol. V.
22 NP, vol. II, p. 15.
23 DN, private correspondence files.
24 DN to Hornsey police, pp. 103–4, Exhibit 19.
25 Ibid., p. 110.
26 Ibid., pp. 111–12.
27 NP, vol. IXA, p. 5.
28 NP, vol. II, p. 75.
29 DN, document written for police entitled 'Unscrambling Behaviour'.
30 DN to Hornsey police, p. 142, Exhibit 21; Statements tendered, pp. 108–30; NP, vol. XV, p. 5.
31 Statements tendered, pp. 39–40; DN to Hornsey police, p. 146, Exhibit 21.
32 Further statements, pp. 1–30; NP, vol. II, p. 52.
33 NP, vol. IXA, p. 6.
34 NP, vol. VII, p. 9.

35 NP, vol. XI, p. 7. 36 NP, vol. XXVII, p. 23.

8 Remand

1 NP, vol. XIX, pp. 2–3.
2 NP, vol. XVI, p. 9; vol. XVIII, p. 24.
3 NP, vol. II, pp. 51–2.
4 NP, vol. XVI, p. 5.
5 NP, vol. V.
6 NP, vol. IXB, p. 20.
7 DN to BM, 30 March 1983.
8 DN to BM, 16 April 1983.
9 DN to BM, 14 April 1983.
10 NP, vol. XVI, pp. 13–14.
11 NP, vol. II, p. 63.
12 NP, vol. XI, p. 13.
13 DN to BM, 3 June 1983.
14 NP, vol. XIII, p. 1.
15 NP, vol. XV, pp. 1–4.
16 NP, vol. II, p. 72.
17 NP, vol. XVIII, p. 17.
18 DN to Hornsey police, 25 May 1983.
19 NP, vol. V, pp. 10–11.
20 NP, vol. II, p. 76.
21 NP, vol. V, p. 1.
22 NP, vol. II, p. 52.
23 NP, vol. IXB, p. 4.
24 NP, vol. VII, pp. 2–3.
25 NP, vol. VI, p. 26; vol. IXB, p. 16.
26 NP, vol. VII, p. 7.
27 NP, vol. IXB, p. 32.
28 NP, vol. V, p. 41.
29 NP, vol. XIII, p. 3.
30 NP, vol. XIII, p. 1.
31 NP, vol. I, pp. 19–20.
32 NP, vol. V, p. 39.
33 NP, vol. IXB, 'Sad Sketches'.
34 NP, vol. IXB, p. 3.
35 NP, vol. XV, p. 7.
36 NP, vol. IXB, p. 4.
37 NP, vol. IXB, p. 3.
38 NP, vol. VI, p. 36.
39 *Times Literary Supplement*, 11 March 1983.
40 DN to BM, 3 May 1983.
41 NP, vol. XVIII, p. 18.
42 DN to BM, 22 May 1983.
43 DN to BM, 19 June 1983.
44 NP, vol. XXXVIII, p. 6; vol. XLIII, p. 1.
45 DN to BM, 9 May 1983.
46 NP, vol. XIII, p. 14.

9 Trial

1 DN to BM, 29 October 1983.
2 NP, vol. XLII, pp. 3–5; vol. XLIII, p. 5.
3 NP, vol. III, p. 15.
4 NP, vol. VII, p. 4.
5 NP, vol. XLVIII, p. 20.
6 NP, vol. XLVIII, p. 19.

10 Answers

1 NP, vol. XLII, p. 6.

2 NP, vol. XXVII, p. 11.

3 Colin Wilson, *Order of Assassins* (Rupert Hart-Davis, London, 1972), p. 21.

4 NP, vol. XLIX, p. 49.

5 NP, vol. XXVII, p. 31.

6 NP, vol. XXVIII, p. 16.

7 Philip Rahv, in *Dostoeivsky, a Collection of Critical Essays*, ed. René Wellek (Prentice-Hall, New Jersey, 1962).

8 Ibid., p. 25.

9 Robert P. Brittain, 'The Sadistic Murderer', *Medicine, Science and the Law*, vol. 10, no. 4 (1970), pp. 198–207.

10 NP, vol. XLI, p. 1.

11 DN to BM, 26 June 1983.

12 N. Blackman, J.M.A. Weiss and J.W. Lamberti, 'The Sudden Murderer', *Archives of General Psychiatry*, vol. 8 (1963), p. 289; J. Satten *et al.*, 'Murder without Apparent Motive', *American Journal of Psychiatry*, vol. 117 (1960), pp. 48–53.

13 NP, vol. XLI, p. 2.

14 Marvin E. Wolfgang and Franco Ferracuti, *The Subculture of Violence* (Tavistock Publications, London, 1967).

15 Anthony Storr, *Human Aggression* (Allen Lane, London, 1969), p. 87.

16 Ibid., p. 88.

17 NP, vol. XXII, p. 21.

18 See Chapter 9.

19 NP, vol. XXI, pp. 39 and 45.

20 NP, vol. XXVII, p. 10.

21 NP, vol. XXXVII, p. 1.

22 NP, vol. XXII, p. 9.

23 NP, vol. XXVI, p. 10.

24 NP, vol. XXVIII, p. 15.

25 NP, vol. XLI, p. 8.

26 NP, vol. XLI, p. 10.

27 Frederic Wertham, *Dark Legend* (Victor Gollancz, London, 1947).

28 Konrad Lorenz, *On Aggression* (Methuen, London, 1966), p. 210.

29 Ibid., p. 94.

30 S. Reichard and C. Tillman, 'Murder and Suicide as Defences against Schizophrenic Psychosis', *Journal of Clinical Psychopathy*, vol. II (1950), p. 149.

31 K. Menninger and M. Mayman, 'Episodic Dyscontrol: A Third Order of Stress Adaptation', *Bulletin of the Menninger Clinic*, vol. 20 (1956), p. 153.

32 Wertham, op. cit., p. 99.

33 J. Satten *et al.*, op. cit., pp. 48–53.

34 Colin Wilson, *Criminal History of Mankind* (Granada, London, 1984).

35 Wertham, op. cit., pp. 96–7.

36 NP, vol. XXXVII, pp. 5–7.

37 Karl Berg, *The Sadist*

(Acorn Press, London, 1938).

38 NP, vol. XXIV, p. 13.

39 George Meredith, 'Modern Love' (Rupert Hart-Davis, London, 1948), p. xliii.

40 NP, vol. XXXVII, p. 8.

41 J.M. Reinhardt, *Sexual Perversions and Sex Crimes* (Charles Thomas, Springfield, Illinois, 1957).

42 P. Friedman, 'The Phobias', *American Handbook of Psychiatry*, vol. I (1959).

43 A. Bartholomew, K. Milte and F. Galbally, 'Homosexual Necrophilia', *Medicine, Science and the Law*, vol. 18, no. 1 (1978).

44 E. Moll, *Handbuch von sexualen Wissenschaften* (1912).

45 NP, vol. XLI, p. 1.

46 NP, vol. XIX, p. 15.

47 NP, vol. XXII, p. 25.

48 NP, vol. XXII, p. 13.

49 C.M. Eddy Jnr, 'The Loved Dead', in *Collected Ghost Stories*, ed. August Derleth (1952). I am grateful to Colin Wilson for bringing this story to my notice.

50 NP, vol. XLVI, page prepared for Dr MacKeith.

51 NP, vol. XLIX, p. 1.

52 NP, vol. L, pp. 7–8.

53 Abraham Maslow, *Motivation and Personality* (Harper & Row, New York, 1954).

54 Colin Wilson, *Order of Assassins* (Rupert Hart-Davis, London, 1972), p. 39.

55 Ibid., p. 3.

56 J. Paul de River, *The Sexual Criminal* (Charles Thomas, Springfield, Illinois, 1958).

57 Martin Israel, *The Spirit of Counsel*, p. 132.

58 Iris Murdoch, *The Philosopher's Pupil* (Chatto & Windus, London, 1983), p. 76.

59 St Augustine, *Confessions*, Bk V.

60 Iris Murdoch, op. cit., p. 511.

61 NP, vol. XXIX, p. 14.

62 NP, vol. XXIV, p. 13.

63 NP, vol. V, p. 26.

64 NP, vol. XLIX, p. 4.

65 NP, vol. XLVII, p. 11.

66 J. Satten *et al.*, op. cit.

67 Stephen Michaud and Hugh Aynesworth, *The Only Living Witness* (1983), pp. 123, 288.

68 NP, vol. XXX, p. 62.

69 Marie Corelli, *Poems* (Hutchinson, London, 1925), p. 8.

70 James Hogg, *Private Memoirs and Confessions of a Justified Sinner*, ed. John Carey (Oxford University Press, 1981), *passim*.

71 NP, vol. VII, p. 3.

72 DN to BM, 4 May 1983.

73 NP, vol. XLIX, pp. 11–14.

74 NP, vol. IXA, pp. 1–2.